A STUDY OF SWINBURNE

By Courtesy of A. M. Philpot (Publishers), Ltd.

ALGERNON CHARLES SWINBURNE
The last and best Photograph

A STUDY OF
SWINBURNE
By T. Earle Welby

BARNES & NOBLE, Inc.
New York
METHUEN & CO. Ltd
London

First published, 1926

Reprinted, 1969
by
Barnes & Noble, Inc., New York
and
Methuen & Co. Ltd, London

Printed in the United States of America

DEDICATION

*

TO

My Brother

Note

THE author desires to make cordial acknowledgment of the generosity with which Mr. T. J. Wise has thrown open to him that incomparable Swinburne collection which is the chief glory of the Ashley Library. He desires also to acknowledge his obligations to Sir Edmund Gosse's *Life*, a book which, as an official induction of a great poet to his place among his peers, is without rival in critical tact.

Contents

CHAPTER		PAGE
	ILLUSTRATIONS	ix
	TABLE OF DATES	xi
I	INTRODUCTION	1
II	APPARITION	14
III	ANTECEDENTS	33
IV	LAUS VENERIS	68
V	SONGS BEFORE SUNRISE	91
VI	THE TROUBLED YEARS	115
VII	PAN AND THALASSIUS	129
VIII	IN SHELTER	143
IX	THE LYRICAL DRAMAS	156
X	THE TRAGEDIES	170
XI	THE POET AS CRITIC	182
XII	LAST DAYS	204
XIII	CONCLUSION	208
	BIBLIOGRAPHICAL NOTE	257
	INDEX	265

Illustrations

ALGERNON CHARLES SWINBURNE — *Frontispiece*
   The last and best photograph: By courtesy of A. M. Philpot (Publishers), Ltd.

SWINBURNE AND HIS SISTERS — *Facing Page* 36
   From the painting by George Richmond in The National Portrait Gallery

ORIGINAL HOLOGRAPH MS. OF "A VIGIL" — ,, ,, 44

ORIGINAL HOLOGRAPH MS. OF "A RECORD OF FRIENDSHIP" — ,, ,, 54

SWINBURNE READING HIS POEMS TO ADAH ISAACS MENKEN — ,, ,, 80
   From a caricature by Burne-Jones in Mr. T. J. Wise's collection

A. C. SWINBURNE IN 1869 — ,, ,, 100
   From a photograph by Elliot and Fry, Ltd.

ORIGINAL HOLOGRAPH MS. OF "AT A MONTH'S END" — ,, ,, 118

ALGERNON CHARLES SWINBURNE — ,, ,, 164
   From a drawing in The Fitzwilliam Museum, Cambridge, attributed to Simeon Solomon

ALGERNON CHARLES SWINBURNE — ,, ,, 178
   From the painting by G. F. Watts in The National Portrait Gallery

TENNYSON'S LAST LETTER TO SWINBURNE — ,, ,, 200

LANDOR'S LAST LETTER TO SWINBURNE — ,, ,, 220

ORIGINAL HOLOGRAPH MS. OF "TO A SEAMEW" — ,, ,, 250

Table of Dates

1837 Born, 5th April, in Chester Street, Belgrave Square, London.
1849 Eton. Holidays spent at his parents' house in the Isle of Wight and Sir John Swinburne's seat, Capheaton, Northumberland.
1853 Leaves Eton.
1856 Balliol.
1857 Meets Rossetti, Morris, Burne-Jones.
1858 Friendship with Pauline, Lady Trevelyan.
1860 Leaves Oxford. *The Queen Mother* and *Rosamund*.
1862 Refused by Jane Faulkner, niece and adopted daughter of Sir John Simon. " The Triumph of Time ".
1864 Visits Landor in Florence.
1865 *Atalanta in Calydon. Chastelard.*
1866 *Poems and Ballads.*
1867 Meeting with Mazzini. " Ave atque Vale ".
1868 Escape from drowning off Etretat. *William Blake.*
1869 " Hertha ".
1871 *Songs before Sunrise.*
1872 Meeting with Watts(-Dunton).
1874 *Bothwell.*
1875 *Essays and Studies.*

1876 *Erechtheus.*
1878 *Poems and Ballads,* second series.
1879 Removed by Watts to Putney.
1880 *A Study of Shakespeare.*
1882 *Tristram of Lyonesse.*
1889 *Poems and Ballads,* third series.
1896 *The Tale of Balen.* Death of his mother.
1903 Attacked by pneumonia.
1909 Death, 10th April.

A STUDY OF
SWINBURNE

Chapter I

INTRODUCTION

IT is sixty-one years since, with the publication of *Atalanta in Calydon*, Swinburne was revealed as one of the great poets of England; sixty years since, on grounds far more literary than those on which Byron's notoriety was based, he became, with the publication of the first series of *Poems and Ballads*, more notorious than any poet subsequent to Byron had been; perhaps fifty years since criticism attained to a lamentable ease about him.

From time to time within the last quarter of a century the general verdict on Swinburne has been explicitly or implicitly challenged with reference to some finding. There have appeared, in that order, Mr. Wratislaw's book, Mr. Mackail's brief and suggestive lecture, the acute criticism by the late Edward Thomas, Mr. Drinkwater's book, my own small volume of 1914, Sir Edmund Gosse's authoritative biography, the thoughtful book by M. Paul de Reul, Mr. Harold Nicolson's volume in the series once edited by Swinburne's severest critic and staunchest journalistic supporter. But the general verdict stands. To write another book on Swinburne, I am assured, is either superfluously to restate it or to argue against it in sheer perversity. There is no Swinburne problem; there is nothing to elucidate. He is the simplest, the most readily and completely understood of our great poets. His appeal is obvious, and ephemeral. He is an intoxicant for adolescence, rapidly outgrown. Three-fourths, or perhaps only two-thirds, of his poetry, for certain spokesmen of the public are disposed to be generous, is of no interest except to students of prosody.

As for the man, never was there a simpler case. The confident summarizing intelligence need not for a moment be exercised by the questions how so very English, and more narrowly so very Northumbrian, a creature was so French, so Italianate, so Greek; how one so very definitely an aristocrat was a revolutionary; how the innovator was reversionary; how one of the most mutinous of men was also one of the most submissive where he deemed submission to be due; how one of the most chameleonic of men was also so rigid and persistent that in essentials he may seem to have been at seventy what he was at twenty; how so spasmodic and anarchical a nature was yet dedicate to purposes pursued over decades; how one in general so absorbed in aesthetic interests and so aloof from ordinary life was yet so acutely aware of the human comedy as the one novel he published proves him to have been; how the Sadist, as he may seem, could yet be our second laureate of the charms of childhood; how he who was incapacitated for love in action could be imaginatively one of our supreme amorists. . . .

I refrain from indicating the further complexities of the problem that is said not to exist. I cannot pretend, though I came under the enchantment of this poet at fourteen, as so very many have done, and have remained under it to forty-four, which is uncommon, Swinburne, by hypothesis, being a poet whom one outgrows, that I have found, in all those years, any one solvent formula to apply to every part of the problem. I take leave to doubt whether any great poet can be made to yield up all his secrets by the use of a ready-made key. My business, for which I claim no qualifications beyond those which the humblest student may acquire in thirty years of constant brooding over the subject, is simply to suggest that we have not attained to finality about Swinburne, and to expose, as far as I can, those qualities in him which I believe to be most characteristic.

The practice of labelling poets, as poets of nature, of love, or what not, is in general to be deprecated, for even if there should be considerable excuse for it in the facts of a poet's production, the significance of his dealings with a preferred subject cannot be discerned without due heed to the whole background against which that subject is made to stand out. Every great poet makes a whole world of his own, and however much emphasis we may rightly choose to lay on some salient feature of it, we must take account of that world in its totality. Or, in a more modest metaphor, our map of this country of the mind must accurately exhibit the level stretches and minor prominences as well as the major contours. But there are poets whose various energies are co-ordinated in some one creative task, whose various experiences cohere in one supreme experience; and to these, with caution and with reservations, we may usefully apply a title. To Swinburne, at any rate, if we can conceive of that title in the most liberal sense, we may accord, without injury and with some advantage, the designation of the poet of liberty.

Not because in a particular volume, on the whole the greatest volume of lyrical verse he ever produced, he devoted himself to passionate commentary on contemporary struggles towards political liberty, or because from boyhood to old age he was ready, on the slightest stimulation, to shriek out incitements to mutiny and tyrannicide; but because liberty, sensual and aesthetic as well as political, was his natural element, because only under that conception of him is he seen to attain to completeness of emotional and imaginative life.

To segregate what are called his political poems from the general body of his work is an error disastrous to understanding of Swinburne. There can be but one error more fatal, that of supposing them to be, except in incidentals, simply the response of a dependent, derivative poet to the influence of Landor, of Hugo, of Mazzini, and to the impact on him of Mentana and Aspromonte and the halt before Rome, the *coup d'état* and the miserable end of Napoleon III. Some of them are occasional, some are derivative, but the ceaseless and vehement aspiration to liberty is no accident, nothing learned from the masters he chose in a proud humility; liberty is the vital principle of Swinburne, animating not only the obviously political verse but all of his work that is truly alive.

Not in one way only did Swinburne live for liberty. He brought to her, in her many manifestations, her splendid or perilous embodiments, all that it was in him to give. She would not have been his liberty if she could have been served more restrictedly, if she could have been contented with a peculiar tribute. He brought her his rebelliousness, which thus ceased to be the random thing it is often taken for; he brought her his singular humility, bowing before her a head else so defiant; the learning that enabled him to enter into the life of her chosen and ancient city of Athens; the ardour with which he entered into the life of her supreme symbol, the sea, and the unhuman ecstasy through which he identified himself with those other symbols of freedom, the sea-birds, " the others " as he called them from boyhood, and his feeling for fire, for light, for all the modes of swift motion. Something else he offered to her also, directly in a mystical sense, as well as in a shattering of conventions which impeded her in one department of life.

It is a regret to me that I wasted the hour of the only long talk I ever had with the late W. H. Mallock in politico-economic discussion for some journalistic purpose, without asking him whether he was wholly aware of what he had suggested in his brilliant parody of Swinburne. For in that parody, whether in mere burlesque of a kind of phrase common in Swinburne, or with a flash of insight, the poet was made to announce to liberty that he would " do unto thee diverse and disgusting things ". Had Mallock divined what has remained hidden from so many, that even Swinburne's sensuality was offered directly to liberty, that her son, her servant, her prophet, was also her lover, not only in the pure, chivalrous ways of certain of his great poems, but also in the ways in which he was the lover of Dolores and Fragoletta and those other " daughters of dreams and of stories ", with a thrilled appreciation, too, of her wounds, and of the blood shed for her?

Swinburne's work, then, is a multiple, many-mooded offering to liberty apprehended in very many ways: in her antique revelation to Greece; in her workings in contemporary Italy; in the dimly descried and exciting future; in her several attitudes of defeat and victory as *mater dolorosa, mater triumphalis*; in her candid virginal grace and strength, as of Atalanta issuing to the destruction of incarnate evil; in her maternal solicitude for her martyred sons; in the implacability of her demands for sacrifice; and also in her wild urgings to the freedom of sensual impulses; and in her great natural symbols of sea and wind and fire and light.

An offering, it has often enough been said, to a chimaera. The most fitting reply is silently to hand the adversary the poems of Swinburne, for no poet ever made real poetry out of unreal experience. But there are other replies, to be made here and hereafter. Freedom for Swinburne is not a riot of impulses in a vacuum. It is that condition in which man becomes the conscious, voluntarily dedicated, unimpeded instrument of the supreme purpose, which is not the hastening of some divine far-off event decreed by a power external to man, for there is no such power acknowledged by him, but complete self-realization for man in obedience to the common human will, in satisfaction of the general aspiration of humanity. By its very nature, this process demands both the utmost freedom and the utmost co-operation. It demands a united and comprehensive republic of free men, but one bearing to the ordinary republic of history or political theory such a relation as the Kingdom of God may be thought to bear to an ordinary kingdom. It is a conception much less political than religious; and because Swinburne says "dear city of man", instead of "dear city of Zeus", the religious character is not thereby taken away from his thought. Indeed, it is because he is, in his own mode, religious that it becomes so urgently necessary for him, besides being very entertaining to him, though not always to his readers, to assail not merely conventional Christianity but every theology which postulates a divinity exterior to man. It is essential to his theology that divinity should be regarded as existent only in man, not that "each man of all men is God", but that "God is the fruit of the whole". Denial of this is a blasphemy, against the divinity of man; and refusal of co-operation in working towards the realization of it is sin, a thwarting of the sole divine purpose operative in the world. The conception, though it transcends politics, includes political life; with this effect, that offences against the State, in the degree to which it may have approached the ideal, become opposition to the sacred will, to be denounced, as by Swinburne they are, in terms which would be preposterous if directed against purely political offences, Napoleon III, for instance, being to Swinburne, as Sir Edmund Gosse has suggested, what Nero was to the early Christian Church.

Aspiration towards such an ordering of mankind in the illimitable republic can look for no satisfaction beyond that of a sense of progress towards the infinitely remote objective. But images in little of that perfection may be, as they have been, fashioned in the impatient mind of man, with some warrant from the history of actual States; and Swinburne, after writing the *Songs Before Sunrise*, created his ideal State, after the historical model of Athens, in *Erechtheus*, that great and severe lyrical drama in which every action and emotion arises from patriotism held as a religious faith. Given a chimerical idea of liberty such as has been ascribed to Swinburne, it would have been the vaguest and most unreal of his works. It is, in fact, the most thoroughly organized and evenly wrought work that ever came from him.

And it is not only in this way, subsidiary to the world-wide movement of his desire, that man may experience liberty. Granted such a temperament and nervous system as were Swinburne's, he may have the sensations of freedom, of escape from the clogged and enclosed existence of the average human being into a life incomparably more spacious and vivid and unhampered, far more frequently and completely than most of us suppose. The liberation of sensual energy, which with Swinburne was apt to be wholly a mental affair, that too is a mode of escape into freedom; and identification of the self with the released energies of nature, with the movement of great waters, with the wind, with fire, with light, with the gull flashing in sunshine over the waves, is an experience of liberty. Swinburne was endlessly responsive to these things. It has been thought strange that one so very lavish with imagery should have drawn it from so few sources, winds and waves, fire and light, and little else, and should so often have neglected to co-ordinate it; but inevitably he relied on images of the life of liberty, and it was in their reference to that life that they were related. It has been thought strange that he was so undefined, but in his constant pressing towards freedom he would have no limiting outline, and far from wishing to " station " himself was eager for speed and the space in which it might have scope.

We need not, and must not, suppose that the mutinous workings in his mind and his blood were always directed against conditions and institutions necessarily to be destroyed in the interests of liberty. He was a virtuoso in revolution as well as a passionately convinced and aspiring revolutionary. In his weaker moments, he enjoyed revolt for its own sake; just as, again in his weaker moments, he enjoyed submission, yielding himself to it with a sensuality of the mind. He found it great fun sometimes to set his little heel on the neck of the tyrant or of some representative of respectability without any particular object except enjoyment of the process; and there were times when he prostrated his arrogant little body before Landor or Hugo or Mazzini or some other of his heroes for the sheer luxury of collapse. But this, though to be noted, does not abolish the truth that in the main his rebellions and blasphemies and acts of adoration were expressive of a profound, essentially original, life-long devotion to a liberty which he had clearly conceived, and which, whether or not to our minds it be wholly desirable or capable of complete realization, is among the noblest ideals set up in even our poetry. I will go farther, and since I propose to deal with what was morbid or eccentric in him rather more plainly than has hitherto been done, I am anxious to say this as soon as possible. I do not know anywhere in our literature a body of poetry, comparable in poetical excellence and in bulk, which breathes out a purer air than the *Songs Before Sunrise* or any drama that maintains a loftier ethical temper than *Erechtheus*. And I will add that, with a considerable knowledge of what he could be in certain relations, and after perusal of letters and verses far too liberally inlaid with irreverence and smut ever to be printed, I cannot feel that there is any poetical personality produced by our country more deserving of reverence, of at least the reverence due to courage, intellectual generosity, chivalry, chastity of honour, the high patrician way of conferring and accepting obligations, of facing enemies and supporting friends. With all his childishness, impishness, extravagance, all his freakishness and weaknesses, he was a very great man and a very great gentleman. The brandy, the flagellation, the frustrate orgies, the excessively naughty schoolboyish rhymes, the absurd violences, the epileptic fits, the beautiful voice raised to a scream of rage, while the little body twitches with an almost excuseless passion, have their place in the record of what he was, but only their place.

Nor can Putney, that opening for cheap irony, be allowed the prominence which it assumes with those who find Swinburne still a great poet so long as he is in the cab, apparently a dying man, but a nonentity the moment he has arrived at an address not poetical enough for the unpoetical. Without denying that his housemate, in a sense his proprietor, Watts-Dunton, gradually exercised over him an influence in several respects rather harmful to his genius, I must deny that, except for the Post Office, he was living merely at Putney. During those last thirty years he lived less in Putney than in Athens, in Elizabethan London, in his native Northumberland, on the wind-swept spaces of the sea.

Age, an isolation from general society consequent on

increasing deafness, separation from the stimulating, though in certain instances detrimental, friends of early days, certainly told on his mind after 1879; and even before that date he had become somewhat inhospitable to new ideas and emotional experiences. But the language usually employed about the last thirty years seems to me rather misleading. Except in degree, there was nothing strange in his inaccessibility to what was novel; few men are truly receptive after forty, and if, on the whole, he was much serener and much less self-willed at Putney than he had been in his tumultuous youth, he remained highly responsive to all the old stimulations. The flame of excitement still leaped in him, only it now seldom communicated its heat to others. It is not so much, except in certain personal and, after all, rather petty matters, a tamed Swinburne that I see at Putney as a Swinburne who has largely lost the power of reaching his public.

The case is one of the most remarkable presented to us by literary history, and with deference to my predecessors I doubt whether it has been carefully enough considered. Here is a man to whom expression is an urgent necessity, who is master of one of the vastest, though most monotonously used, of vocabularies, and who is unrivalled in his command of the metrical instrument. Yet from time to time, between 1879 and 1896, when he suddenly recovered the full power of communication in *The Tale of Balen*, though only to lose it again, he is found to be addressing a public to which he communicates hardly anything. The loss of ability or inclination to establish a sympathetic relation with readers was by no means so nearly total as is hastily assumed. There is not a volume of verse issued by Swinburne in his last thirty years, unless it be *A Midsummer Holiday*, in which there are not certain successes in communication, and even *A Midsummer Holiday* contains the " Ballad of Appeal " to Christina Rossetti. But the failures are frequent, sometimes very irritating. For we feel of such a writer as the author of the elaborate and breathless " Word with the Wind " that he is a poet, that there is something fine in his experience if we could only get at it, and we cannot turn away as placidly as we do from, say, Wordsworth's worst failures, certain that we are missing nothing of the smallest value.

What, we ask in dismay, has happened to him or to us ? What has happened to him it is extremely difficult to say. We may reflect, however, that in other ways and from an earlier period Swinburne had occasionally shown a curious inability to understand the mind of the reader. I will return to this later, when noticing the unhappy constitution and sequence of his publications, which seriously affected contemporary regard for him, though that will matter very little to posterity. For my immediate purpose it is enough to point to his invariable assumption, from the early and most admirable essay on Ford to the latest of his posthumously published studies of Elizabethan and Jacobean dramatists, that the average intelligent reader would be intimately acquainted with the obscurest writers of that age. In Swinburne's belief, every adult in this country carried in his head the text of *Arden of Feversham* and was as cognizant of the humour of *Lingua*[1] as of *Pickwick*. It was not only knowledge that he assumed. He quite seriously supposed that a natural and effective method of persuading more readers to approach Landor and Hugo was to eulogize them in enormous and cryptic odes, each strophe and antistrophe of which would be packed with circumlocutory references to the least generally studied of their works. Now, as it seems to

[1] Was not Swinburne justified in rejecting on grounds of style the persistent attribution of *Lingua* to the author of *Albumazar*?

me, it was, on the whole, less a decline in sheer poetical energy than a growth of this incapacity for judging what would and what would not get through to his readers that resulted in the least enjoyable of his later poetry.

Naturally not well qualified at any time for reaching the public, Swinburne, if he was to reach it, needed some very strong motive. In no unworthy sense, he needed a propagandist purpose, an additional motive for desiring his readers to share his experience. In the earlier years he had such motives. There was the desire to shock the public by making it a sharer of his imaginative sensual experiences, sometimes merely an impish desire to shock, sometimes a serious passion for sensual liberty. There was also the desire to secure sympathy for an Italy aspiring to freedom in unity, for a France ruled by Napoleon III, and above all that, for the sublime idea of universal liberty. When these desires had been worked out, Swinburne, I suppose, no longer felt the compulsion to make his readers sharers of his experiences. The gods, giving him in so lavish a measure every gift for the making of great lyrical poetry, had denied him the instinctive desire to communicate experience simply because he had had it. Born to isolation, Swinburne had come out of it when tempted by Mrs. Grundy or inspired by Italy, or to speak more to the level of the argument, in the service of liberty, of that which can be established only by *co-operation*. He retired into his natural isolation when there was no longer a special motive for intimacy of relation to other minds, and his raptures became solitary.

It seems to me, then, that the later poems, though the exceptions are fairly numerous, should be regarded simply as impassioned soliloquies, not addressed to the reader. They must have meant much to Swinburne, though they do not mean much to most of us. Yet even to us they can mean something, if we will take them in the spirit in which we listen to the sea and watch the swift movements of sea-birds.

Though, as I began by saying, I neither offer nor trust any single formula in dealing with a great poet, it does seem to me that by regarding Swinburne as primarily the poet of liberty we attain to two things, a sense of the coherence of his finer work and a partial explanation of the difficulty of his less fine work. So far as it does cohere, it is chiefly in service, various as that is, to the ideal of liberty; so far as it is, as in later years it often was, deficient in the power of communicating real enough experiences to us, that is largely because he is without a compelling motive to effect full communication. But a guiding principle is only a guiding principle. God has not been so concerned for the convenience of critics as to make any of His poets in simple and exact illustration of any principle that they can discern. The facts of Swinburne's production are the facts, where they contradict any theory of mine or another's as well as where they corroborate it, and I hope to recognize his best whenever I encounter it.

Chapter II

APPARITION

HE broke in on that rather agreeably tedious Victorian tea-party with the effect of some pagan creature, at once impish and divine, leaping on to the sleek lawn, to stamp its goat-foot in challenge, to deride with its screech of laughter the admirable decorum of the conversation. The disorder that followed remains indescribable; and, knowing what we do of the real character of many of the startled company, it is not now quite easy to understand. Few of them were really so tame as they seemed, in that August of 1866, when the summer was so suddenly smitten with strange air, and keen, wild scents and hot, artificial odours of the alcove overwhelmed the temperate perfumes of the insular garden. Even their typical poet, Tennyson, if you considered him closely, when he was off duty, had in him, at any rate as a man, something farouche and acrid, a reminder that, if he now wrote *Enoch Arden* and the like, he had been, not so long ago, in his lucky, unguarded hour, the author of *Maud*. But, for the time being, he was complacent, and rather somnolent, and a trifle official. There was rather too much suavity in the setting he and they had contrived for themselves, too even a gloss on that cultured society. It had genius and talent in abundance, and was concerned with many high matters, of which, however, it now spoke with the emphasis of habit rather than of constantly renewed conviction; but it had become inhospitable to new ideas, suspicious of all instincts which did not bring with them a certificate from some reputable authority. Admirably, it had decided, with the Laureate, to let the ape and tiger die, at any rate as subjects of discussion, but it had fallen into a certain zoological confusion, whereby many permanent, if you like deplorable, human characteristics had been assumed to be simian or feline, and it was sure they could be eradicated by a conspiracy of silence.

The intrusion startled them so much partly because they were unprepared. A few, and in particular Ruskin, had been aware for some time that some invasion was possible. For several years Ruskin had been on terms of friendship with Rossetti and most of his circle, and he had known Swinburne since they met in 1858 at the house of Pauline, Lady Trevelyan, the young poet's wisest and most devoted protector. But even to Ruskin the literary intentions of the group were still rather obscure, and most of the others knew hardly anything of its ardent poetic activities. True, years earlier there had appeared the *Germ*, containing, with other significant things, so consummate a piece of work in the new temper as Rossetti's " The Blessed Damozel "; that poem, revised, together with " The Burden of Nineveh " and " The Staff and the Scrip " had been printed in 1856 in the *Oxford and Cambridge Magazine*, to which William Morris had contributed his early romantic tales in prose and one of the most beautiful of all his shorter poems. Morris had issued his wonderful first volume of verse, *The Defence of Guinevere*, in 1858; Swinburne had put forth his two early plays in 1860. But the *Germ* and the *Oxford and Cambridge Magazine* had been short-lived coterie periodicals; Morris had attracted very little attention from his general public with *Guinevere*, though it contained some of the very finest, and certainly the most intense, poetry he was ever to produce; and Swinburne's first book, after some twenty copies had been given away to reviewers and friends, had become, what for half a decade it remained, lumber in the publisher's stock room. Rossetti's one volume had not fared so very much better, and in any event was translation from the early Italian poets, to whom might be referred certain peculiarities of sentiment and style: his volume of original poems was to be delayed till 1870 by his impulsive burial of the manuscripts in his wife's grave.

The proceedings immediately after the sudden, deeply tragic death of that beautiful, gifted woman assist us to realize how incurious the general public was about members of the group. On the evening of the 10th of February 1862 D. G. Rossetti, his wife, and Swinburne had dined together at the Sablonière Hotel, Leicester Square. Rossetti had taken her home, gone out again, and returned to find her dying of an overdose of laudanum. An inquest was necessary, and Swinburne was a witness of great importance, not only because he had been the last person except her husband to see her alive, but because he had been for the two years since their marriage her closest friend and the most frequent visitor to their home. For many months before this, as Lord Houghton's guest at gatherings frequented by almost every distinguished writer and by many people of fashion, he had been a figure conspicuous by his extraordinary appearance and a talker the most stimulating that most of the company had ever heard. Yet not one paper reported his evidence.

In 1862 Swinburne was nobody. Almost as much might be said of other poets in the group, with one exception, though Pre-Raphaelite painting, so far as it was still represented by the accommodating Millais, had begun to secure some favour. Christina Rossetti alone had managed, or rather chanced, to make a stir with her poetry. But her exquisite first work, though definitely related to her brother's, won its way by qualities altogether its own. It did not prepare the public, to any considerable extent, for the poetry of Dante Gabriel, and still less for the poetry of Swinburne. And Swinburne himself had done very little to fit the public mind for the reception of the first series of *Poems and Ballads*. Success with the general body of readers, but by no means to the extent suggested in most accounts of his career, had been achieved by him in 1865, with *Atalanta in Calydon*, on which had followed the much earlier conceived *Chastelard*; not by any volume of lyrics which, revealing personal emotion and the several facets of his character, might have enabled readers to anticipate the nature of those new poems which threw literary England into paroxysms.

The first that most people learned of the *Poems and Ballads* was from the very lengthy and extremely hostile criticism in the most influential literary periodical of the period, the *Saturday Review*, a criticism which appeared before copies of the book were readily obtainable, which at once fixed the general attitude towards Swinburne, and which continued to be echoed, often no doubt unconsciously, for at least thirty years.

This notorious, and in its consequences very important, criticism was anonymous, but, as has long been known, the work of John Morley. It was the more damaging because here and there it showed, and still oftener seemed to show, willingness to leave the artist a reasonable liberty in choice of subject and method. "It is mere waste of time", it began, "and shows a curiously mistaken conception of human character, to blame an artist of any kind for working at a certain set of subjects, rather than at some other set which the critic may prefer. An artist, at all events an artist of such power and individuality as Mr. Swinburne, works as his character compels him. If the character of his genius drives him pretty exclusively in the direction of libidinous song, we may be very sorry, but it is of no use to advise him and to preach to him." Such as Swinburne's bent is, he follows it, and in the eyes of this critic he at least "deserves credit for the audacious courage with which he has revealed to the world a mind all aflame with the feverish carnality of a schoolboy over the dirtiest passages in Lemprière". Not everyone would so readily avow interest in "the practices of the great island of the Ægean, in the habits of Messalina, of Faustina, of Pasiphae". Were he simply a rebel against the "fat-headed Philistines and thin-blooded Puritans" who insist that all poetry should be fit for perusal by girls of eighteen, he would have all generous minds on his side. But there is a vast difference between a healthy paganism and "an attempt to glorify all the bestial delights that the subtleness of Greek depravity was able to contrive". No condemnation could be too strong for "the mixed vileness and childishness" which presents "the spurious passion of a putrescent imagination" as the chief glory of life. This poet, certainly, has power of imagination and mastery of the music of verse; he is capable of "variety and rapidity and sustention", of music if not of thought; he can achieve sometimes, as in the hendecasyllabics, "perfect delicacy and beauty", and he is deeply poetical in such a piece as "The Sundew" (certainly one of the most charming of his minor successes, the present writer would say, but also one of the least characteristic). But for the most part, in Morley's view, he is addicted to "the most violent colours and the most intoxicated ideas and images". Even his best work is excessively pessimistic. "The bottomless pit encompasses us on one side and stews and bagnios on the other. He is either the vindictive and scornful apostle of a crushing iron-shod despair, or else the libidinous laureate of a pack of satyrs." He is thin in thought, and totally without perception of the pure, peaceful, kindly aspects of life.

A very just view of the intruder, it was pretty generally agreed on the desecrated lawn, though here and there some mild dissent revealed itself. Ruskin, for one, declined to join the general and furious remonstrance. But it is easy to make too much of that. For one thing, he had been persuaded to countenance the *Poems and Ballads* before they appeared, and could hardly withdraw from the position he had taken up. For another, if he would say nothing against the peccant volume in public, he adopted in private a tone of melancholy wonder at the perversity of his young and gifted friend. To one who had urged him to denounce Swinburne he could write: " He is infinitely above me in all knowledge and power, and I should no more think of advising him or criticizing him than of venturing to do it to Turner if he were alive again. . . . I'm *righter* than he is—so are the lambs and the swallows, but they're not his match." To Swinburne himself he wrote in the month after the appearance of the book:

" For the matter of it—I consent to much—I regret much—I blame or reject nothing. I should as soon think of finding fault with you as with a thunder-cloud or a nightshade blossom. All I can say of you, or them, is that God made you, and that you are very wonderful and beautiful. . . . There is assuredly something wrong with you—awful in proportion to the great power it effects, and renders [you] (nationally) at present useless. So it was with Turner, so with Byron. It seems to be the peculiar judgment-curse of modern days that all their greatest men shall be plague-struck."

Maintaining this attitude, modest, generous, affectionate, Ruskin could only refrain from condemnation, could not champion the volume or its author. Among literary journalists Swinburne had backing from Joseph Knight, whose friendship he had won a year earlier, whose wide reading in dramatic literature made him congenial company, and with whom he remained intimate for another seven years, when there was an unfortunate quarrel, one of the quarrels of Swinburne's worst and least characteristic period. Socially, since Pauline, Lady Trevelyan, whose shrewd, amused, maternal interest in him had been so helpful, died shortly before the publication of the *Poems and Ballads*, and Lord Houghton now showed signs of an only moderately benevolent neutrality, and moreover was out of England at the most critical moment, Swinburne was in need of support.

For, inevitably, with the notoriety of the *Poems and Ballads* stories began to circulate. Gossip that was contemptible when fresh is not less so when stale, but the baser part of the Swinburne legend cannot be ignored, for it provided in the middle 'sixties reasons for discounting his work. Setting aside stories of another kind, it was passed about, correctly, that Swinburne from time to time was the victim of a singular kind of seizure, epileptic no doubt, but unlike anything recorded of anyone else. Then, inaccurately but with excuse, it was passed about that he drank heavily, the truth being that with his high-strung, indeed abnormal, nervous system, he was overcome or frenzied by what for the normal man would have been a very moderate amount of wine. Evidently a maladive, disordered creature, whose impulses and opinions might to some extent at least be referred to disease and drink, though the real Swinburne, when he was himself, was full of vitality, tireless in walking and swimming, free from all the usual minor ailments, and as radiant, witty, courteous, and dignified a companion and conversationalist as could be desired, the best talker of sense and nonsense to be found in any company.

Then, there was his appearance, as of an elf, some said, as of a character escaped out of some story by Poe, a French observer thought. There was no cultivation of eccentricity in appearance. The young poet dressed in the precise mode of the moment, and, great gentleman that he was, scorned all affectation; but nature had set him apart from all other men. Take Guy de Maupassant's impression of him, three years after the date of the first *Poems and Ballads*:

"Le front était très grand, sous des cheveux longs, et la figure allait se rétrécissant vers un menton mince ombré d'une maigre touffe de barbe. Une très légère moustache glissait sur des lèvres extraordinairement fines et serrées, et le cou qui semblait sans fin quissait cette tête, vivante par les yeux clairs chercheurs et fixes, à un corps sans épaules, car le haut de la poitrine parassait à peine plus large que le front. Tout ce personnage presque surnaturel était agité de secousses verveuses. Il fut très cordial, très accueillant; et le charme extraordinaire de son intelligence me séduisit aussitôt."

This strange, brilliant little being, with that incredible hair and those grey-green-blue eyes full of abstract excitement, his small body quivering with enthusiasms, angers, and spasms of mischievous amusement, his tiny hands fluttering or keeping time by jerking movements at the wrist to some inner pulse of agitation, his words pouring forth in elaborate eulogy of his strange literary gods or in mockery of the whole apparatus of British respectability, was eminently disconcerting.

But far more serious than any of these obstacles to comprehension and sympathy was the difficulty of divining the centre from which radiated all those raptures and furies and screams of mocking laughter. At

Oxford, even so acute and sympathetic an observer as Jowett had been perplexed by the saltatory and apparently illogical movements of Swinburne's thought. Two or three years later George Meredith, seeing much of Swinburne, admiring his gifts, grateful for his championship of *Modern Love*, was confessing his inability to discover this poet's intellectual base. And in truth there was excuse for the puzzled. The " daemonic youth " of Ruskin's mournful praise, the " little mad boy letting off squibs " of the ignoble abuse that was to come later from Robert Buchanan, drew sustenance from remote sources, many of them foreign, many of them suspect, some of them hardly known even by name to the public of that day. It was one of the distinctions of Rossetti, Morris, and Swinburne, a valuable part of their service to English poetry, that they imported so many exotics into it: the early Italian poets of Rossetti's natural admiration, Villon, mediaeval French romances, Omar Khayyam, discovered in FitzGerald's translation by Rossetti and Swinburne, and so forth. Of the three, Swinburne ranged both most widely and farthest back; he accompanied his two elder brothers in art with delighted sympathy almost wherever they went, but he was also, if not exactly in the academic sense, a profound classical scholar, and he had elsewhere, in contemporary France, particularly, his private objects of adoration. And, at almost every point, even on ground that might be supposed common to himself and the best part of his public, his attitude was unusual. Thus, in regard to the classics, far from sharing the Virgilian enthusiasm of Tennyson and so many others, the Horatian temper still cultivated to some extent by statesmen and men of the world, he cared for no Latin poet except Catullus, but for him passionately, and of the Greek dramatists fantastically hated Euripides while prostrating himself before Æschylus. But, of course, for the most part he nourished his imagination on writers very much less frequented by his contemporaries than any classic; on the Elizabethan dramatists, on Landor, on Hugo, on the vaguely infamous Baudelaire, on Gautier, on the just re-discovered William Blake. Had he not played a prank, hereafter to be described, on the *Spectator*, but continued writing criticism there from 1862 to 1866, or had he been able to find what between those years he repeatedly desired, a regular and independent journalistic outlet for criticism, the public might have been provided with some means of relating him to the world's literature. As it was, he appeared suddenly as a solitary portent, a flower of evil whose roots could hardly be conjectured.

And, then, there seemed to be various contradictions in his literary personality, though these were not very readily or widely noticed. Under one aspect he was obviously revolutionary in literature, in politics, in his theology, if he might be credited with a theology, in morals. What was much less evident but essential was a reversionary tendency in matters of art, causing him already or a little later on to strike back through all adaptations, corruptions, improvements, in lyrical drama to the true Greek model, in other drama to the authentic Elizabethan play, in the ode to the principle of strict correspondence of parts and that other principle by which the subject of an ode must be that of some actual or imagined national celebration, in the ballad to the starkness of the great originals. Of all this, readers in 1866 had hardly the dimmest suspicion. Six years earlier if they had looked at *The Queen Mother and Rosamund*, as they did not, they would not have seen that in the former play Swinburne was going back, mainly, to George Chapman, occasionally to a forgotten poet, then still living, Charles Wells, author of the utterly neglected *Joseph and His Brethren*. They had looked at *Chastelard*, to be impressed, certainly, but to be taken aback by the treatment of love there, after so long an experience of Tennysonian poems in which the lovers of old time had been presented as Victorians actuated by the impulses of latter-day chivalry and controlled by a nice sense of what modern society expected of ladies and gentlemen. They could not see that, however much Swinburne might be delighting in the presentation of love as a devouring insanity, in the presentation of a hero who was an epicure of its sensations and willing to pay for them with his life, the poet was doing a perfectly legitimate thing in filling a play of that period with the emotions of its period. So also the readers of " Anactoria " could not perceive that if Sappho is to be revived in modern poetry at all, it must be on her own terms, and not as the slightly over-wrought head mistress of an academy for poetical young ladies.

The more serious part of Swinburne's intention, the independence of his resolve to deal with antique or contemporary but abnormal modes of emotion in a spirit of loyalty to truth, escaped, it seems, the great majority of his readers in the 'sixties. So did the peculiar mischievousness which prompted a good deal of his work. They saw, and proclaimed with shrieks, that there was devilry in certain things; and what cries would have gone up to too patient heaven if they had seen such unpublished and unprintable verses of his as I have had pass through my hands I dare not try to imagine. But they were rather too ready to suppose that he was definitely on the side of the devils. I am not sure that even to-day quite everyone has the right attitude towards a certain part of Swinburne's early work, which is to be taken morally much as aesthetically we take things like Poe's " Ulalume ", Rimbaud's sonnet on the vowels, and perhaps, on its lower level, Wilde's " Sphinx ", not jestingly, not seriously, balancing ourselves where we can get the maximum of enjoyment out of them.

The younger of Swinburne's readers took him too literally, over-stressing certain elements in the first *Poems and Ballads*; the elders whose hair had uncurled thought it perfectly damnable that anyone should pray in public to be redeemed from virtue, and took such steps as seemed proper to them severally.

One man, who made Swinburne very happy for months, wrote to inform him that, when he least expected it, a bag would be put over his head in the street, and an operation performed on him with a view to diminishing his interest in such subjects and obviating all risk of a dynasty of amorous poets. Another, later on, showed how far senseless hatred of Swinburne could be carried by having a portion of a picture by Legros, which he had bought, painted out simply because Swinburne, in the notes on the Royal Academy of 1868 written with W. M. Rossetti, had praised it. *Punch* called the poet " Mr. Swineborn ". And so on, and so forth. There were compensations, however, in the clergyman who sent his sermons to the poet as to a fellow-worker for righteousness, and in the lady at Florence who wrote verses describing how the seven principal angels in heaven were entirely occupied in singing the praises of the poet to the Almighty. More mundane comfort was also proffered to Swinburne, whose head, " bright and insubmissive " as his own Marlowe's, was by no means bowed in penitence, though he was upset by the cowardice of his publisher, Moxon, represented by Bertram Payne, who had abruptly withdrawn *Poems and Ballads* from circulation the moment the fierce article in the *Saturday Review* appeared![1] Bulwer Lytton communicated with Swin-

[1] The criticism in the *Saturday Review* was contained in the number dated 4th August 1866; Payne notified cessation of supply

burne, invited him to Knebworth, discussed the situation, and through Joseph Knight found him a new publisher, John Camden Hotten.

The choice of publisher can be defended only on the supposition that no choice was really possible, that the condemned book had to reach the public by a drain in the absence of any reputable channel. Swinburne's opinion of Hotten, at a later date, may be gathered from his comment on the rumour that the publisher had died of a surfeit of pork chops; irrefutable proof, said Swinburne, of Burton's error in contending that cannibalism was a wholesome mode of diet. However, to Hotten were transferred all Swinburne's works. These included *The Queen Mother and Rosamund*, originally issued through Pickering; *Atalanta in Calydon*; *Chastelard*; and the sheets of *William Blake* (which, according to a letter from Swinburne to Hotten, Moxon had in " second or third proofs "). Hotten was later to cause Swinburne a great deal of annoyance and loss. From a letter from Swinburne to Watts-Dunton, written at the end of 1872, which I have examined in Mr. Wise's collection, it appears that over a period of " several years ", presumably from the date of the transfer of the works just mentioned, the poet had received from him no more than £40, " obtained with much difficulty after repeated demands ". Considering that the sum was supposed to represent about six years' dues on the most sensationally successful volume of verse since Byron's *Childe Harold*, to say nothing of what should have accrued to the author of *Atalanta*, it is obvious that Hotten robbed him. Further, at least once, Hotten issued an edition without

---

to the trade on the 5th. Later on, when *Poems and Ballads* had been transferred to Hotten, he was guilty (letter from W. M. Rossetti to Swinburne, in Mr. Wise's collection) of selling odd copies he had held back to private collectors at a premium and without accounting for them to the author.

authority, for when, in 1868, " Siena " was published in America in *Lippincott's Magazine*, only six copies [1] were struck off in England for purposes of copyright, but Hotten took it upon himself to issue the well-known pamphlet, which he vended at an indeterminate price of between five and ten shillings. In 1870, when Swinburne was giving his great volume of political poems to Ellis, Hotten set up the plea that all future writings had been promised him, orally, in 1866. It is true that during this period Swinburne was employing as in some sort his agent that brilliant, ingenious, unscrupulous adventurer, Charles Augustus Howell, to whose charm and fluency in fiction he had succumbed, and for whom he long felt a very real affection. But there is no reason to suppose that he plundered Swinburne, as he did Rossetti; and I deprecate harshness towards a man whose lies entertained two great poets until they were so unlucky as to find him out. My friend Miss Violet Hunt tells me she has discovered that Howell was descended from Charles II, and surely a certain amount of divinity should hedge him on that account. But in time Swinburne came to hate and despise Howell beyond measure, and there was no relenting when Howell came to his miserable end in 1890, a few days after having been found, with his throat cut and a ten shilling piece between his clenched teeth, in the gutter outside a Chelsea public-house. What peculiarly incensed Swinburne was Howell's traffic in his letters, a batch of which, passed into the hands of Mr. George Redway, were recovered, by a bargain very distasteful to Swinburne in

[1] Hotten's unauthorized issue is often taken for the first edition, which is worth about £150. The true first English edition and this issue are indeed very similar, but they may most easily be distinguished by looking at the title-page. The genuine first edition has a full stop after the publisher's address, " Piccadilly ". The unauthorized issue has no stop there. The colour of the cover also differs, in a readily perceptible degree.

1866.[1] But whatever the sins of Howell, the dishonesty was Hotten's, and whatever the subsequent conduct of Hotten, at the moment, in 1866, he was not unhelpful.

It was Hotten who suggested to Swinburne the prose defence which presently took shape as *Notes on Poems and Reviews*. This, though weakened by some special pleading and disfigured in one or two passages by an excess of arrogance, had in abundance the qualities of a retort that would tell with all but the incorrigibly prejudiced. The professions of inability to understand the charges brought against him were no more than amusing; the firm insistence on the right, which indeed had been conceded by Morley in the *Saturday Review*, of the artist in literature to address an adult public was salutary. The prose of this pamphlet is among the lightest and most entertaining ever written by Swinburne, though even here he cannot wholly avoid the ponderous alliterative antithetical passages which were presently to become far too common in his work. But, on a historical view, the importance of the *Notes* arises from the fact that it gave public evidence of what hardly anyone outside Swinburne's inner circle of friends, and not everyone inside it, had so much as suspected: evidence that he was not wholly a poet " without a conscience and an aim ", that he could give reasons, good or bad, for his faith and unfaith, his choice of subjects and of methods. William Michael Rossetti's friendly and judicious *Swinburne's Poems and Ballads* was of considerable assistance, and

[1] Swinburne, who was advised by Watts-Dunton, and dealing with R. H. Shepherd as representative of Mr. Redway, yielded up the copyright of " A Word for the Navy " for the nominal sum of one guinea to Mr. Redway in order to recover the eighteen letters, which contained a good deal of unseemly chaff. The entire correspondence is now in Mr. Wise's collection. Parts of it are shocking, but nothing in it is seriously discreditable to the poet. It covers the whole period of Swinburne's intimacy with Howell—1865-1877.

the *Examiner*, so far as its influence extended, was a useful support. Altogether, before the end of 1866 there was in several literary quarters, though by no means among the general body of readers, a certain reaction from the extreme hostility of August. On the other hand, vulgar abuse of Swinburne was to be found where it was not to be expected. Thus, the *Spectator*, in September, published over the signature, " Caliban ", some rhymes written by Robert Buchanan directly charging Swinburne with drunkenness, and a dozen years later the baser prints were still active in insinuations sometimes more serious.

The attitude which Swinburne soon took up and, except for a few spasms of irritation, steadily maintained was one of great dignity. The best statement of it is not in any surviving correspondence of the time but in a letter written later to Watts-Dunton, who had very properly reported some libel to him.[1] His position, and none could have been wiser, was simply this. He wished to be acquainted with any allegation so dishonouring that self-respect would necessitate its definite refutation; but, for the rest, he preferred to remain in ignorance of libels. For the weakness which led Byron to catalogue the infamies attributed to him, Swinburne expressed contempt; at the weakness which, after 1870, left Rossetti's peace of mind at the mercy of every hostile scribbler, he expressed astonishment. And towards worthier opponents he was prepared to exhibit magnanimity. It has been assumed by a distinguished authority on Swinburne that he was resenting Morley's most damaging attack when he wrote, in some not very effective couplets [2] directing the satirical muse:

[1] Letter to Watts-Dunton dated April 1876; holograph original in Mr. Wise's collection.
[2] Holograph original of these unpublished lines in Mr. Wise's collection.

"Then, before she find her art stale,
  Flog some Morley at the cart's tail;
  Or expend a few stray kicks on
The bruised breech of Hepworth Dixon."

But these rhymes, written on the reverse of a page carrying some verses to the one girl loved by Swinburne, unquestionably belong to 1862, not 1866. Thus they afford no evidence at all of Swinburne's knowledge of the identity of his most formidable assailant. He wrote about the time when the controversy over *Poems and Ballads* was raging several satirical pieces which were left in manuscript, but these were not aimed at Morley. The bitterest and best, "A Study", was directed against Froude, who had nothing to do with the condemnation of his lyrics. So admirable is this Dryden-like exercise in invective that I cannot refrain from interrupting myself to quote a few lines of it:

"First in manure of hot religion hatched,
  And fattening on the tit-bits that he snatched,
  Then with gorge heaving at the daily cram,
  And dreaming he had soul enough to damn,
  The hybrid, fit for neither man nor priest,
  Skulked into light, a ruminative beast.
  With foul mouth mincing on the skirts of sin,
  With dubious nose and academic chin,
  Fetid and flatulent, he snuffed and sipped,
  Lapped at thoughts' stagnant pools, but rose dry-lipped;
  With shreds of doctrine delicately sliced,
  For tender thinkers served up half a Christ. . . .
  He with meek brows of martyrdom upraised,
  Praised God for making what God never praised,
  (For if indeed He who made man made this,
  He mixed into the dough no flour of his,
  But, kneading to a lump the refuse bran,

Spurned into life the mockery of a man,
A bastard halting soul of sexless shape,
Not half a human, and not all an ape)."

But this immortalizing lash (" where my lash stung a little life shall throb ") was not employed on Morley.

Yet that he had penetrated the anonymity of the *Saturday Review's* notice of *Poems and Ballads*, and adopted a nobly generous attitude towards an antagonist worthy of it, is proved by a letter of later date [1] in which he distinguished sharply between the ignoble pseudonymous slanders of a Buchanan and the honourably anonymous hostility of a qualified and conscientious critic like Morley, and in refusing to keep company in any publisher's list with the former alluded to the cordiality of his relations with the latter:

" Now I am not childish enough either to suppose it any man's business to dictate to another what and for whom he shall publish, or to entertain any slightest feeling of ill will or reluctance to be associated, whether nearly or remotely, with men who may have attacked my writings in the course of their literary functions as critics or reviewers; in proof of which I may refer to the terms on which, as a contributor to his Review, I have stood for six years almost with relation to my friend Mr. John Morley; who, on the publication of my *Poems and Ballads* was one of the most violent, as he assuredly was the most effective, among my assailants. But I did not wait for any expression on his part of regret for the very grave damage his attacks had inflicted upon me in purse and in character, to show by plain proof that I bore no ill will for the expression, however strong and unmeasured, of any man's opinion as to my literary demerits or offences."

[1] Holograph letter from Swinburne to Watts-Dunton, dated 6th December 1872, in Mr. Wise's collection.

Magnanimity of this kind, however, was characteristic of Swinburne in youth and age rather than in the period, say 1876-79, to which this letter itself belongs, and during which, as occasionally rather later, he was decidedly too quick to take offence and unduly arrogant in his general attitude towards all but a few of his idols and intimates. Certainly he was ungentle in his handling of Churton Collins, who, having animadverted severely on his prose in an anonymous article in the *Quarterly Review* without evoking protest, was foolish enough to think himself entitled to boast, in avowing its authorship, that it had not disturbed his friendship with Swinburne. The quarrel with Furnivall is not to the point, for there Swinburne was provoked by gross insults. As a rule, except during the years when his nervous system was strained by his mode of life, and when temporary doubts of his future as an artist drove him to a not unpathetic self-assertion, Swinburne showed little or no animus towards those who assailed him legitimately. The real dignity, which at one time was suffered to show itself as arrogance, the abundant common sense which underlay his extravagances, made him incapable of the anxious waiting on popular verdicts that he observed with surprise and disdain in certain of his eminent contemporaries.

In 1866 he was a portent, as I have said, because so little was known, except within a small group, of the earlier stages of a development that had proceeded obscurely and under very peculiar influences. Even now, perhaps, there are not very many people who realize the precise auspices under which his genius developed between his twentieth and his twenty-fifth year; and, indeed, some of the evidences of that development still remain unpublished or have only been given to a minute public of specialists.

Chapter III

ANTECEDENTS

WHEN the first series of *Poems and Ballads* was published, Swinburne, though it amused him to encourage the belief that he was twenty-six, was four months past his twenty-ninth birthday: he had been born in a still unidentified house in Chester Street, Belgrave Square, on the 5th April, 1837. Only the accident of a brief sojourn made London his birthplace; his parents, Admiral and Lady Jane Swinburne, lived in the Isle of Wight, at East Dene, Bonchurch, and it was between Bonchurch and the ancestral seat of the Swinburnes, Capheaton, Northumberland, that Algernon's time was divided when not at school.

The facts of his ancestry are not quite what the poet supposed them to be; but for us his suppositions are very much more important than the facts, for he was profoundly influenced by them, pride of family counting with him for almost as much as it did with Villiers de l'Isle Adam. For all the certain antiquity of the Swinburnes and their probable turbulence as a Border family, they were not exceptionally distinguished from the earliest times for reckless adventurousness. They did not, as their descendant supposed, pour forth blood like water and lands like dust in the cause of the Stuarts. When Mary Queen of Scots crossed the Border, they seem to have done little more than meet her. In the 1715, they played but a minor part, the then head of the family, Sir William Swinburne, being too grievously afflicted by gout for campaigning, though some other members of the family saw fighting. The exile in France to which the poet's mind reached back fondly again and again, and the loss of land to which he referred with a proud regret, amounted to little more than this, that his great-grandfather found it necessary to become a wine merchant at Bordeaux, and on succeeding to the baronetcy had a somewhat smaller territorial basis for his dignity than his predecessors. But Swinburne was repeatedly inspired as a poet by the generous errors of his own version of the family's history. The author of the great trilogy on Mary Queen of Scots and of so many ballads in the Border manner and spirit, the poet who, saluting Victor Hugo in exile, claimed to be himself "born of exiles", owed much to the Swinburne legend as shaped by his imagination. It pleased him to be able to say that as his ancestors had given their lives for Mary Queen of Scots, so he had given her the twenty years of his life devoted to the three plays. W. M. Rossetti, who was on terms of intimacy with Swinburne longer than any other observer, even thought that Swinburne's republicanism was given edge at times by a Jacobite desire to gird at a dynasty of Hanoverian origin. And, to consider the broader effects of Swinburne's pride of family, there is ample evidence in his correspondence, especially in one of his letters to E. C. Stedman and one to Watts-Dunton, that he was confirmed in moral and artistic defiance by the belief that he came of a family eminent for the waywardness and courage with which its members had chosen causes and held to them in the face of general opposition. It would have been strange, he said, if such a family as his, when it produced a poet, had produced one timidly obedient to the dictation of the public or content to live by licence of the critics of his day.

If Swinburne unconsciously exaggerated the wilder elements in his ancestry, he had some excuse. On the assumption that his grandfather, Sir John, was a typical Swinburne, exaggeration was scarcely possible, for that extraordinary old man, with his prodigious vitality even in extreme age, his violent political opinions, his great physical courage, was a locally notorious "character", he and his horse being, as they said in Northumberland, the two maddest things in the country. Sir John was hardly so close a friend of Mirabeau as Algernon supposed, but he had known Mirabeau; and though Algernon's belief that Sir John was partly French in blood was also mistaken, being due to confusion between the first and second wives of that Dillon whose daughter by the first wife married a Swinburne, early years in France had left Sir John with something, reproduced to a certain extent in Algernon himself, of the elaborate and proud courtesy cultivated by French aristocrats of the pre-revolutionary era.

With the exception of certain physical characteristics, the strange colour of his fiery hair from his father, his voice from his mother, Algernon derived very little from his parents; and except that his mother, by teaching him Italian from a very early age, laid unwittingly one basis of his enthusiasm for the liberation of Italy, he was not influenced intellectually by them, by his two sisters, or by his brother. The fervent Anglo-Catholicism, so to call it, of his mother and sisters, though shared by him, it seems, for part of his boyhood, became embarrassing to him by the time he was fifteen; the devotion to music in his home caused him off and on for many years an exasperation which he was at pains to hide, for he had a delicate consideration for all the nearer of his relations; and he became aware, as his own power matured, that the pride taken in his successes was not accompanied by any very sensitive appreciation of the qualities of his or other poetry. His reverence for his mother was boundless, his respect for his father very sincere; he was charming to his sisters; and on the death of his brother, an unsatisfactory and unfortunate person, he wrote a letter to Watts-Dunton which it is impossible to read without realizing how strong in him were the simple human affections. But from boyhood he went his own way intellectually, and nowhere did it run with the ways trodden by his parents, his sisters, or his brother.

From his grandfather, however, he had ample, superfluous, encouragement in every wildness. His rebelliousness was fortified, unnecessarily, by Sir John's recitals of his own acts of political defiance, and the boy's flame-like vitality was afforded ample outlet at Capheaton, where he tore about the countryside on his grandfather's horses. The young Swinburne rode as a poet, with an ardent delight in speed, but no great attention to the dull business of remaining on the horse. He acquired, all the same, a certain amount of the knowledge on which the average youth of his class, brought up in a great country house, prides himself. Years later, he was greatly incensed by descriptions of how the future author of *Atalanta* had ridden through " honeyed leagues of the northland border " on a shaggy pony—" Shaggy pony! *Blood* mare! " And this is to be noted because to the end of his life, amidst what seemed an exclusive devotion to aesthetic interests, there would surprisingly be revelations of the boy who had been at Eton, who had galloped about his grandfather's estate on horses of breeding and mettle, and who came of a county family, revelations also of the adult but still young Swinburne who, though only for a while, had observed the social comedy reproduced with so much pungency in *A Year's Letters.*

Swinburne was fond of tracing the parallel between his own career, up to a point, and Shelley's. Late in life he wrote to his sister, with reference to Shelley and

SWINBURNE AND HIS SISTERS

*From the Painting by George Richmond
in The National Portrait Gallery*

himself: "I must say it is too funny—not to say uncanny—how much there is in common between us two!"[1] Both, as he would point out, were born in the one class; both were educated at, and encouraged or ordered to leave, Eton and Oxford; Shelley was drowned at sea at almost exactly the age at which Swinburne was so nearly drowned; and so forth. But, he would add with justifiable pride, he had never been accused of borrowing from Shelley; and, in truth, except for a few lines and phrases in the "Ode on the Proclamation of the French Republic", nowhere does Swinburne become imitative of Shelley. Here, however, what I would emphasize among the differences between the two poets is that Swinburne, for all his aloofness, abstract rapture, extravagance, absorption in purely aesthetic matters, had in him, hidden away for the most part, as Shelley had not, some of the qualities which make the man of the world. When he chose to exercise it, he had abundant common sense, which could issue in almost Johnsonian maxims, and a keen sense of character, with an ironical appreciation of much that was extreme in his own conduct. Enthusiastic and unsuspicious as he was, he had few illusions, and was well enough aware, as a rule, how his own attitude might strike a detached and humorous intelligence. At no period of boyhood or youth did he exhibit the silliness which characterized the immature Shelley.

At Eton, so far as can now be discovered, he made no deep impression. His extraordinary appearance was noticed, and his habit of reading Elizabethan and Jacobean dramatists; and he had his success in winning the Prince Consort's prize for French. But the diminutive, dainty-featured boy, with his immense head and flaming hair, and his volubility in the recitation of verse, was not of much account. He played no cricket,

[1] Letter dated 1902.

though, from an allusion in one of his letters, it would seem he took some pleasure in football. Out of class, he was either taking long walks with his cousin, afterwards Lord Redesdale, or reading the dramatists and English lyrists. His developing literary faculty seems to have enabled him to achieve Latin verse which in one instance had high official commendation, but he was not, at that stage, appreciably above the average in Greek or Latin scholarship. In somewhat obscure circumstances he was withdrawn from Eton in 1853, after four and a half years of study there, to avoid trouble with his housemaster. He never resented this disguised and considerate expulsion; kept up a certain amount of Etonian slang and technical phrasing; and was delighted by the invitation to write his Eton ode of 1891.

Against Oxford, however, though his withdrawal thence was under pressure so friendly as Jowett's, he nursed considerable ill-will. His visits to it in later years were solely to Jowett, not to an *Alma Mater*, and his refusal of the honorary degree offered him by Lord Curzon in 1907 was very decisive. He matriculated at Balliol in January 1856, rather more than two years after leaving Eton, and having, apparently, though information is here very scanty, spent most of the interval in riding, swimming, and unacademic reading at Capheaton or in the Isle of Wight. It was a long break in formal education, at a very important period of life, but Swinburne, who had only some rather casual tuition from a neighbouring clergyman in Northumberland, seems to have emerged, at the end of it, a scholar. For it cannot have been almost wholly at Oxford that he acquired his mastery of Greek literature. He was too busy writing at Oxford to concentrate on classical studies; though it would appear (and this early and marked preference for the Greek dramatic poets over all classical lyrists except Sappho, existent chiefly in Swinburne's imaginative expansion of her fragments, and Catullus, is significant) that he did devote much time to Æschylus and Aristophanes.

With the general life of the University he had no sympathy, and his time there was to end in what he himself called total and scandalous failure; but it was at Oxford that he made almost every important friendship of his life, only not his friendships with Burton, with Powell, with Sir Edmund Gosse, with Watts-Dunton. Two Oxford men, one in academic authority, the other senior in years though contemporary at the University, exercised over him a very strong influence: Jowett and John Nichol. Jowett, always quick to discern high promise, tempered his encouragement of Swinburne with some sharp, characteristic criticism: "a very brilliant youth, it's all youth", is one of his somewhat dubiously reported sayings, and, on Swinburne telling him he had made a bonfire of all his boyish verse, "someday you will make another". But Jowett's greatest services to Swinburne were rendered much later, in those critical years, 1873-1879, when Swinburne, on getting temporarily out of touch with most of his early friends, seemed adrift. Nothing could exceed the indulgence with which Jowett treated the occasional indiscretions of the poet in later years. It was with an admirably tolerant smile that he would recount how he had conveyed the not completely sober poet back from a party, in a cab whence issued the voice of Algernon chanting "bad songs, very bad songs", and it was with great kindliness that, years later, he would reply, "Thank you, Algernon, thank you", when the deferential but very candid critic of his translation of Plato cried out over the work, "Another howler, Master". They were the happiest of collaborators in an edition of the Bible for children, a task to which Swinburne, for all his audacity and delight in verbal impropriety, brought the same good sense that he showed in his defence of Bowdler's Shakespeare.

The influence of Nichol on Swinburne, except in so far as in the earliest days of their acquaintance he confirmed Swinburne's devotion to literature, I cannot but regard as much less happy. Swinburne, with an important qualification presently to be noted, was very impressionable, even chameleonic, and such natures benefit most from contact with those who, however, authoritative, are not rigid and persistent. Nichol was the kind of man who dominates his juniors while still young himself in years, but gets left behind. With his strong, set, Scottish mind, he toughened Swinburne rather than broadened or enriched him. He had also a strong Scottish head for liquor, a thimbleful of which was too much for his high-strung friend. The poet's visit to him in 1878, at Glasgow, where Nichol was Professor of English Literature, was among the least fortunate of his expeditions; and over what happened when Nichol lodged for a short while at Putney, where Bacchus could be honoured only in the Professor's bedroom, I must draw a veil. But Nichol's loyalty to Swinburne was never in question; it was very warmly appreciated by Swinburne, who, in a letter I have examined, contrasted it pungently with the fickleness of such former supporters as Lord Houghton and D. G. Rossetti.

The full force of Jowett's influence, as has already been suggested, was not felt till long after the poet, in submission to his tactful pressure, had left Oxford. Nichol's influence, strong as it was, did not direct Swinburne to the particular poetical work that was to be his. The strictly artistic impulse from without came from such of the Pre-Raphaelites as visited Oxford in the autumn of 1857, to paint the luckless frescoes on the walls of the Union. That, for about two years,

William Morris should have had more effect on Swinburne's tentative verse than Rossetti is surprising but not inexplicable. Rossetti, more than any other man of his period, had a natural authority, an inborn, casual, compelling power over his fellows, the easy habit of command; and over the next decade he showed a juster and livelier admiration of Swinburne's poetry than Morris could feel. But, for one thing, Rossetti, at that moment, was somewhat disposed to hold himself aloof; he did not admit Swinburne to real intimacy till 1860. For another thing, Swinburne, at that time, was deeply engaged in the reproduction of archaic models; and, with his mind full of the early French work he had seen in the superb library of his uncle, the bibliophile Earl of Ashburnham, and of the border ballads he had studied in the congenial atmosphere of Capheaton, he responded at once to the author of *The Defence of Guinevere*. That wonderful volume, rich in promise of perhaps a greater, certainly a more intense poet than Morris in fact became, was still unpublished; but certain of the pieces destined for it were made available to him by Morris, and his own essays in that kind drew from Morris the most encouraging praise. But, though this has seldom been realized by writers on Swinburne, the Pre-Raphaelite phase was mainly an interruption in the natural development of Swinburne's genius.

At the time when the stimulants provided by Morris, Rossetti, and Burne-Jones began to act on him, he was voluntarily bound to as curious a literary apprenticeship as any of which we have record. The lyric instinct must have been immensely urgent in him, but with an astonishing self-discipline, almost incredible when the ebullience of his temperament is considered, he was holding it in check. Not only was he not allowing himself to be, except at very rare moments, a lyric poet; he was, for the most part, not allowing himself to be a poet at all. What he was working at was the precise reproduction of Jacobean drama, especially as represented by Fletcher; an effort involving, of course, metrical exercise, but not allowing of any personal handling of metre, any expression of personal emotion. From the age of twelve, when he had read an excerpt from the *Duchess of Malfi* in Campbell's anthology,[1] he had been an enthusiastic student of as much of the Elizabethan and Jacobean drama as a boy could lay hands on. He had become owner of Dyce's edition of Marlowe when he was thirteen; he had known Marston, and, still more surprisingly, Nabbes, from the age of twelve; and before he was fourteen had read, in whole or in great part, every considerable dramatist of the period. His earliest serious ambition had been to do something in the same line not unworthy of a countryman, as he afterwards put it, of Marlowe and Webster. In 1858-59, however, the model, rather oddly, was Fletcher.

In those patient, self-sacrificing mimetic dramas, *The Laws of Corinth* (which doubtless had its title from his predecessor's piece, *The Laws of Candy*), *Laugh and Lie Down*, and *The Loyal Servant*, composed between some early date in 1858 and some date in the winter of 1859-60, Swinburne is found attempting an exceedingly unusual task. He is not doing what almost all poets do in early youth; he is not trying to express a personal sense of the world before he has created a personal style, and therefore in the manner of an earlier poet. He is labouring, and that with marvellous success, to reproduce both the qualities and the defects, at times even the spelling, of his model; to produce pieces which in substance and style, in temper and metrical peculiarities, shall be simply such as Fletcher might have written but forgot to write. They have less dramatic worth than perhaps even the very worst works of the great romantic

[1] Letter from Swinburne to William Poel.

opportunist; they have not much poetry; but the drama, what there is of it, is Fletcher's; the poetry his also; not a single outburst of modern or distinctively Swinburnian lyricism being permitted, not the slightest endeavour being made to avoid any of the blemishes of the master. By the kindness of Mr. Wise, who owns the manuscripts of these plays, I have been enabled to examine them minutely, and I have not found a single passage, hardly a separate line, which might not be mistaken for Fletcher's. There is, however, one startling qualification to be made: *The Loyal Servant* is less like the Fletcher of literary history than like what Fletcher would have been if born twenty or thirty years earlier. It leaves one with a wild suspicion that the accepted dates are wrong, and that Beaumont's partner came to the achievements we know of by way of a series of dramas, now lost to us, in which his genius worked more tentatively on matter less ductile. Swinburne, in this piece, is not following the actual Fletcher but anticipating him.

Apart from these plays, Swinburne in Oxford days, and perhaps for some few months after he left Oxford, was producing, not the ebullient lyrical poems we should expect, but, for the most part, work in the nature of romantic narrative. Whatever he may have written before going to Oxford,[1] in 1858-59 and perhaps part of 1860, he was writing, besides the imitative dramas, hardly anything in verse that was not after the model of simple antique romance with more or less of colour derived from William Morris. The earliest extant piece,[2] "A Vigil", is peculiarly interesting because it is the first draft of the poem afterwards entitled "The

[1] The only piece surviving from Eton days is the very immature and characterless set of verses, "The Triumph of Gloriana", 1851.
[2] Original holograph manuscript in Mr. Wise's collection, the paper water-marked 1857.

Leper" and included in the first series of *Poems and Ballads.* As originally conceived, it was simply the reverie of a man beside the dead body of the woman he had loved. In substance it might, perhaps, though distantly, be compared with an early poem of Rossetti's, "My Sister's Sleep", though there is in it nothing like Rossetti's subtlety in rendering sensation, and might even, on account of the last of the eight stanzas, retained in the final version,

> "I am grown blind with all these things,
>   It may be now she hath in sight
>   A better knowledge; still there clings
>   The old question: 'Will not God do right?'"

be regarded as a remote, naïve echo of something in Browning. But the general manner of it, so far as it is not derived from old English poetry at large, is borrowed from Morris. Two or three years later, the motive of disease, and of the consequent isolation of the lovers from the world, was worked into it, out of an old French story,[1] and the piece was so much rewritten that only the fifth and the eighth stanzas of the original survived.

We are still near, perhaps nearer to, Morris in the piece called "Rudel in Paradise", the manuscript of which has been inserted by Mr. Wise in a volume privately printed in 1918, containing the quite distinct poem, "The Death of Rudel". I will quote the first two stanzas of the former:

> "Is this God's own house I see
>   Builded with much gold to be
>   Like a place of sleep for me?
>   And always over it

---

[1] In the "Annales des Gaules", 1533: Swinburne's letter to Charles Carrington, in Mr. Wise's collection.

A Vigil

The night grows very old; almost
One hears the morning's feet move on.
That flower is like a lily;
One lily glimmers like a ghost
On the black water—only one.

I thought she was not dying; feel
How cold her naked feet are grown!
But I dare not sit nor kneel;
The flesh is stiffened to the bone.

I kissed the feet; never again
Now she Will she kiss me or any man.
She seems so quiet, tho' the pain
Has left her very forehead wan.

I fear that she will turn or speak
To me, as yesterday she did;
There are not tear-stains on her cheek,
No wrinkles on her eye's white lid.

ORIGINAL HOLOGRAPH MANUSCRIPT OF
"A VIGIL"

> The angels go like birds, and here
> Wind blows a noise of singing near
> To comfort me, and make me cheer
> With singing very sweet."

So also is some verses written later, presumably in 1859:

> " As she sits in her father's house,
> Full many thoughts there lie asleep
> Under the patience of her brows,
> Under her eyes so dear and deep.
> Her father groweth white and thin;
> The fame is wasted from his house.
> No horseman ride there out and in;
> Nought stirs there louder than a mouse.
> His life was sound without a sin,
> And yet the face looks very sad.
> Her heart grows sick and her hands thin;
> There comes no love to make her glad.
> Pale is she, and too weak to move
> But slowly as a hurt bird may,
> This is my lady that I love;
> And she will die, the people say. . . . "

Morris is found affecting other work of his also, "The Queen's Tragedy", which remained in manuscript from 1859-60 till printed for private circulation by Mr. Wise in 1919 in an edition of thirty copies, being obviously influenced by the elder poet's " Sir Peter Harpdon's End " and " The Haystack in the Floods ", though by that time Swinburne's own poetical personality has begun to emerge. The influence of Morris, indeed, is felt everywhere outside the three early plays, except in those sonnets written in 1859, seven out of eight of which are exact reproductions of the temper, diction, and style of the sonneteers of the last years of Elizabeth's reign, the eighth, however, being an exercise after Rossetti.

In the amplest non-dramatic piece of work done by Swinburne during his Oxford period, "Queen Yseult", which was intended to consist of ten cantos, but of which only six were actually written, we are still in the world of mediaeval romance into which Swinburne had, to some extent, ventured on his own initiative, but which, from the moment of his contact with Morris to that of his decision to stand independently, from some date in 1857 to some in 1860, he gazed upon through the convention of Morris.

Only one canto, the first, of "Queen Yseult", was published by Swinburne, in the periodical which his Oxford set, the "Old Mortality", so called in jesting reference to the health of some of its members, issued in 1858, *Undergraduate Papers*. This magazine, which is perhaps the most interesting of all such more or less private productions, is more alluring to the collector of rarities than any except *Stockdale's Budget*.[1] John Nichol was the originator and editor of *Undergraduate Papers*; the motto for it, "And gladly wolde we learn and gladly teach", was given him by Birkbeck Hill, afterwards so distinguished as a Johnsonian expert; the principal contributors were: George Rankine Luke, a young man whose early death by drowning cut short a career of promise, and whose memory was long cherished by Swinburne; T. H. Green, the philosopher; A. V. Dicey; Bryce; Swinburne himself. The poet was modest about "Queen Yseult", despite the very high praise lavished on it by Morris.[2] The poem, however,

[1] There exist, I believe, only six perfect sets: that owned by Mr. Wise, who has allowed me to inspect his copy; the Birkbeck Hill copy, now at Harvard; Mr. Spoer's copy; the copy formerly owned by Mr. Forman, sold in New York in 1920 for $725; Mr. Huntingdon's copy; and Mr. Falconer Madan's. The British Museum possesses only the first two numbers.

[2] "In reperusing my cantos, I think they are too imperfect to appear for a year or two."—Swinburne to John Nichol, 1857.

though too stiff, too deliberately ingenuous, too slow-moving, to be really characteristic of Swinburne, has not only considerable merit but a certain small measure of individuality.[1]

There is more of the Swinburne we know familiarly in a piece, one of several attempts towards a poetical version of Boccaccio made by him in 1858, entitled "The White Hind". All that remains of the enterprise, presumably all that was ever carried out, for Swinburne, after the burning of his schoolboy verses, seems never to have destroyed a page of his writing, consists of versions, the original manuscripts of which are in Mr. Wise's collection, of parts of the eighth and ninth stories, and of the prologue, of the Fourth Day, and this poem, "The White Hind", which last was later developed into "The Two Dreams", and published in the first series of *Poems and Ballads*. Here, though to nothing like the extent to which "The Two Dreams", itself not entirely characteristic, reveals him, we have a recognizable Swinburne. The variations between the first and the final draft are not uninstructive, but the two differ so widely after the opening that comparison is difficult without more space than can here be allowed, and I content myself with the examination of the first lines of the two. Taking the third line of each, we find

" for the spring,
Has bitter fits of pain to keep her sweet "

changed into the alliterative

" for the spring,
Has flecks and fits of pain to keep her sweet."

---

[1] There is still more individuality in the piece, also on the subject of Tristram, entitled "Joyeuse Garde", which exists in a holograph manuscript owned by Mr. Wise; but this was certainly a later composition.

The couplet

> "Dead sorrow is not sorrowful to hear
> As the harsh noise that comes in weeping were"

becomes before 1866

> "Dead sorrow is not sorrowful to hear
> As the thick voice that breaks mid weeping were."

A little later on in the poem,

> "The cool thick leaves smelt sweet of rain and dew,"

turns into

> "The leaves smelt sweet and sharp of rain and blew
> Sideways with tender wind."

But we need not wait for the revision of "The White Hind" to discover Swinburne himself. He is plain in that unsuccessful, carefully suppressed prize poem, "The Death of Sir John Franklin", submitted for the Newdigate of 1858. Naturally, it is not quite the mature Swinburne that we have there. For its author, the movement of the verse is not rapid, is a trifle stiff now and then; and the use of undefined natural symbols is not yet habitual. But this poem, which would have been totally lost to us if Admiral Swinburne had not preserved a copy, now in the British Museum, is no juvenile performance to be commended as meritorious for its writer's age; it is authentic and accomplished poetry, with many touches of feeling and turns of phrase thoroughly characteristic of Swinburne, and it would have done him no discredit if included in the first series of *Poems and Ballads*. Take this passage:

> "What praise shall England give these men her friends?
> For while the bays and the large channels flow
> In the broad sea between the iron ends

Of the poised world where no safe sail may be
And for white miles the hard ice never blends
With the chill wasting edges of dull sea,—
And while to praise her green and girdled land
Shall be the same as to praise liberty,—
So long the record of these men shall stand,
Because they chose not life but rather death,
Each side being weighed with a most equal hand,—
Because the gift they had of English breath
They did give back to England for her sake,
Like those dead seamen of Elizabeth,
And those that wrought with Nelson or with Blake,
To do great England service their lives long."

There are Shakespearean echoes almost everywhere in the poem, and once or twice a tinge of Pre-Raphaelite colour, but the movement of the verse is of a noble originality, the temper of it utterly noble. In it is begun that praise of great men, that song of honour, which was to be heard from Swinburne all the remaining years of his life; a song that was often to be more vehement, more elaborate, more lavishly enriched with splendid offerings, but seldom more gravely beautiful.

The academic judges gave the Newdigate prize to another competitor, Mr. Lathom, subsequently of some note as a lawyer in India, and Swinburne lost the chance of securing whatever little attention the outside world pays to Oxford prize poets. That he was sharply disappointed is shown by his endeavour to conceal the fact that he had ever competed; and his resentment at the general failure of his University career, which had been brightened only by his success in taking the Taylorian scholarship for French and Italian, and which would almost certainly have culminated in formal expulsion if he had not gone down at Jowett's suggestion, is established by the fact that for years he kept his name on the books, in mere assertion of his right, without the least intention of return to Oxford. But he was by no means in haste to justify himself before the general literary public. To be sure, he was not driven to write for a living. After some negotiations from Capheaton, whither he had retired on leaving Oxford, he was granted by his father an allowance which, according to Sir Edmund Gosse, was eventually increased to the then quite adequate sum of £400 a year. Later on, his income was much smaller; I have perused a letter[1] from Swinburne stating that he had no more than £200 a year in 1876 (and could not count on making as much by the entire body of his then published writings). But whatever the facts of his financial position, they are of little importance. If not obliged to earn a livelihood with his pen, the young Swinburne might have been expected to be urged by ambition.

Swinburne, however, when he came down from Oxford and for perhaps nearly four years thereafter was oddly undecided in purpose. His lyrical production continued to be scanty.[2] It may, I think, be assumed that Swinburne had either not yet understood how predominantly lyrical his genius was or that he was by sheer will-power checking the lyrical impulse of which he was

[1] Letter from Swinburne to Watts-Dunton, dated 22nd January 1876, chiefly with reference to £42 due to him from the *Examiner*, the late editor of which, Fox Bourne, had asked him to treat the amount as a private and personal obligation. It was apparently not till the Putney days that Swinburne derived any substantial income from his books.

[2] Of the sixteen pieces in the first series of *Poems and Ballads* which Swinburne, in a letter to his publisher, Chatto, dated 1876, now in Mr. Wise's collection, described as "early", four or five may have been produced before 1860, but internal evidence and his preoccupation with numerous other tasks, in verse and prose, inclines me to believe that most were written a year or two after that date. In any event, sixteen poems was not a lavish production for a writer of Swinburne's exuberance and with Swinburne's facility.

conscious till his other tasks should be completed. His energy, at any rate, was given chiefly to the completion of the short play, *Rosamund*, which he had begun at Oxford before the end of 1857,[1] but which he revised radically, putting immense labour into it, before its publication with *The Queen Mother* in 1860. He was also, between 1860 and 1863, occupied with the prose tales which were to have constituted the " Triameron " projected by him when he abandoned the already noticed attempt to render Boccaccio; with translation and appreciation of Villon, whose " Complaint of the Fair Armouress " he did into superb verse in 1861, and on whom he wrote an essay, still in manuscript, in 1863; with two exceedingly naughty skits on French treatment of English life, of which *La Fille du Policeman*, 1861, survives in the manuscript owned by Mr. Wise, though the preposterous drama[2] which presented Lord John Russell as the too warmly favoured lover of Queen Victoria exists no longer, having been destroyed under Watts-Dunton's urging; and on the composition, from 1862, of Border Ballads.[3]

[1] Letter from Swinburne to Edwin Hatch, dated 17th February 1858, stating that the play is admired by Morris, and is " verging on a satisfactory completion ". When under tuition by Stubbs, the historian and future Bishop of Oxford, at Navestock in 1859, Swinburne read him an early draft of *Rosamund*, was dismayed by his mild objections to its moral tone, tore up the manuscript, and then sat up all night reconstructing the piece. So the story goes. But the existing manuscript is certainly not the work of one night.

[2] Its title was *La Sœur de la Reine*, as recorded in a letter, in Mr. Wise's collection, written by W. M. Rossetti to Watts-Dunton shortly after Swinburne's death.

[3] Swinburne wrote no Border Ballads of his own till, probably in consequence of the appearance of Aytoun's *Ballads of Scotland*, 1861, he most unnecessarily and unfortunately abandoned the edition of *Ballads of the English Border* on which he had been employed from 1859 to 1861. His intense sympathy with the spirit of the ballads, and the great independence and sure feeling for primitive diction shown by him in the reconstruction of the texts, make it most

It was, apparently, as a dramatist, as a writer of romantic tales after Boccaccio and of short satiric novels and dramas which should at once expose the ignorance of French novelists and flutter British prudery, as a translator, and as an editor and unservile imitator of the makers of border ballads, that Swinburne, from his twenty-third to his twenty-fifth year, conceived of himself, not, except secondarily, as the lyrist he was later to prove. Dramatic ambition, it need not be said, remained with him till at the very end of life he published, in 1908, the *Duke of Gandia*. The ambition of the novelist died down only very slowly. He returned again and again to that strange, still unpublished novel, in prose with incidental verse, *Lesbia Brandon*, between 1859 and 1867, had it set up in type in 1877, and presumably would have issued it then if it had not been for the extraordinary confusion of the manuscript delivered to the printers and Watts-Dunton's inability to find the four missing chapters. *A Year's Letters*,[1] issued serially in 1877, was revised and published as a book in 1905, some forty years after the inception of that acute, ironical study of temperaments. As a translator, too, he brooded for years over projects as ambitious as almost any that could present themselves to artists in this kind with the much ampler freedom from the original work of a Frere or a FitzGerald. The intention of doing the whole of Villon into English was with him from 1861 to somewhere near 1877, when he expressed to Norman McColl, Editor of the *Athenaeum*, lamentable that this work was not completed. The skill with which he made "The Jew's Daughter" out of the various ballads of Hugh of Lincoln and the unhesitating recognition by him of the great poetic worth of "The broom blooms bonnie and says it is fair" are extraordinary in so young an editor.

[1] The original holograph manuscript, owned by Mr. Wise, is on paper bearing watermarks from 1862 to 1866; but there was some subsequent revision.

his willingness to allow certain of the renderings to appear in that paper though he had always meant, he said, to hold them back till they could be issued with the essay he had begun in 1863. He was also, though between quite what dates I have not been able to ascertain, pondering the translation, whether of choruses or of whole plays, of his beloved Aristophanes, "the half divine humorist in whose incomparable genius the highest qualities of Rabelais were fused and harmonized with the supremest gifts of Shelley".

Swinburne, it must be repeated, was slow to realize that his genius was pre-eminently fitted for the production of such lyrical poetry as he wrote in abundance between 1864 and 1878, and with less frequent success to the end of his life. The point has not, I think, been made in any critical study of his career, but I am convinced, after careful examination of his early work and of his correspondence, that his realization of his true bent would have been delayed for several more years if the first series of *Poems and Ballads* had not created a public sensation extremely stimulating to his mischievous and defiant nature, and if events in Italy, the country of his adoration, and contact with Mazzini had not aroused in him an enthusiasm for which even his lyrical poetry was a barely sufficient outlet.

But all this was in the future, though not far off. In the early 'sixties he was, to those outside this circle of friends who knew of him at all, a young man of very peculiar appearance and very unusual enthusiasms, who was writing, prose mostly, for the *Spectator* and who was consorting with the still rather mysterious Pre-Raphaelites. Good and gifted Mr. Hutton of that respectable paper had admitted his chivalrous and admirably argued defence of George Meredith's *Modern Love*, and even his long review of the great French poet whose name, spelled wrongly, was to be later on a journalistic term of abuse. The readers of the *Spectator* had been allowed to peruse the eulogy of Baudelaire. They had even, with Mr. Hutton's acquiescence, had inflicted on them the critic's own poem, "Faustine". But something the vicarages of England were spared. When Swinburne, who had invented an English poet, Ernest Wheldrake, at Oxford, in order to review his poems in *Undergraduate Papers*, proceeded to create those deplorable decadents, Félicien Cossu and Ernest Clouët, and to use his own extremely clever and excessively naughty French verses as a pretext for wagging a moral and mournful head over their sins, Mr. Hutton protested. It was not that he suspected a hoax, but that he was perturbed by his reviewer's tone in condemnation. " There is a tone of raillery about it ", Hutton wrote [1] to Swinburne when the Clouët review was in type, " which, I think one should hardly use to pure obscenity. I confess your tone on Art is a little unintelligible to me. What is poetry and Art? Are they all ' flowers '? Are they all to be judged by smell and sight?" A letter which you can see Swinburne reading, his impish little body quivering with mirth. May it have consoled him in some degree for the failure of Clouët to get beyond that stage of the proof " which is no guarantee of acceptance "!

Cossu and Clouët closed the *Spectator* to Swinburne, and since nothing came of a proposal that Moxon should found a literary periodical for him to edit, he remained without any means of reaching the public that reads reviews until, much later, Morley opened to him the pages of the *Fortnightly*.

But by now, with lapse of time and under the stimulus provided by D. G. Rossetti, in whose house, 16 Cheyne Walk, Chelsea, he had gone to live in 1862, Swinburne

[1] Letter from Hutton, dated 16th December 1862, to Swinburne in Mr. Wise's collection.

A Record of Friendship

De mortuis nil nisi verum

At the beginning of the year 1862 I had been for a little more than four years acquainted with Mr. Dante Gabriel Rossetti. When first introduced to him, I was an Oxford undergraduate of twenty. For about a year past we had lived on terms of affectionate intimacy; shaped & coloured, on his side, by the cordial kindness & exuberant generosity which to the last, I am told, distinguished his recognition of younger men's efforts or attempts: on mine, I can confidently say, by gratitude as loyal & admiration as fervent as ever strove & ever failed to express "all the sweet & sudden passion of youth toward greatness in its elder". During this year, also, I had come to know, & to regard with little less than a brother's affection, the noble lady

ORIGINAL HOLOGRAPH MANUSCRIPT OF
"A RECORD OF FRIENDSHIP"

was finding himself. He was at various periods during the next two years at work on the first play of the great trilogy devoted to Mary Queen of Scots, *Chastelard*, with which he had made some sort of beginning before leaving Oxford, and which had occupied him off and on since 1860.[1]

He was producing also, in what order it is impossible to say, but with rapidity, for all but sixteen of the pieces seem to have been composed in 1862-1865, the first series of *Poems and Ballads*. And, at some date in the summer of 1863, which he spent in Cornwall with Inchbold, the painter, he had made a beginning with *Atalanta in Calydon*; it was finished while he was staying, from October of that year to February 1864, in the Isle of Wight with his aunt, Lady Mary Gordon, and her daughter.

Meanwhile, that rather too placid literary society which he was presently to startle had begun to be aware of him. Probably through his friend Pauline, Lady Trevelyan, for eight years, from 1858 to her death, his wisest helper, he had received in 1860 an introduction to Lord Houghton, then, as Monckton Milnes, a dominating figure in those circles in which men of letters mingled with people of fashion. "The Young Man's Guide", as Swinburne called him, had hastened to acquaint the young poet with various persons of literary celebrity. Thus at Houghton's town or country house he met with some frequency not only Ruskin, whom he had known through Lady Trevelyan for some time, but Browning, Matthew Arnold, Herbert Spencer, Froude, and G. H. Lewes. Houghton, whom Carlyle wished to establish as President of the Heaven and Hell Amalgamation Society, was a lion-hunter with catholic tastes, and experience of his hospitality must

[1] Letter from Swinburne to Lord Houghton dated October 1860: "I have done some more work to *Chastelard*."

have been broadening in its effect on Swinburne. The point here, however, is that certain of these new acquaintances spread reports about Swinburne which prepared alike for the triumph and the scandal that followed in 1866.

Few can have been indifferent to the strange personality presented to them. The appearance, the conversation, of the young poet were much too extraordinary to escape attention. Just under five feet five inches in height, slightly built, with markedly sloping shoulders, and with a neck that seemed at once too thick for those shoulders and barely adequate to support the magnificent head with its weight of dense, fiery hair, Swinburne was an astonishment to the eye. Art had nearly anticipated his features in Uccello's picture of Galeazzo Malatesta at the battle of Sant' Egidio; nature was nearly to match them in the person of M. Paderewski; but in general effect, as in some curious details, he was unlike any other man of whom we have record. The great beautifully shaped forehead; the strange, level, grey-blue-green eyes, full of abstract passion; the narrowing underface and weak, subtle, sensual mouth, the mouth of one in whom sensual competence never matched sensual desire; something elfin and something bird-like in the appearance of the vivid, tremulous creature; with the alternation of barely sane exaltation and barely human mischievousness, of an excitement that could set him darting and fluttering about the room and of an almost trance-like immobility in which only the flash of the eyes and the quivering of the lips revealed the inner energy; the voice that fluted so beautifully till anger or rapture carried it up into a scream; the disconcerting screech of the laugh which announced what fools these mortals be: these could not but surprise, charm, shock, and infuriate people who saw him often enough to have experience of all his moods and idiosyncrasies yet not often enough to grow accustomed to them.

And his conversation, though it at once commanded respect by the speaker's evident familiarity with five literatures, and at its best could not but stimulate by the generosity of its enthusiasms and amuse by its wit, must frequently have agitated his audience by its mutinous tone, the audacious irony with which it treated the institutions of British respectability, the extravagance of the claims it confidently made for poets and artists either little known to the hearers or profoundly suspected by them.

Above all, those who met him in these years, 1860-1865, like so many who have read him since, were at a loss to conjecture the source of all those rhapsodies and invectives. Where his opinions were not summarily rejected as fantastic or perverse they were taken literally, crudely, separately, as, by the most of us, they have continued to be taken. For example, his strong, and sometimes preposterously enunicated, republicanism was, and still usually is, supposed to be simply a passionate preference for a particular type of political machinery; and his toleration of existing British institutions, his eventual readiness to celebrate the jubilee of "a blameless queen" and eagerness to resent a Russian insult to her, have been regarded as inconsistent. It has even, and quite lately by a writer of no ordinary ability, been contended that Swinburne should have championed the Boer States, since they were republics, instead of releasing his invectives against them in 1899. It did not dawn on those who met him in the early 'sixties, and something still hides it from most of those who read him now, that Swinburne's republic was a spiritual institution. Swinburne's republic, it cannot too soon or too emphatically be said, exists only in our retrospective and idealizing vision of Athens, our reading of his *Erechtheus*, and our hope for some remote future. Again, the remarkable people gathered at Lord Houghton's table, listening with amazement to the fiery-haired little youth who poured forth such floods of eloquence with fluttering, distracting gestures, hardly guessed what lay behind and beneath his passionate conviction that, for the artist at any rate, in a deeper sense than Marvell's,

> " All beauty, when at such a height,
> Is so already consecrate,"

the conviction that liberty is the condition of the only millennium conceivable in Swinburne's philosophy, the complete self-realization of man, and, with all this, an impish delight in the most luckily necessary enterprise of clearing the way for liberty by the subversion of so many admirable, atrophied conventions. They took his political revolt too superficially, his sensual revolt at once not seriously enough and too seriously.

Society was still, in the main, aristocratic in leadership, if not to any great extent in composition. That Swinburne was revolutionary was, therefore, no obstacle to understanding. Aristocracies, having produced nine out of every ten valid revolutionaries, can always understand a revolutionary of any high type. That he mocked at respectability was no hindrance, for an aristocracy is always more or less antinomian. It was not at this stage that Swinburne was to feel the opposition of bourgeois prejudices. It was, simply, that the secret core of his convictions, the base from which he operated, the mainspring of his revolt, was not perceived. His wit, roguishness, excitability, helping, he was pretty generally taken to be irresponsible.

And, as we have already noticed, there were facts about him which discouraged the inquiry whether the sources of all that eloquence might not lie deeper than in the moods of the moment. Constitutionally incapable of carrying more than a glass of light wine, Swinburne was apt, without anything that for the normal man would have approached excess, to become a speaker whose enthusiasms might be referred to Bacchus rather than Apollo. Further, he was the victim of nervous trouble. From early childhood he had been liable to an agitation in which he would very curiously strain down his arms, with the gestures of one who was seeking to touch the ground with his fingers without bending the body or of one who, having fallen into a hole, was trying to lift himself out of it with stiff arms. Members of his family always contended that it was this dragging down of the shoulders that gave them their very marked slope. But, whatever the effect on his figure, his health had been little affected till 1863 by the frequent spasms in which he pressed downwards with his rigid little arms, his fingers working convulsively. In that year he had the first of those mysterious epileptiform seizures which would cause him to fall to the ground and lie there as if dead, but from which he would emerge, it sometimes seemed, the better for his dreadful experience. Some of these attacks were witnessed by many, and in their minds there was no doubt that the vehemence of Swinburne, when not due to wine, proceeded from a morbid condition of his nervous system.

His brilliance, his exquisite courtesy when he was not carried away by resentment of some slight to his idols, the very real dignity of his usual attitude, the sound sense which he could and quite often did show, did not fail to win him some new friends and supporters in these years, but in the absence of any solid proof of intellectual and emotional self-mastery, many others besides Meredith feared that he was destined to notoriety gained by a fitful display of talents rather than to the fame earned by positive and ample achievement.

The appearance of *Atalanta in Calydon*, in April 1865, temporarily allayed doubts and suspicions. It has been customary to say that it took the public by storm, but that is an exaggeration. The first edition, it is true, was at once exhausted, but it consisted of no more than one hundred copies, and the second edition sold at no rapid rate. However, *Atalanta* aroused enthusiasm far outside Swinburne's own circle; the reviewers were virtually unanimous; and there were very few acknowledged judges who would have disputed Ruskin's summing up—"the grandest thing ever done by a youth, though it is Demoniac youth." The final epithet indicates a reservation made in several quarters. Extraordinarily beautiful as the tragedy on the Greek model was declared to be, with its stately and novel blank verse, its rapturous and still more novel lyrical choruses, some of those who praised it were perturbed by the temper it revealed. The arraignment of the Gods, Hebraic rather than Greek in its spirit, far from seeming to have been dictated by dramatic necessity, appeared to be the result of the poet's personal desire to make an opportunity for it. There was, too, a kind of delicate excess in many passages, very delightful to some tastes, less so to others, but in any event pointing to something unstable and un-English in its author. *Chastelard*, which had been seven years in preparation, followed speedily; and though it had no mutinous questioning of the Gods, it had very much more of that excessive way of dealing with sensation, and for subject a suicidal passion, perfectly clear-eyed and yet inflexibly, even delightedly, set on its ruinous course. Not one in a hundred of the readers *Chastelard* found can have realized, for all contemporary conditions were unfavourable to such realization, with what imaginative fidelity to the truth Swinburne had revived the romantic emotional modes of his chosen period. They had been accustomed by Tennyson and others to seeing the persons of mediaeval legend or Renaissance history endowed with the virtues and circumscribed by the moral preferences of Victorian English gentlefolk, and they could but gasp incredulously at this play in which love, instead of being an honest sentiment operative under sanction of the conscience, is a devouring madness, and the hero an epicure of its sensations content to pay for them with his life.

But worse, much worse, was to come; and, unfortunately, towards the end of this time a good many people knew it. In 1864 Swinburne, whose residence in Cheyne Walk, though broken by the visit to Italy during which he had laid the dedication of *Atalanta* before Landor, and by other absences, had tired both Rossetti and Meredith, had moved to rooms of his own, at first at 124 Mount Street, later to 22a Dorset Street. He had done nothing very shocking in Cheyne Walk, merely irritated Rossetti by leaping or fluttering about the studio during his ecstatic recitations and Meredith by emulation in epigram and by sliding down the banisters of the staircase. He had not deserved the somewhat abrupt intimation that Rossetti wanted the whole house for himself, an abruptness that was recalled to mind years later when the breach with Rossetti came. But the point is that Swinburne was now making acquaintances outside those circles in which the Pre-Raphaelites and Lord Houghton's friends were respectively the principal figures. For a surprising length of time he had been content with the sympathy of a very few auditors or readers. Now, living in his own rooms and accepting overtures from outside those groups, he was letting others know that there was very explosive matter in him. He was getting into contact with younger and less distinguished and less critical persons, where there was no slangy, authoritative correction from the sympathetic but very candid Rossetti, no growl of friendly but emphatic dissent from Morris, no worldly warning from Lord Houghton. He recited " Dolores " to a number of these new admirers, and under the influence of the poem, of the flute-like voice, of the strange, convulsive gestures, of the rapt face, the wonderful eyes, the fiery halo of hair, they sank to their knees in worship. A thrilling tableau, but rumours of the appearance of the divinity in the guise of the devil were not likely to prepare a smooth way for the forthcoming poems.

Meanwhile, Lord Houghton, genuinely anxious to help, and at certain earlier stages truly helpful to Swinburne, had injudiciously begun a kind of referendum on the question whether the poet should or should not publish the pieces constituting the first series of *Poems and Ballads*. Palgrave appears to have been consulted; Rossetti, Burne-Jones, Whistler, and Burton certainly were. The matter was talked about to weariness, and there was probably a good deal of leakage. Lord Houghton, in an access of benevolent officiousness, submitted the volume, without the poet's authority, to Murray, by whom it was rejected with speed and vigour. With the best intentions, everything was done, said, and looked that would arouse expectation of a great scandal.

The sole gain to the poet was the securing of the rather unexpected and decidedly influential, though in the event not very active, support of Ruskin. Having listened in Dorset Street to a certain number of the pieces, Ruskin accepted their paganism with " frankness ". But it is improbable that the poems read to him included " Anactoria ", or " Dolores ", or

> " To say of Shame—what is it?
> Of Virtue—we can miss it,
> Of Sin—we can but kiss it,
> And it's no longer sin."

After the appearance of the book Ruskin, generous, affectionate, as we have seen, was a good deal taken aback.

George Meredith was anxious on the eve of publication, and there exists a letter in which he warned Swinburne:

"As to the Poems . . . if they are not yet in the press, do be careful of getting your reputation firmly grounded. For I have heard 'low mutterings' already from the lion of British prudery; and I, who love your verse, would play savagely with a knife among the proofs for the sake of your fame; and because I want to see you take the first place, as you may, if you will."

Pauline, Lady Trevelyan, the wisest and most consistently helpful of his women friends till her death in 1866, shortly before the publication of the *Poems and Ballads*, was writing to him even more solicitously:[1]

"Now, do, if it is only for the sake of living down evil reports, do be wise in which of your lyrics you publish. . . . It is not worth while, for the sake of two or three poems to risk the widest circulation of the whole. You have sailed near enough to the wind in all conscience in having painted such a character for a hero as your *Chastelard*, slave to a passion for a woman he despises, whose love (if one can call it love) has no element of chivalry or purity in it; whose devotion to her is much as if a man should set himself to be crushed before Juggernaut, cursing him all the while for a loathsome despicable idol. . . . Don't give people a handle against you now."

The poet's friends, with few exceptions, were tremulous with anxiety, but the most of them had no

---

[1] Holograph letter from Pauline, Lady Trevelyan, to Swinburne, dated 6th December 1865, in Mr. Wise's collection.

clear idea of the probable occasions of offence. They suggested or acquiesced in a preliminary test of the public's endurance being made with so comparatively innocuous a poem as "Laus Veneris", in which the questionable matter might be supposed to have been made obligatory by the legend. That piece was accordingly issued by Moxon "a few months"[1] before the main volume appeared, but as the edition was very small and most of the copies seem to have been given away to friends, it is difficult to see how it can have tested the forbearance of the general public. Certainly, it remained unknown to those whose complacency was presently to be so disturbed by the *Poems and Ballads*, and who, under the rush and blare and blaze of that incursion into their tame garden and drowsy atmosphere were to develop so unprecedented a panic.

Their rallied forces could not frighten the young intruder, who kept his suddenly won place on the desecrated and abruptly unpeopled lawn, and was no whit abashed when Morley, under cover of anonymity, called him "a fiery imp from the pit", "the libidinous laureate of a pack of satyrs". But Morley alone sufficed to scare his publisher into retreat. The notorious unsigned criticism by Morley appeared in the *Saturday Review* of the 4th August 1866; Moxon, as represented by Payne, next day notified the cessation of supplies of the book to the trade. The effects of Morley's article and of Payne's craven action were felt by Swinburne to the end of his life.

Sir Edmund Gosse, who, with so many other critical gifts, has an extraordinary instinct for the detection of the external influences which shape literary reputations, has dwelt with emphasis on the immediate consequences

[1] Swinburne's own statement. There is no other evidence of the date of issue. The type is apparently that used for Moxon's edition of the *Poems and Ballads*, in which the piece was included.

of the notice in the *Saturday Review*. The most of us take a perverse pleasure in dilating on the crimes of our peccant ancestors, but, I will ask the reader to believe, it is not through the journalistic equivalent of that sort of piety that the obscurest Saturday Reviewer of to-day attaches to Morley's attack even more importance than Sir Edmund has done. Its appearance was one of the greatest misfortunes of Swinburne's career.

It appeared before the offending volume of poems was generally on sale in the bookshops. Payne's cowardice arrested supplies next day, and the reading public was largely without the means of forming its own opinion. Meanwhile other papers commented on the *Poems and Ballads* only by echoing the *Saturday*. Ten, twenty, thirty years later the phrases brought up against Swinburne were almost invariably those which had been quoted with fierce disapproval by the Saturday Reviewer; and to this day, as far as I am aware, there has never been public condemnation of those which escaped him, as, for instance, the supremely audacious allusion to perhaps the most candidly physical love-lyric in Catullus.

But it may be doubted if Swinburne fully foresaw how Morley's attack, repeated by so many others at the time, and then reproduced in paragraphs at third or fourth hand for years to come on the lower levels of criticism, would prejudice his future even after he had abandoned the themes and modified the methods to which Morley so strongly objected. Though this does not seem to have been observed even by recent writers on Swinburne, Morley's article, in the reverberations to which it gave rise, did more than bring down on his head in the middle 'sixties the wrath of those who were by temperament the enemies of sensuality and extravagance; it made it certain that, decades later, the born admirers of Swinburne's earlier verse should lament disproportionately over the serener and aloofer lyrics of his old age.

Presently there was a lull in the storm, but it had by no means blown over. The malignant and pseudonymous Robert Buchanan was to come, with his essay on "The Fleshly School of Poetry"; Mortimer Collins, whose hostility to Swinburne has escaped notice, but was pronounced and hurtful, was to appear; and there were periodically to be journalistic echoes of Morley's article. Swinburne, to be sure, was finding supporters. The youth of England was largely with him, and at Oxford and Cambridge copies of the *Poems and Ballads* were accepted in certain sets of " golden books of spirit and sense", and paid the compliment of being mingled with other explosives in 5th of November fires. The poet had homage nearer home also, as he recorded with ecstasy; a young cousin of his suffered the extreme penalty of birching rather than comply with tutorial orders to leave the magical volume unread:

" I must say though I was sorry for him, I was much tickled (otherwise tickled than he was, and elsewhere) at the idea of the blood from a young disciple having already watered the roots of the Church planted by me; and we know that ' Sanguis martyrum semen (so to speak) ecclesiæ.' "

But, with Burton and Whistler abroad and Lord Houghton assuming a kind of neutrality, Swinburne felt somewhat solitary. Refreshing himself, after the over-excitement of his life in London, by a sojourn in Wales with a new friend, George Powell, he began, however, to prepare for a further assault on British prudery which was to take shape in a novel, Balzacian to a certain extent, with inlaid poems; he began to ponder the eventually completed, never published, *Lesbia Brandon*, which was meant to scare Mrs. Grundy out of her remaining wits. Meanwhile his old political enthusiasm, quickened by contact with Mazzini,[1] was issuing in *A Song of Italy*, completed before he met Mazzini, but dedicated to him with profound reverence.

Though Swinburne probably did not realize it, he had been labelled already and so far as the general public was concerned permanently. Five of his greatest works, *Songs before Sunrise*, the second series of *Poems and Ballads*, *Bothwell*, *Erechtheus*, *Tristram of Lyonesse*, were still to come, but his poetical character was popularly fixed. *Atalanta in Calydon* was to remain the most generally honoured of his achievements; that first book of poems and ballads, the most notorious; the eulogies and objections heard in the middle 'sixties were to be repeated, with diminishing energy, for the next forty years.

[1] Swinburne was introduced to him by that odd journalist, Purnell, through Karl Blind, in accordance with an amiable conspiracy between Jowett and the future Earl of Carlisle, who both wished to divert him from the exclusive worship of the more startling pagan deities.

Chapter IV

LAUS VENERIS

IN English poetry, for the most part, love is an honest sentiment, without fear, except the fear that it will not be returned, without doubt, except the lover's doubt of his worthiness, without more power over the lover than his conscience gladly allows to it, and the coming of it is by no means the approach of a desired enemy terrible with banners. But in classical poetry, in certain great instances, and not infrequently in the modern poetry of Latin peoples, love is a disease or an insanity, a fever of which the victim would not be quit if he could, an enthusiasm for that which the intellect may scorn and the possession of which may be more ruinous than its loss. The examples range from the *odi et amo* of Catullus to the duel of sex in Baudelaire's sonnet. We have not much to put beside these things, but we have something: certain of the sonnets of Shakespeare, several poems of Donne, in a way some passages of the less familiar Coventry Patmore, some passages out of Meredith's *Modern Love*, some slighter and more perverse pieces by Mr. Arthur Symons. Two or three other English poets might be partially brought into the argument: the Keats of the letters and poems to Fanny Brawne; Browning sometimes; Rossetti perhaps.

Much as they differ from each other, in qualities and in rank, these are poets in whom, at times, love is not what the English mind ordinarily recognizes as love. The Shakespeare of the sonnets remains enigmatic, and not only because the identity of the friend, of the dark lady, is uncertain. Donne is that disconcerting poet who writes, alternately, the most minutely truthful poetry of lust and the most minutely truthful poetry of transcendental love that we have, and the average English mind has never been at ease about his sensual ardours and sick revulsions and inhuman superiority to the flesh. Patmore is another contradiction, the most sacred of our modern poets with a quite unholy knowledge of the way love as a sensation comes and goes along the nerves. Rossetti is sensual and mystical, obviously Latinate. Keats, with all the fevered fainting and luxury of his imagined lovers, has seemed as unmanly in one way as the cry of his hysterical jealousy made him seem in another way in his personal poems of love.

For the typical English mind there is something the matter with all these poets in such portions of their work as come into this argument. They seem love-sick rather than in love; or they are too fantastical about love; or slaves to a love which, condemned by their intellects, should have no power over them; or they are confusing love and lust; or they are the prisoners of their own perversity. There is something else the matter with Shelley, who is almost sexless, and who grows dizzy in his flight into some region in which he can

> " Nurse the image of unfelt caresses,
> Till dim imagination just possesses
> The half-created shadow ".

And, certainly, from the average English point of view, there is something very serious the matter with Swinburne, who stands between some of those other poets and Shelley.

Love comes to Swinburne as cerebral excitement, with the metres throbbing in his head. He is extremely sensual, but with a sensuality very curiously mental and self-sufficing. The love poetry of Browning, subtle as it often is in introspection, is eminently the poetry of the relation, desired or achieved or destroyed, between two individuals. But in Swinburne, with an exception or two to be noticed hereafter, there is hardly any sense of such relationship. He may superficially be almost as physical as Donne, but he has no fear that " else a great Prince in prison lies ": he will " nurse the image of unfelt caresses " with an ecstasy that needs no sharing. Though experience as well as imagination went to the making of the first series of *Poems and Ballads*, Swinburne was perfectly justified when, in the beautiful dedication to Burne-Jones, he wrote of his loves as " daughters of dreams and of stories ". Almost all the energies and languors of love in that intoxicating volume are such as can come only to a man whose love is given to a creature of the imagination or to the mere idea of an actual woman, the raptures and dejections being unhindered, unhelped, by anything outside himself, in the independent volition of a loved human being. In a sense very modern in his conception of love, though with a modernity partly as old as Catullus, he is altogether free from that anxiety, of having trusted all to after all a stranger, which was torture to Keats, and in one way or another has harassed so many Latinate, decadent lovers.

" *Toujours ce compagnon dont le cœur n'est pas sur!* "

But he has really yielded nothing to her keeping. He sings often enough of the insecurity of love, but, singularly, without fear or cynicism. Whether it be in that song " At Parting "—

> " Now let him pass, and the myrtles make way for us;
> Love can but last in us here at its height
> For a day and a night "—

or in the verses he inscribed in the album of Adah Isaacs Menken [1]—

> " Combien de temps, dis, la belle,
> Dis, veux-tu m'être fidèle ?—
> Pour une nuit, pour un jour,
> Mon amour.
>
> L'amour nous flatte et nous touche
> Du doigt, de l'œil, de la bouche,
> Pour un jour, pour une nuit,
> Et s'en fuit "—

the impermanence of love is accepted, with no more regret, as a rule, than a man may feel at the passing of any fine sensation. The experience is in itself enough, or too much:

> " A month or twain to live on honeycomb
> Is pleasant; but one tires of scented time."

This lover, having his memory of what was, is but little moved generally by the thought that it will or will not be again, and rarely is he concerned, and then only out of curiosity, to wonder what the experience may seem to the beloved.

An entirely human, not wholly self-regarding love comes into the love poetry of Swinburne perhaps only once, in one of the most beautiful and much the most personal of all the poems, " The Triumph of Time ". It was composed in Northumberland in 1862, and is strictly written out of experience. Shortly before that

---

[1] They were not written for her, though the contrary has often been asserted. Swinburne merely took them from his unpublished novel, *Lesbia Brandon*, when in 1867-68 he was called upon to contribute to Adah's album. In 1883, in the *Pall Mall Gazette*, in a moment of forgetfulness, he denied the authorship of the lines, but they are in the manuscript and in the unique proof of *Lesbia Brandon* owned by Mr. Wise.

date he had become acquainted with Sir John Simon, whose wife was one of Ruskin's most intimate friends and one of the firmest early supporters of Burne-Jones. At their house he had met and instantly fallen in love with their niece and adopted daughter, Miss Jane Faulkner, familiarly known as " Boo ". He had written to her verses, of which an unpublished set entitled " To Boo " survives and has been read by me. The lines are of no great poetic merit, but tender and with a wistful tentativeness:

> " You should love me a little, my one love,
>   One love for a week and a day,
>   For either has hardly begun love,
>   For the space of a sickle-sweep, say.
>   Suppose we should settle to try love,
>   It may be as sweet as its fame;
>   Set your love again beside my love
>   They may be so nearly the same."

She had been gracious to him; had given him flowers, for which he was always delicately avid; had played music to him, and though, like most poets, he was ignorant of music, he had been even more deeply affected by it than he was later by the singing of Mrs. Sartoris at Vichy, which he celebrated in enthusiastic verse nearly thirty years after hearing it. Carried away on some occasion, Swinburne had proposed to Miss Faulkner, prematurely, and she, no doubt out of mere nervousness, had burst into laughter. There had followed the kind of scene to be expected when Swinburne thought himself derided; and he had flung away to his favourite Northumberland, where anger quickly died down, and where he produced " The Triumph of Time ".

It has one of the finest stanzaic forms in Swinburne, and, what is rarer than beauty or originality of stanza construction in this poet, the form is exactly appropriate, with a kind of buoyant yet weighty recoil on itself as of a baffled wave. But the point for us here is that desire in this poem is for something truly human, the possession of which would have yielded a natural content and the loss of which matters to the heart, not merely to nerves insatiable of sensation. It is the nearest that Swinburne ever got to the expression of what people in general understand as love, but everywhere it has his own poetic idiosyncrasy stamped upon it, nowhere more clearly or with nobler effect than in the miraculous verses which describes the poet turning for consolation, inevitably, to the sea and soothed by anticipation of a life made one with the life of great waters. And " The Triumph of Time " has another distinction, among so many poems that acknowledge no limit, that cry out for subtler, fiercer, and more prolonged delight than life can yield, or proclaim an eternity of pain; it admits, and owes much of its pathos to admitting, that a term is set to passion and grief.

" And grief shall endure not for ever, I know.
As things that are not shall these things be;
We shall live through seasons of sun and of snow,
And none be grievous as they to me.
We shall hear, as one in a trance that hears,
The sound of time, the rhyme of the years;
Wrecked hope and passionate pain will grow
As tender things of a spring-tide sea."

There is another piece in the first series of *Poems and Ballads* which presents love, not as an isolated sensual ecstasy, but through the defined relation of two lovers. " Félise " is the utterance of a man to a woman he loved and loves no more, who did not love him then and has learned to love him now. The two personalities are kept dimmer than they would have been in Browning, but they are adequately suggested, and there is a setting for their emotions, not particularized, for that was never the mature Swinburne's way, but brought before us with his peculiar feeling for the needs of the poem as a whole, as in that line which summons up " a fire of flowers and glowing grass ". With no more than the memory of desire left in him, the man can muse quietly, wistfully, without rebellion, on the impermanence of love. His thoughts are allowed to wander a little too widely, but they circle back to the mystery of passing passion through many delicately beautiful and musical ways of return.

And there is one other poem in Swinburne, considerably later in date of composition, expressive of a deeper experience than that of " Félise ", which is also a poem of definite relationship in love. I refer to that deeply felt, pitilessly clear-eyed, severely and intricately wrought masterpiece, " At a Month's End ", in the second series of *Poems and Ballads*. It is a study of profound incompatibility. The man who speaks in it has loved a splendid soulless creature, without illusion, and knows that neither can hold the other. He will not allow himself to be deluded by sentimentality into the belief that he can change her, or she change him.

> " For a new soul let whoso please pray,
> We are what life made us, and shall be.
> For you the jungle and me the sea-spray,
> And south for you and north for me."

That panther-like woman must be accepted simply for what she is, or left wholly alone, and he is leaving her, at a month's end, on a night of marvellously evoked storm in the world and in their hearts—

> " Our hearts were full of windy weather,
> Clouds and blown stars and broken light."

But this one thing he throws her, his song as a feather of a tameless seabird, which, in the magnificently imagined circumstances of her after-loving, may fall on her fiery sleep as the northern sea-mew's on tropic sands. The hold on the situation, the resolute masculine recognition of its true nature, no less than the curious compression of the endlessly undulating verse, as if each line were overtaken before its natural subsidence, give this poem, to my mind, a place with " Hertha " and " Ave atque Vale ", among the very highest of its author's achievements.

But it is not of such poems as " The Triumph of Time ", " Félise ", and " At a Month's End " that any reader thinks first at a mention of Swinburne the amorist; rather of those pieces in which the poet, fevered with an abstract excitement, is the celebrant of an uncircumstanced, unrestrained passion for figures of which he realizes hardly anything but the sex. Morley and others in the 'sixties threw at this Swinburne the reproach of boyishness; we may call this part of his work boyish without any implication that it has puerile pruriency in it. Shelley's love is often enough a boy's, the enthusiasm of a boy who is unaware of sex or who has not related it to his emotion. Swinburne, in these poems, or many of them, is intoxicated with sex, but with an apprehension of it such as comes to a boy in a dream of fair women. He touches lips that are not less ideal because they are infamous, bosoms that have pillowed no head but a dreamer's. If you look in this poem or that merely to what is called the subject, or merely to the recurrence of certain words, Swinburne is what in the scandal of the 'sixties and early 'seventies he was summed up as being, " fleshly ". But the subject of a poem, apart from its expression, is a critical figment, and words in a poem have not their separate dictionary values but the value that comes from their adjustment to the metrical pattern and their suffusion in the imaginative atmosphere of the whole poem. And because Swinburne had genius for this in general no doubt questionable enterprise, the things that lay inert in the frigid hand of lust were redeemed by him, vivified, set back with all other beautiful things burningly in the divine hand of Browning's phrase, and the words that might have been those of cold coarse physical inventory were made to lilt and gleam and dance in the rapturous ritual of a service, religious *à rebours*, but religious all the same. A prose synopsis of "Anactoria", done badly enough, might be a piece of pornography, but "Anactoria" itself is a poem exalting every mind capable of receiving it. With these things we are in the region of that paradox by which evil, conceived with enough intensity, becomes, by that intensity, a kind of good. Fire is the symbol of purification, and wherever it truly burns there is an altar. It is callousness, dead coldness that is the distinguishing characteristic of lust.

But, in defending these poems, it is necessary to be on guard against attributing too serious an intention to their writer. In his mere intention there was undoubtedly rather often a youthful desire to disturb all the solid, somnolent respectability he saw about him. Not a few of the peccant pieces horrify us because they were designed to horrify us. The prime impulse was now and then indistinguishable from that which we have all felt in the company of the perfectly earnest, to hazard a risky anecdote or take up a position against which all the most reputable authorities can be quoted. Swinburne was not Donne, torn by the desire of the body because his soul was destined to be enamoured of holiness; he was not Baudelaire, wounding himself as he deliberately, ironically violated that exact and rigid and almost mathematical relation of things which, in his sense of it, was morality. But, far less deeply concerned as he consciously might be for the eventual significance of his poems of sensual revolt, he could seldom write a line before his genius was involved in the naughtiness, before a gesture intended to flatten out the bourgeois intelligence became a salute to the eternal principle of beauty. I have read unprinted and utterly unprintable verses of his in which, though his purpose was no more than Rabelaisian jest, devilment turns into an unintended evocation of the devil, who, it has been well said, is nearer to God, by the whole height from which he fell, than the average man.

It is, naturally, of " Dolores " that one thinks, at the right age, when there is a question of Swinburne as the defiant amorist. It is, in its way, a wonderful poem. It has a metre, brilliantly developed out of light examples in Gay and Praed, which is the very daughter of Herodias among metres and can dance away any young head that is not wholly deaf. The rush and spin and flash of the poem are astonishing. But if one has been persistent enough to live to forty, one loves it perhaps rather for what it was to one, once, than for what it is at that sober age. For all the technical excellence of it, it comes in time to seem comparatively ingenuous in technique. That, however, only shows that the years do not necessarily bring wisdom. For, though the thing, an example once provided, may seem easy to do, the " Dolores " metre and stanza have difficulties proved to be almost insuperable by a multitude of parodies and even by some of Swinburne's own subsequent attempts. In three dedications, that of the first series of *Poems and Ballads* to Burne-Jones, that of *Astrophel* to William Morris, and that of *A Channel Passage* to the memory of Morris and Burne-Jones, he again used the form finely, showing in the first of these dedicatory poems at any rate that it was capable of yielding an effect quite other than that of " Dolores ". But Swinburne was guilty of something like unintentional self-parody when he employed the " Dolores " form in " The Garden of Cymdoce ", and no intentional parodist, not even H. D. Traill, has ever been able to capture the inner secrets of that obvious-seeming form.

" Dolores ", with an element of boyish paradox, has an admixture of perverted mysticism not common in Swinburne. It is, in a way, the sensual and excited reply to such a lament as George Herbert's

> " Though there were forty heavens or more,
> Sometimes I rise above them all;
> Sometimes I hardly reach a score,
> Sometimes to hell I fall."

Swinburne's grief is that, though sometimes he can sink below the fortieth hell, at times he can hardly descend lower than the twentieth, and in his human frailty he occasionally rises into heaven. " Come down and redeem us from virtue ", is the cry of the poet of " Dolores ", a cry, after all, of the spirit.

Very far as " Dolores " is from being Swinburne's finest lyric, it does, in some respects, deserve the prominence it has had from the time of its first appearance. The manner of its construction, by the accumulation of appropriate imagery round a central motive, here the refrain, in every alternate stanza, " Our Lady of Pain ", instead of by the development of an idea, which each stanza shall carry farther, is typical of much of Swinburne's work, and it may be doubted whether he ever used that method with greater assurance. More narrowly, with reference to the small group of frenetic amorous poems, " Dolores " is typical of one section of his poetry in a discontent with the worst matching the discontent of some saints with the best of which humanity is capable. The poet of " Félise " could boast:

> "But there is nothing, nor shall be,
> So sweet, so wicked, but my verse
> Can dream of worse."

The poet of "Dolores", and less explicitly the author of some other pieces in these first *Poems and Ballads*, can but lament that the dream must remain untranslated into reality, and in other pieces that there must be the anti-climax of waking from it.

> "Ah, do thy will now; slay me if thou wilt,
> There is no building now the walls are built,
> No quarrying now the corner stone is hewn,
> No drinking now the wine's whole blood is spilt;
> Ah God, ah God, that day should be so soon." [1]

There are lighter and sweeter moods of love in that initial volume of lyrics, put into swift, light-footed metres; and, unique in Swinburne, there is the tender, half-rueful, half-smiling, very boyish "Interlude":

> "And the best and the worst of this is
> That neither is most to blame
> If you've forgotten my kisses
> And I've forgotten your name."

But it is to the other and much more startling poems that the discussion turns back.

Do they correspond with his own experience? A question to be treated with some of Swinburne's contempt, and yet perhaps to be answered with the object of preventing its repetition. Swinburne himself said, looking back on these poems in his old age, that some were direct reproductions of fact and others pure excursions of fancy, and that critics had frequently

---

[1] Swinburne doubtless took this refrain from the thirteenth-century Provençal poem with the burden:

> "Oy dieus, oy dieus, de l'alba tant tost ve!"

found realism in the latter and mere fantasy in the former. We should need to be God's spies to distinguish, with any confidence, between what came to him out of his physically limited but very curious experience and what came to him in dreams or after reading Catullus, Gautier, Baudelaire, and his half, but only half, ironically admired *Justine*.[1] But something, though it may only be negative, should be said of the woman who has sometimes, quite absurdly, been given a great place in his life.

Adah Isaacs Menken, by no means the only woman with Semitic connexions among Swinburne's more bohemian friends, for these included Rebecca Solomon, Simeon's sister, afforded the poet and certain of his circle a good deal of amusement for a while, and he was not insensitive to the pathos of her wretched end. He made himself pleasant to her, allowed himself to be photographed with her, wrote some lines in her album, glanced through the proofs of her sprawling poems, but except in so far as the poor, beautiful, tawdry creature may have suggested to him the thought of how the modern world limits the opportunities of lights o' love, she meant little enough to him.

Adah was two years older than Swinburne, and Burne-

---

[1] For this work, to which perhaps (though Mr. Wise favours an earlier acquaintance) Lord Houghton introduced him in 1860, Swinburne had a smiling yet fanatical passion. He quoted it constantly for some years, and he lavished reproaches on friends who did not share his Sadist raptures. Thus he wrote to Watts-Dunton as late as 1874: "I deeply grieve at the incurable blindness and stiff-neckedness of a new Pharaoh which keeps you still in the gall of prejudice and the bonds of decency, and debars you from the just appreciation of a Great Man . . . a deeper study of whose immortal work would have shown you

> 'How charming in divine philosophy;
> Not harsh and crabbèd, as dull fools suppose,
> But musical as is Priapus' pipe '".

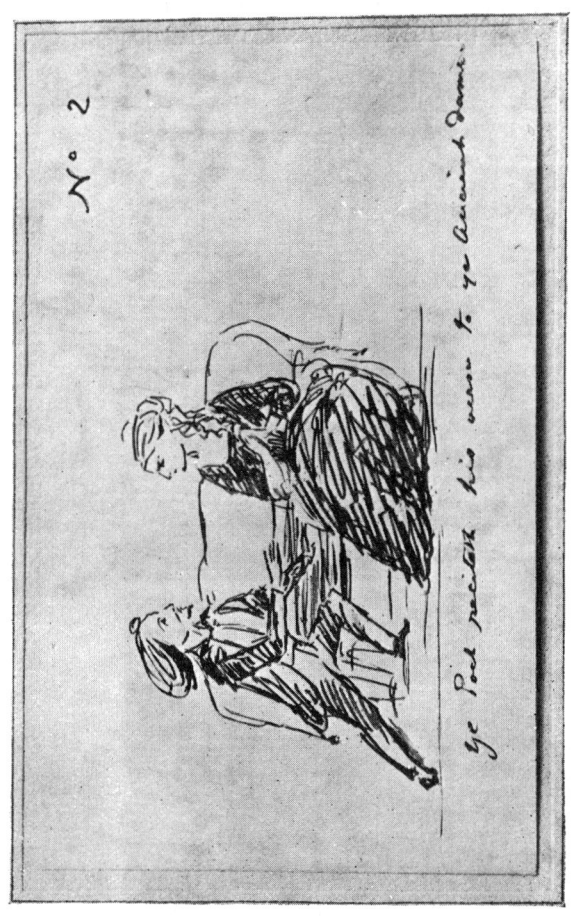

SWINBURNE READING HIS POEMS TO ADAH ISAACS MENKEN
From a Caricature by Burne-Jones in Mr. T. J. Wise's Collection

Jones, in some cartoons he made of her in relation to the poet, called her " ye Ancient Dame ". Authorities, if there can be said to be any where almost every fact is tinged with fiction, differ as to her parentage. She may have begun as plain Adelaide McCord; more probably, she began as Dolores Adios Fuertes, the child of a Spanish Jew and a French mother. Her birthplace was Chartrain, now Milneburg, near New Orleans, U.S.A. She was precocious, and in addition to French and Spanish, which she knew from early childhood, had acquired some Greek, Latin, and Hebrew before she was twelve. She and her sisters were put on the stage, and marrying, at the age of seventeen, a Jewish musician, Alexander Isaac Menken, she turned to journalism in defence of her husband's people, and elicited from Lord Rothschild the declaration that she was " the inspired Deborah of her race ". She soon divorced Menken, but always retained his name, altering Isaac to Isaacs. In 1859 she married Heenan, next year the opponent of Sayers in one of the most famous of all prize fights; but he divorced her in 1862. She had anticipated her liberty by going through a form of marriage with the now half-forgotten American humorist, Orpheus C. Kerr,[1] and had returned to the stage. Her first real success came with her appearance in 1861 at Albany as " Mazeppa "; her figure and her daring as a horse-woman were her only considerable assets as a performer, and she belonged to the circus rather than the stage. She first came to London in 1864, to Astley's. By that date Swinburne had written most of the poems in which we have been invited to trace her influence. As regards her own irregular, often quite preposterous, work in

---

[1] He divorced her in 1865. Next year, having returned to America from England for a while, she married in New York one James Barclay. Her one sincere, utterly unselfish lover was Thomson, Swinburne's secretary.

verse, though internal evidence against Swinburne's part authorship is overwhelming, it may help to kill a persistent theory to record that the late G. R. Sims had cuttings from the American papers showing that nearly every piece Menken published in *Infelicia*, 1868, had appeared in American journals long before she was in touch with Swinburne. It was Thomson, for a while Swinburne's secretary, who introduced the poet to her, and it was she, in that infatuation which Purnell has described in a letter, who forced on the friendship. When she had died, in that miserable fifth-floor room of a lodging-house in Paris, Rue de Bondy, opposite the stage-door of the Porte St. Martin, and had been buried in the Jewish cemetery of Mont-Parnasse, with two words of Swinburne's " Ilicet " over her, " Thou knowest ", the words of her actual appeal to divine judgment from human, it was spread about that she had been Swinburne's Egeria. He did not publicly contradict any of the allegations then made, any more than he had contradicted the pleasant Parisian report of an earlier month that he was to appear as Cupid in a ballet with her. But he left no room for doubt in the minds of his friends. The terms in which he corrected error on the point would have been appreciated by the public which applauded Restoration comedy; they are difficult to reproduce, even with prudent omissions, for the public of to-day. The general tone of these denials may, however, be surmised from a condensed paraphrase of one of them, in which he hinted that other than distant relations with her would have been as disagreeable to him as intimacy with the lady then occupying the highest position in the country.

What she and her like did for Swinburne, and others more than she, for Adah Isaacs Menken, in cultivating Gautier, Dumas, Dickens, and Swinburne, and setting up as poet, put herself in a false position, was to offer him, sometimes, the subtlest of all forms of flattery to a creative artist—the assurance of the truth of some vision of his. It has happened with many poets, many painters, that they have invented a type before meeting it in actual life; and I do not doubt that it was so with Swinburne. He responded with such transfiguring generosity of imagination to every woman of the half-world or under-world who carried, unconsciously, some sign of descent from the ancient or mediaeval queens of her order because his mind was haunted by the image of Cleopatra or Messalina in degradation. No special intimacy was needed to set his imagination working in a poetic restoration of such dynasties, and we know from his own statement, in *Notes on Poems and Reviews*, that the mere sight of a beautiful, vicious face in a London crowd, a face that recalled the features of Faustina, sufficed to inspire " Faustine ".

For the rest, all that can be said by anyone respectful of the dignity of life and of literature must be said in Swinburne's own words, in quotation from his autobiographic poem, " Thalassius ". It presents to us the experience of one who, foiled in the higher ways of love, has gone down, sick at heart, to the no longer consoling sea, and there is suddenly involved in the riot of the Bassarides:

" So came all those in on him; and his heart,
  As out of sleep suddenly struck astart,
  Danced, and his flesh took fire of theirs, and grief
  Was as a last year's leaf
  Blown far down the wind's way; and he set
  His pale mouth to the brightest mouth it met
  That laughed for love against his lips, and bade
  Follow; and in following all his blood grew glad
  And as again a sea-bird's. . . .
Till on some winter's dawn of some dim year

> He let the vine-bit on the panther's lip
> Slide, and the green rein slip,
> And set his eyes to seaward, nor gave ear
> If sound from landward hailed him, dire or dear;
> And passing forth of all those fair fierce ranks
> Back to the grey sea-banks,
> Against a sea rock lying, aslant the steep,
> Fell after many sleepless dreams on sleep."

"Hesperia", in the first *Poems and Ballads*, is a poem expressive of the desire for such escape from the fever and cruelty of passion, but by way of a nobler and tenderer love, not by way of a return to nature. The speaker there looks back on his self-chosen servitude to Dolores, to our Lady of Pain, to cry out against the peril of return to it.

> "She laughs, and her hands reach hither, her hair blows hither and hisses,
> As a low-lit flame in a wind, back blown till it shudder and leap;
> Let her lips not again lay hold of my soul, nor her poisonous kisses,
> To consume it alive and divide from thy bosom, Our Lady of Sleep."

But "Hesperia" ends with the question whether escape be possible, and for Swinburne certainly, as a poet, it was not easy. Whatever in that first volume of lyrics may be ascribed merely to "the light fire in the veins of a boy", behind portions of the book was the curiosity of the mind that would taste forbidden or ambiguous fruit. The sonnets, written during a visit to Paris in March 1863, when he made friends with Fantin-Latour and Whistler and met Gautier, in which he dealt with that "sweet marble monster of both sexes ", as Shelley had called it, the Hermaphroditus, and the poem entitled "Fragoletta" are wanderings into a doubtful region in which Swinburne undoubtedly took a perverse personal interest, and " Anactoria " was not born simply of admiration for the poetry of Sappho, though its origin was in attempts to translate such fragments as we have of her work. The confusion of that which in nature is normally divided, the inversion of normal human instinct, had its attraction, intellectually, for Swinburne. It was not, we may be sure, just to round off his mischievous assaults on a Philistine respectability that Swinburne wrote these poems, and indeed their perversity is, in Gautier's words of Baudelaire, so learned and so veiled in the forms of art that it has remained barely intelligible to many casual readers. I do not say that the sonnets written at the Louvre or "Fragoletta" are poetically of special importance, but they and "Anactoria" are in motive more serious, nearer to the spirit of Baudelaire, than most of the poems which fling an obvious challenge to accepted morality. It would, however, be an error to suppose that everything in the first *Poems and Ballads* which sets us thinking of Baudelaire was in fact due to his influence. It is, at any rate, certain that " Les Femmes Damnées ", which might seem answerable for a good deal in Swinburne, was not known to him till 1864, when, through Mr. W. M. Rossetti, he became possessed of the original and speedily suppressed edition of *Les Fleurs du Mal*.

"Anactoria", though it has at least one very bad couplet, and though it exhibits something of the character of a mosaic of verse in which a number of couplets might be transposed without seriously affecting the general impression, will always deserve prominence in this poet's work. Simply as a piece of versification it is of extraordinary interest. The basis, clearly, is Dryden, but the modulation is of extreme originality, even when, as in one of the most magnificent of these couplets,

> " Take thy limbs living, and new-mould with these
> A lyre of many faultless agonies ",

the basis is most evident. Every secret of flow and check and recoil and onward rush had been mastered by Swinburne before he produced such things, such miracles of versification, as:

> " I would find grievous ways to have thee slain,
> Intense device, and superflux of pain;
> Vex thee with amorous agonies and shake
> Life at thy lips, and leave it there to ache;
> Strain out thy soul with pangs too soft to kill,
> Intolerable interludes, and infinite ill;
> Relapse and reluctation of the breath,
> Dumb tunes and shuddering semitones of death,"

and as,

> " Bound with her myrtles, beaten with her rods,
> The young men and the maidens and the gods,"

and as,

> " But in the light and laughter, in the moan
> And music, and in grasp of lip and hand,
> And shudder of water that makes felt on land
> The immeasurable tremor of all the sea,
> Memories shall mix and metaphors of me."

Sapphic up to a point, with a rare skill in the utilization of what among the fragments of Sappho was to the purpose, the poem is modern and Swinburnian in the expression of the cruelty of passion, but it is with a superb energy of imagination that it seizes on the pretext given by the famous phrase, " Thee too the years shall cover ", for the final assertion of her immortality put in the mouth of Lesbian poet.

Begun in an endeavour to render Sappho's so-called " Ode to Anactoria ", begun again, perhaps, chiefly with the desire to analyse a type of forbidden passion, " Anactoria " became a celebration of poetic immortality rather than of passion. We may turn back from it, for the essential part of Swinburne's thought about passion, to the poem from which I have taken the title of this chapter. It is not explicit there, but " Laus Veneris ", as he explained in the *Notes on Poems and Reviews*, originated in the idea of Venus " grown diabolic in ages that would not accept her as divine ". If Swinburne had not been so confidently summed up long ago, if people in general were not so sure that there is little for the intellect in the frenzied amorousness of the *Poems and Ballads*, one might be more hopeful of bringing home to them the simple truth that this idea is of higher value than nine-tenths of the ideas on which poets have been promoted or degraded into the company of philosophers or moralists. Deceive ourselves as we may, the prime instincts of humanity are invincible, and the only choice open to us is a choice whether they shall be satisfied in an abandonment to the divinity or indulged in a dishonouring surrender to a power which becomes diabolic because we so conceive of it.

The Victorians had agreed to believe, while their pens were in their hands, that the way of a man with a maid either left her a maid or converted her into the angel in the house. Swinburne made a violent end of that, and it was more of a service than is now quite easy to realize. It is not only in that respect that the poet of the first series of *Poems and Ballads* has the right to complain of our ingratitude. The volume, it must be conceded, is by no means its author's chief claim on us. The finest of the second series of *Poems and Ballads* and of the *Songs before Sunrise* arise out of a greater depth of life, use a purer diction and maturer technique, exhibit nobler qualities of intellect. But the first *Poems and Ballads* cannot be dismissed as little more than the brilliant escapade of an exceedingly naughty boy.

It is a book, we have been told to weariness, that one outgrows. Well, of course, " the breasts of the nymphs in the brake " occupy a great deal less of one's attention at forty than they did at twenty; and it is not only a particular kind of ardour that dies down in us with the passage of the years, for we become in time incapable of adherence to the melancholy of youth. " Happy days or else to die " means less and less to us, as we come to desire significance rather than happiness in our living. But no man who has read the first *Poems and Ballads* at the right age, which may very well be nearer fifteen than twenty, is quite what he would have been without that experience. He may disparage the experience, he may even forget it, but what the book did to him is not thereby obliterated.

Nor will I subscribe to the assumption that those old agitations of myrtles and roses must be for all of us in maturity beyond recovery. If I may venture to be egotistical, and here, surely, a man can but speak for himself, I have but to take up the volume to feel much of the excitement it gave an electrified and partly terrified boy of fifteen. I do not now think it the most precious book in the world or even of its author's. I am not now always in the mood for so insistent a music. But I should suppose myself unfitted for the enjoyment of all poetry whatsoever if I had outgrown the book in the sense of having become irresponsive to the flushed beauty and pulsing metres of it. To read it is to recover, though incompletely, one's youth: and a book which can restore something of his youth to the reader is not a book which he can afford to outgrow. Nor will he wholly outgrow it unless he has been cursed with total lack of imagination, total inability to enter into emotions other than those aroused by his present circumstances and recent experiences. " From ourselves we pass away "; some of us no doubt do; but the reproach is on us rather than on the work of art which once meant so much to us if it shall thus have become meaningless.

A golden book of youth, it is also the book which more than any other single volume of our poetry exposes the variety of our English prosodical resources. It is indeed true that, when compared with portions of his later work, this first volume of Swinburne's lyrics seems here and there almost coarse in technique. Now and then it is overcharged with a rather too obvious metrical energy. But it has that which no poet may possess except in the first hours of his discovery that he is a lord of language, a master of the science of his instrument —an ecstatic joy in the use of all the means at his command. Metrical perfection has not yet become a habit with Swinburne; almost every poem in this wonderful initial volume is an astonishment to its author as well as to the reader at a first perusal. He riots in his mastery. He goes to the extremes of complication and simplicity in stanzaic forms, crowds his rhymes together and then separates them more widely than almost any predecessor, sets the lines dancing, and then, as in the admirable " Stage Love ", makes them move with a slow, emphatic, scornful stamp; he invents new stanzaic moulds with amazing facility, and then shows that he can be just as original in adaptation, as of Dryden's lyric scheme in the famous song from *The Spanish Friar*, or of FitzGerald's quatrain.

The book that is so thrilling a revelation at once of the life of the senses and of the resources of English metre can never cease to take captive the minds of successive generations of boys with a poetical temper.

But the day is already past when it was evident what that first volume of Swinburne's lyrics had done for English poetic diction, bringing into it not only the sumptuousness that might have been expected, but also a powerfully effective element of what had been deemed prosaic words—"bloat", "wince", and so forth. The delightful shock of such novelty inevitably disappears as the novel word is incorporated into the language of poetry. But the service to poetry is not diminished by ceasing to be easily discernible, and it was in the first series of *Poems and Ballads* that Swinburne rendered it.

Chapter V

SONGS BEFORE SUNRISE

THE political opinions of Swinburne were almost all formed at an extremely early age; and so far as they derived from any external source, were drawn from minds not only much older than his own, but of an obsolescent cast. Here, as so often elsewhere in Swinburne, account must be taken of a marked reversionary tendency accompanying his revolutionary ardour and visions of progress. Revolt was in his blood, but he received a strong bias from his vehemently rebellious grandfather, and well before he left Eton was confirmed in devotion to a turbulent, old-fashioned, superficially very simple republicanism by his very precocious enthusiasm for Landor and Hugo. As it happened, not very fortunately, Hugo did more than strengthen his boyish admirer in a faith essentially that of 1848 when it was not that of 1789. The chance that put into Swinburne's hands, when he was sixteen, such a volume as *Les Châtiments*, determined, in certain respects, what was to be almost invariably in the 'sixties and 'seventies Swinburne's tone in expressing the stronger of his political opinions. From that moment it became inevitable that arrogance and elaborate over-emphasis should weaken those portions of his magnificent political verse in which the attack was directed against causes or persons already lashed by the many-corded and somewhat too widely flourished scourge of the master. But though there was this kind of emulation of Hugo, there was never, and the fact is testimony to Swinburne's originality as an artist, any imitation of

Hugo's substance. The most careless reader of the two must observe that the contents of the most nearly comparable poems of the great French and the great English poet differ very widely. Hugo is frequently, and to the satisfaction of the ordinary reader, in some sense or the other personal, occasional, a particular man or god calling or hurling down fire from heaven on particularized heads. Swinburne, eminently justified in saying that *Songs before Sunrise* was himself whereas his other volumes were books, is yet almost always in a way impersonal, thrilled with abstract passion, denouncing crowned or mitred criminals who may indeed have human names but who are images of evil rather than definite historical personages with limitations in their capacity for wickedness.

The Eton boy who had decided, once for all, that Napoleon III was the vilest and most cruel of creatures, was provided at Oxford with confirmation of his beliefs, notably by John Nichol, but also by several other distinguished members of the " Old Mortality ". At Oxford, too, his sympathy with Italian aspirations developed with fiery exuberance. At an early stage of his Oxford career he had installed a portrait of Mazzini in his rooms, and begun to pay it honours far exceeding those which Catholic piety might lavish on the relics of a saint. His general devotion to Italy, due to his mother, who had taught him Italian in early childhood, had been directed by republican rapture into a worship of Mazzini; of which the " Ode to Mazzini ", composed early in 1857, is the earliest extant expression.[1] About a year after the production of this poem Orsini, unconsciously obeying the Providential directions to give Swinburne a

[1] Complete text first printed in *Posthumous Poems*, 1917; original holograph manuscript in Mr. Wise's collection. Unlike the mature odes of Swinburne, this piece is irregular: Pindaric in the conventional and bad sense.

new and strong reason for relating his French and Italian enthusiasms, attempted to assassinate Napoleon III. His portrait was at once added to the republican shrine in Swinburne's rooms; and years later, when Swinburne was living in Great James Street, in London, the poet got a good deal of healthy exercise by leaping up in generally unsuccessful efforts to kiss the likeness of the would-be tyrannicide.

There were other expressions of republican zeal during the Oxford years, but acquaintance with Rossetti, Morris, and Burne-Jones diverted Swinburne for eight or nine years from the writing of the mass of political poetry he would otherwise have produced as soon as he was free of the experiments after the Elizabethan dramatic model. During this fortunate interval, Swinburne's political thought was clarified by Mazzini, to whom he was introduced in 1867, by events in Italy, and most of all by his natural intellectual development.

That development did not take the form of progress beyond the political principles which he had adopted with passion as a boy. On the surface, what he wrote in maturity was what he would have written, with less technical assurance, in adolescence. But beneath the superficial simplicity there was, by the time he began writing the *Songs before Sunrise*, a body of profound and subtle thought, hardly yet acknowledged by criticism.

With his abstracting intellect, Swinburne in the late 'sixties had learned to see contemporary events in his beloved Italy under the aspect of eternity. It has been said by a critic that the *Songs before Sunrise* need elaborate historical notes: that is precisely what it would be most undesirable to append to them. They take incidents or weary intervals in the struggle for Italian freedom and unity as their occasions, but what they give us is a series of sublime hymns to a freedom such as no warrior in that cause conceived of, and the ideal of a republic which no mere political machinery could ever realize. In those incomparable poems every excellence of Swinburne has its finest opportunity. To the speed and splendour which were ever at his command there are added a lucidity, a purity of diction, a chastity of style far less common with him, and his reliance on undefined natural symbols was never so well justified as in poems which relate the highest passions of which humanity is capable to the prime energies and the sublimest phenomena of nature. Of this poet, in these poems, as of no other the modern world has known, we may say what we said of his ideal man:

" His heart is equal with the sea's
And with the sea-wind's, and his ear
Is level to the speech of these,
And his soul communes and takes cheer
With the actual earth's equalities...."

This proud poise, of an attitude, utterly natural, utterly noble, in which man accepts his position in the universe, without a suspicion of the cringing and the insolence summed up complacently by a later poet in the antithesis of

" Magnificent out of the dust we came,
And abject from the spheres ",

gives to the finest portions of the *Songs before Sunrise* an elevation and a rightness for which it is idle to seek anywhere else in modern poetry. The moralist and the uplifter may make the claims of their kind for aspiration, but in art there can never be any comparison between the soul that has goaded itself up alien heights and the soul that reaches them with the composure in excitement of one entering on his heritage. As in the life of religion there can be no parallel between those who earn heaven, by no matter what good works, and those elect spirits, a St. Francis or a St. Catherine or a St. Teresa, who breathe heaven's as their natural air, so in art it is altogether impossible to liken the poet of no matter how strenuous and ambitious and successful spiritual endeavour to the poet of immediate natural spiritual attainment.

The religion of Swinburne, and, if we discard the conventional meaning of the term, he is in the *Songs before Sunrise* a profoundly religious poet, acknowledges no creative or moral energy external to the universe. Theism of any kind is impossible for him because he denies not only the possibility of any revelation, but the possibility of the human mind conceiving of any God who shall not be made in man's likeness. Divinity, for him, is diffused through the universe, conscious of itself in man, to be apprehended in its totality in the conception of the world-soul, Hertha, as in the central and supreme lyric of his philosophy.

His religion and his political faith are never to be considered apart, the intimate relation of them being the explanation of the devotional note heard again and again in his appeals to the principle of liberty and of the ferocity with which he denounces any failure, as it seems to him, by an individual or a nation to discharge what, on this view, is the religious duty of furthering the conscious effort of mankind to realize the central and sacred purpose of the divinity innate in the universe. That republic of his, as I have already said, is to what is ordinarily meant by a republic much what, under another conception, the Kingdom of God is to what is ordinarily meant by monarchy. Liberty is to be sought with such rapture because it is immensely more than the politician takes it to be, because without it man cannot further the purpose of the universe of which he is part. However much, on a lower level, Swinburne may incite men to the winning of merely political freedom, as conceived by semi-materialistic revolutionaries, his real call is to the removal of all which, shackling the full development of the individual, the nation, the whole body of mankind, hinders the progress of the universe towards complete expression. There is no definite divine, far-off event to which the whole creation moves; growth has "no guerdon but only to grow",[1] and no conceivable limit. There is no salvation, except for those who have been, in their degree, saviours of man, and have thus accomplished their part in the endless task. But the demand of duty is inexorable, the dedication of himself to the common service the supreme obligation laid on every man.

Man comes to a sense of this only very slowly, and at various stages of his progress towards truth has need to embody his imperfect ideas of it in temporarily valid theologies; his error is to suppose that these have worth beyond their natural life.[2] To assail theologies that, in unnatural survival, hold man back from freedom is the duty of the poet, and Swinburne, with his impishness and his virtuosity in invective, finds it a delight, and too often allows the suggestiveness of his metaphors and the urgency of his metres to carry him to indefensible extremes; but he is not incapable of that wiser and more magnanimous attitude in which, as in his noble sonnet on the deaths of Newman and Carlyle, night's childless children are bidden to go honoured hence and leave man with the sun.

A religious poet does not become irreligious because instead of saying "dear city of Zeus", he says "dear city of Man"; but when his thought is too novel to be easily apprehended, when it is conveyed not in calm expository verse but in ecstatic lyrical measures, when it

---

[1] "Hertha".
[2] "Hertha", "The Hymn of Man", in *Songs before Sunrise*: and, thirty years later, "The Altar of Righteousness".

is accompanied by unguarded and superficially blasphemous assaults on all theologies which assume the existence of an entirely external divinity, he will have to wait for understanding. And he will have to wait the longer if his religion is everywhere interwoven with his politics, if his capital expression of it, like Swinburne's "Hertha", is perhaps less a religious poem than a rapturous deliverance of the politics of that city of Man; nor will his politics be more fortunate in their immediate reception if in a volume which, like the *Songs before Sunrise*, appears to be a commentary on the events of his time, the real theme is one transcending those events, and if some of the profoundest of his political emotions come to us in what seems to be a merely dramatic way, and in drama on a subject so remote from us as that of *Erechtheus*.

Sir Edmund Gosse, who has read everything, who forgets nothing, and who can at once put his hand on the exception to every generalization, has recorded the fact that the higher and less obvious politico-religious thought of Swinburne was divined by Professor W. K. Clifford in the work that writer published in 1877, six years after the appearance of *Songs before Sunrise*. But Clifford was almost alone in that period, and to this moment it is common to find the *Songs before Sunrise* crudely referred to nothing more than events in the Italy and France of those days, while the lofty "Prelude" and "Epilogue" to the volume are commonly not seen to be expressions of a proud patience under the postponement of hopes which neither Mazzini nor any other individual, but only the age-long efforts of all men, could fully realize.

There are, of course, strictly occasional poems in the great book. For first instance, there is the "Ode on the Insurrection in Candia", which was written in response to a definite appeal to the poet, by supporters of the insurrectionaries.[1] George Meredith wrote to him on its appearance that it was "the most nobly sustained lyric in our language", adding, "broader, fuller verse I do not know".[2] But Swinburne himself later on felt a considerable and on the whole justified distaste for it. It has that learned structure which was thenceforth to distinguish his odes, but its author has not taken fire from the theme. Far otherwise is it with the rapidly, clearly, and strictly argued lyric, "An Appeal", written in the autumn of the same year. The thing could not be more direct and pertinent and telling if it had been a forensic effort on behalf of the Fenian prisoners for whom it pleads, but it is pure song throughout, and I do not think it too much to say that, more than any other of his lyrics, it shows the prose intelligence of Swinburne feeding his poetical faculty with material which is at once and completely absorbed into the imaginative flame.[3]

Between the few strictly occasional poems and those more typical competitions, the "Prelude", the "Epilogue", "Hertha", "The Pilgrims", "Mater Trium-

---

[1] The original of this appeal, dated 8th January 1867, is in Mr. Wise's collection. The ode was printed in the March issue of the *Fortnightly Review*.

[2] Letter in Mr. Wise's collection.

[3] The bibliography of this item in the *Songs before Sunrise* is interesting. The poem was composed, as the dated manuscript shows, on the 20th November 1867. It appears in the *Morning Star* on the 22nd. A broadside, on which Swinburne's name was spelled "Swinbourne", was published simultaneously (probably distributed a day earlier) from the offices of the paper. An issue in pamphlet form followed speedily, but on quite what date is uncertain. These, of course, were authorized issues. But in December, as appears from the unique copy in Mr. Wise's collection, the *Northern Daily Express* printed a broadside containing both Swinburne's poem and "England's Reply", by an anonymous writer. The poem must not be read as an expression of sympathy with Fenianism, which Swinburne detested, but simply as a plea for clemency.

phalis ", " Tiresias " for chief examples, in which man and nature are contemplated under their eternal aspects, there are certain pieces which might in a sense be called occasional, since they are ostensibly, and up to a point actually, celebrations of the triumphs and disasters and delays in the Italian struggle, but these, too, have in truth a wider subject than Mentana or Aspromonte, the acts of the Vatican or the halt outside Rome. It is necessary to understand this lest it appear that Swinburne is guilty of greater and more frequent exaggeration than can justly be charged against him.

The picture that seriously needs a title, the poem that truly requires to be hedged about with critical warnings and supplemented with notes, may well be suspected of failure. Not so this volume of *Songs before Sunrise*, for all the cautions it is even now necessary to prefix to it. The book is the superb achievement of our admiration because Swinburne deliberately eliminated from it those things which would have made it, no doubt, easier to understand and more popular. For all the passion of his propaganda, he was never more strictly an artist than when in 1867-69 he was working on the chief poems in this book. When it was virtually complete he determined, as he wrote to D. G. Rossetti in February 1870,[1] " to pass it through a crucible of revision that I may be sure it is thoroughly pure of any prosaic or didactic taint, any touch of metrical stump-oratory or spread-eagleism, such as is so liable to affect and infect all but the highest political or polemical poetry". An examination of such of the original manuscripts as are available suggests that this process was hardly necessary, but it was carried through, and for various reasons certain pieces were excluded from the volume. One of these, long afterwards, gave rise to a blunder by Watts-Dunton, whose knowledge of Swinburne's work from

[1] Original holograph letter in Mr. Wise's collection.

1872 onwards was minute, but who knew less than he thought of the poet's earlier compositions.

In October 1867, in circumstances which Sir Edmund Gosse has described for the private limited issue of the poem at Mr. Wise's instance, Swinburne wrote a piece entitled " In the Twilight ". This was, in effect, a passionate enquiry of Garibaldi whether he would submit to restriction by Victor Emmanuel or strike a blow for the liberation of Rome. Forty-two years later, when the manuscript came to light, Watts-Dunton took it to be an address to the Deity, written at Oxford, and affording proof of Swinburne's piety at that period! Besides this piece, which too nearly resembled " A Watch in the Night " to appear in the same volume, Swinburne had by him " The Italian Mother ", composed probably in 1869, and a piece ten years older, " The Ride from Milan ". All these, however, were left in manuscript to the end of his life. He had by him also some of the sonnets eventually printed in the *Examiner* in instalments in 1873 and reprinted as " Dirae " in *Songs of Two Nations* in 1875. It would appear from Swinburne's correspondence that the four sonnets entitled " Intercession ", which in the book are dated 1869, existed, at least in a first draft, a year earlier, and we know from a letter [1] of Swinburne's to Rossetti, dated December 1869, that it was then he fitted twelve introductory lines to a couplet which had excited Rossetti's admiration:

" But let the worm Napoleon crawl untrod,
  Nor grant Mastai the gallows of his God."

It might be supposed that he had also at his disposal for *Songs before Sunrise* the elaborate and only half-successful *Ode on the Proclamation of the French Republic*,

---

[1] Original holograph letter in Mr. Wise's collection.

Elliott & Fry, Ltd., Photo

A. C. SWINBURNE IN 1869

which he composed on the 5th, 6th, and 7th September 1870, and issued separately in the same year. But the dates are deceptive.

Songs before Sunrise is not the work of a period closing a few weeks before the publication of the volume in the spring of 1871. With a few exceptions, and some of these doubtful, the book is the work of a period ending with the last weeks of 1869, and indeed the book, almost complete in the autumn of 1868, had been placed, after revision and with additions, in the hands of a new publisher, Mr. F. S. Ellis, for issue in October 1870. What postponed its appearance till the spring of 1871 was the strong objection made by Swinburne's previous publisher, Hotten, who, incensed by the *Ode on the Proclamation of the French Republic* being given to Ellis, was infuriated by the prospect of the *Songs before Sunrise* appearing through that firm, and who pleaded earlier oral agreement with the poet for all his writings. The details of the quarrel and of Hotten's peculiar business methods are recorded in correspondence between Swinburne and the two Rossettis, and, as regards a slightly later period, in letters from Swinburne to Watts-Dunton. All that matters here is that *Songs before Sunrise* is somewhat earlier work than might be supposed, and that the Ode could not have been included in it.

In one sense it may be said that Swinburne had prepared the way for it: he had issued *A Song of Italy* in 1867, " Siena " in 1868, the Ode, as we have seen, in 1870. But *A Song of Italy*, despite the great beauty of part of it, had on the whole prejudiced the public against him by its remoteness and volubility. The Ode had been, on the whole, justly received with some coolness as a poem, and within four months it had been stultified as a prophecy. As for " Siena ", the grave beauty of which is so welcome to readers of *Songs before Sunrise*, the authorized English issue had consisted of only half-a-dozen copies, struck off for purposes of copyright on the inclusion of the poem in an American periodical, and though Hotten had taken it upon himself to put forth another issue, that was presumably something of a hole-and-corner business. At any rate, Swinburne's public was not very ready to welcome the flushed, exuberant, morally audacious poet of the first *Poems and Ballads* on his return five years later as the austerely impassioned celebrant of such hopes and griefs as inspired the *Songs before Sunrise*.

The marvellous lyrical qualities of the volume have never been denied, and indeed it is impossible that the almost unprecedented élan of this verse, unencumbered as it is with the occasionally excessive efflorescence of the first *Poems and Ballads* and undisfigured by the mannered elaboration which sometimes appeared in Swinburne's later work, should be missed by any reader. But *Songs before Sunrise* remains one of those great books which have done little to widen their author's audience. Even where, with a strictly literary public, its qualities of exalted thought and generous passion and purified utterance have been most thoroughly recognized, it is common to find explicit or tacit reservations, even a sort of embarrassment in praise. Thus even Sir Edmund Gosse, writing of certain aspects of the book the noblest words ever written on the subject, confesses himself mystified by the ardour of Swinburne's concern about movements outside his native country and without effect on the position of a British citizen; even he is troubled by what seems to him " the vain violence as of a whirlwind in a vacuum ", and can describe the liberty hymned by Swinburne as " largely a chimaera ". But since when, I would ask with the utmost respect, has a poet been precluded from ardent sympathy with movements that cannot touch him as a citizen, whether because they are remote from him in space or remote in time? In what way does Swinburne's imaginative association with contemporary foreign causes differ from, and become inferior to, that whereby a poet identifies himself with the long since won or lost battles of freedom and feels pulsing through his heart the blood poured out for liberty a hundred or a thousand years before his time?

Taken literally as comments on the course of affairs in Italy or France in the 'sixties and early 'seventies, Swinburne's poems may be here and there based on error, and there may be much exaggeration in his eulogy and censure of historical personages. His frequent assumption that kings and priests are the joint authors of most human ills is clearly puerile. His failure to foresee that democracy, which even then had its future behind it, would become with every development of its power grosser, more stupid, more selfish, more dangerous in itself and in the reactions which it would provoke, is patent. But neither Swinburne's aloofness as a British citizen from continental politics nor the fallibility of his judgment in matters of statecraft diminishes in the smallest degree the human and aesthetic value of his magnificent testimony to the eternal truths he supposed to be embodied in this or that contemporary movement or character. In no vacuum is that whirlwind which sweeps thrillingly, cleansingly, through the souls of men, and no chimaera is that liberty which, never to be established through any political machinery, is the condition of spiritual life, and which, in one of the purest and loftiest of its forms, is realized here, before us, in the very verse that cries out for it. Chimerical is an epithet not for that which parliaments and administrators cannot create among us, but for that which, falsely imagined, inconsistent with itself and with the spirit of man, can never be set up in his mind. It is an epithet for a prosaic mechanical Utopia, not for that which springs into existence at the bidding of the poet though it remain out of our physical reach.

But we argue idly when almost any page of the *Songs before Sunrise,* read in the right temper, is immediate proof of all we could claim for it. If not Italy, man is risen from the sepulchre as " Super Flumina Babylonis " sends its solemn jubilant music along our " nerves of delight ".

" Whoso bears the whole heaviness of the wronged world's weight,
And puts it by,
It is well with him, suffering, though he face man's fate;
How should he die?

Seeing death has no part in him any more, no power
Upon his head;
He has bought his eternity with a little hour,
And is not dead.

For an hour, if ye look for him, he is no more found,
For one hour's space,
Then ye lift up your eyes to him and behold him crowned,
A deathless face.

On the mountains of memory, by the world's well-springs,
In all men's eyes,
Where the light of the life of him is on all past things,
Death only dies. . . ."

If Hugo, by turns divine and pompous, is hardly Orpheus, and France issues from hell largely at summons other than his and into a doubtful day, the testimony to the spiritual power of great poetry remains. " Mentana: First Anniversary " is the lament of an immortal over her mortal and sacrificed servants, and can never cease to echo in the world's ears. " A Marching Song " is for all great movements, and " Quia Multum Amavit " is the pardon in every age of those who have seen and loved light, and fallen into darkness, and then yearned to light again.

Far from being chimerical, liberty is the most real thing in Swinburne's experience. It is in the service of liberty that all his energies are brought into harmonious relation, and in the imaginative attainment of liberty that all his aspirations are satisfied. His natural rebelliousness becomes, in this relation, a generous and earnestly motived activity; his equally natural submissiveness attains to a greater dignity than when it was a luxurious bowing down before great men. His sensuality is transformed, by a process similar to that at work in some of the lovers of God, into mystical passion. His delight in the sea, in the wind, in light, in the life of the seabird giving its wings to the storm, acquires deeper significance, since these are among the symbols of liberty. All his loves and hates gain intensity in ministering to a liberty apprehended successively as *mater dolorosa*, *mater triumphalis*, the mother, the beloved, the bride of man's soul, the infinitely bountiful, the implacable goddess demanding bitter sacrifices of man. She is rejected of men, and his chivalry is fired; she is triumphant, and with proud and humble joy he claims his share in her triumph. She justifies his measureless eulogies of her. She sanctifies his measureless invectives against her enemies. Incomparably holy, she is no aloof divinity awaiting a peculiar tribute; he can give to her all that he gave to Landor and Hugo and Mazzini, all that he gave also to Atalanta and Mary and the " daughters of dreams and of stories".

Towards her, and without the check that must elsewhere be felt, he can be by turns filial and passionate, her son, her servant, her lover, her prophet. In relation to her, and nowhere else, can he be wholly himself. In this book alone he attains to completeness of life, with much in him transformed, but nothing excluded or repressed.

Swinburne, who justly preferred *Songs before Sunrise* to all his other volumes of verse, was well aware, when he collected its constituent poems for publication, how widely it differed in temper from his previous work. The " Prelude " is his *apologia*. In it, he figures the conversion of youth to a faith which cannot allow of longer dalliance with the things that have so far delighted it.

" ' Yet, between death and life are hours,
To flush with love and hide in flowers,
What profit save in these? ' men cry."

He has no rebuke for this hedonism; only, for himself, there has been made manifest the truth that pleasures fade, and there abides the duty of self-dedication to the service of liberty. It is gravely, without expectation of easy and early success in high endeavour to loose the chains wherein manhood suffers wrong, that he enters on the new life. His equipment is

" Knowledge and patience of what must
And what things may be, in the heat
And cold of years that rot and rust."

And it is in this insistence on patience, on willingness to stand free of " swift hopes and slow despondencies ", on contempt for facile faith and cheap scepticism, that the poem attains to its noblest moral quality, attaining simultaneously to a severe nobility of style for which readers of the exuberant *Poems and Ballads* were utterly unprepared.

Already, on the earliest pages of *Songs before Sunrise*, there is exemplified that which is the chief purely literary distinction of the book, a power, never before exhibited by Swinburne, and to be exercised by him thereafter only in a few of the second series of *Poems and Ballads*, and in *Erechtheus*, of purifying his style without loss of élan, of achieving solidity without depriving himself of buoyancy. There are, indeed, redundancies in the volume, with certain extravagances of phrase, certain surrenders to merely metrical impulse, but they are fewer than in any other volume of Swinburne's, and there are in this volume many successive pages wholly clear of them. The notes sounded in *Songs before Sunrise* are for the most part clearer, more ringing, than those in the first *Poems and Ballads*. The poet, under the compulsion of his solemn passion for liberty, is less tempted to use the whole of the instruments in his orchestra without regard for artistic propriety, simply out of delight in his command of them.

If there is anything which this great body of poetry lacks, it is the relief of a particularity to which Swinburne was very seldom given. Yet it does not lack it entirely. I have perused a letter from W. M. Rossetti to the poet, in which, acknowledging the book, he said he found " Before a Crucifix ", on a first reading of the poems, " soothing ". An odd word, but I think I know what he meant. In localizing, in rendering more personal in the ordinary sense, the emotions of the poet, that poem differs from most of the others. Again, " To Walt Whitman in America ", with its splendid eulogy of that

> " Strong-winged soul with prophetic
> Lips hot with the blood-beats of song,
> With tremor of heartstrings magnetic,
> With thoughts as thunders in throng,"

brings a certain needed relief to all but the fittest readers of *Songs before Sunrise*.

No similar relief is afforded to readers of the great and severe lyrical drama, *Erechtheus*, in which Swinburne embodied his political ideal, and on which it is proper, indeed necessary, to touch here, though something will be said of it when dealing with *Atalanta*. But before examining that culmination of his political thought it is well to notice the *Songs of Two Nations*, poems composed, for the most part, in the very years in which the *Songs before Sunrise* were written.

The praise of transcendental liberty was followed, not very fortunately, by a volume in part, as regards *A Song of Italy*, less mature, in part, as regards the *Ode on the Proclamation of the French Republic*, less inspired, and on the whole much less universal in application. Why the book into which these were gathered, together with the magnificent sonnets entitled "Dirae", was delayed till 1875 is not quite clear. The two long poems had been issued separately in 1867 and 1870; the sonnets had appeared in the *Examiner* during May 1873; and except for the quarrel with Hotten, which had not prevented the publication of the *Songs before Sunrise*, through Ellis, there was seemingly nothing to delay the volume. Its appearance had been preceded by controversy. Not only the general public, but, in certain instances, Swinburne's own friends, had been taken aback by the ironical salutation of Napoleon III as Saviour of Society. That Hutton, of the *Spectator*, was eventually shocked was merely the kind of gesture of alarm to which Swinburne was by this time accustomed, and he had cared nothing for Hutton since, thirteen years earlier, they had fallen out over the poet's reviews of imaginary and indecent French poets. But much earlier D. G. Rossetti, after seeing the proofs, had taken alarm, and had written to Swinburne:

" I have just happened to see the proof-sheet of your Sonnets, 'The Saviour of Society', glorious pieces of poetic diction, as none knows better than I. But they resolve me to risk even your displeasure by one earnest remonstrance as to their publication. I cannot but think absolutely that a poet like yourself belongs of right to a larger circle of readers than this treatment of universal feelings can include. You know how free I am myself from any dogmatic belief, but I can most sincerely say that ... I do myself feel that the supreme nobility of Christ's character should exempt it from being used ... not as a symbolic parallel to other noble things and persons in relation with which dogmatists might object to its use ... but certainly in contact of this kind with anything so utterly ignoble as this.... You have no right to imperil your sacred relation to the minds of many men worthy to profit by your mind, by using one form of metaphor rather than another when its use involves such disproportionately grave issues." [1]

Rossetti, like so many of those who protested against the sonnets three years later, seems to have thought that Swinburne had invented the title he applied with fierce irony to Napoleon, but it had been used in compliment rather commonly in France ever since that adventurer's seizure of power. A much more serious objection, still widely felt, and the present writer will confess, formerly shared by himself, prompted the question whether the greatest of men with the most generous reasons for indignation is entitled to pursue even the vilest with such utterly ruthless wrath to the grave and beyond it. But to argue thus is to be the victim of that uncritical habit of mind whereby a work of art is condemned in advance on some plausible general ground. The prayer that Napoleon III may live till

[1] Original holograph letter in Mr. Wise's collection.

life seems worse than death, and beyond that, till death seems worse than life, the whole of that terrible supplication to death, culminating in the ferocious exultation over " the descent into hell ", ought to be intolerable. But is it? What has this poet really to do with the wretched ex-Emperor who died early in 1873 at Chislehurst? It is not the shifty, flashy, essentially mediocre criminal, with, after all, certain partly redeeming political virtues, who is here allowed nothing for the years of physical suffering, of mental suffering, too, in survival of all his hopes; it is the incarnation of unmitigated evil that is stamped upon, and by a divine avenger. We can but speak in this matter each for himself; but for myself, I can now only wonder that, writing of Swinburne a dozen years ago, I did not see that a more measured and earthly hatred would have been more wounding to the mind of the reader, being the exhibition of a merely human passion which, however directed, is after all never free from a certain grossness, whereas this measureless anger, if you will forget names out of history, and remember against what it is turned in the poems themselves, purifies, exalts, and is an inverted tribute to a measureless mercy. Swinburne did not desist when the grave had closed upon the exile; no, but immortal hate of immortal evil can take no count of mortality, and this is a judgment in heaven, against that which Napoleon III was too small, and on certain sides of him not evil enough, to represent fully, but which, for Swinburne, he symbolized.

If any further defence be required, it may be found in Swinburne's own *apologia*:

" For chill is known by heat and heat by chill,
And the desire that hope makes love to still
By the fear flying beside it or above,
A falcon fledged to follow a fledgling dove,

>And by the fume and flame of hate of ill
>The exuberant light and burning bloom of love."

The great doxology of the cities of Italy to Mazzini, the almost innumerable outbursts of passionately loyal love towards the leaders of liberating movements, would mean so much less if the lips from which they issued were incapable of being embittered by this merciless wrath. Some of the rapture with which the city of liberty is hymned in *Erechtheus* would be lost if we were not aware of this poet's power to castigate the forces of tyranny.

Erechtheus is, among other things, an answer to those who fancy Swinburne's liberty to be but anarchy. For him, as he showed in " The Hymn of Man " and elsewhere in the *Songs before Sunrise*,

> " Not each man of all men is God, but God is the fruit
>   of the whole ";

and for him the co-operation of men in civic or national life is not merely expedient and for such ends as the politician has in view, but essential to the realization of the divinity of man. The State, thus loftily conceived, republican in a spiritual even more than the ordinary political sense, and by the poet's, the scholar's, preference conforming to the antique Greek ideal, is therefore very much more to him than an organization for even the worthiest material benefits.

It is at least as much as the Church is to the faithful. In truth, it is still more indispensable, for it is only in it that the individual, sacrificing at need everything to it, but voluntarily, can attain to perfect liberty and the divine life. Union and a willingly accepted discipline in the service of the institution whereby man enters into this sublime and ample life are the conditions, not the negations, of liberty. To be united in devotion to the common will is the supreme joy:

> " There is no grief,
> Great as the joy to be made one in will
> With him that is the heart and rule of life "

says Praxithea in the hour when the salvation of Athens has been secured by the sacrifice of her daughter, the death of her husband.

A recent and capable writer on Swinburne, having chosen to approach him with one peculiar key which is to open all his doors, one test that shall separate his greatest from his less great works, is constrained to depreciate *Erechtheus* because it is a drama of submission, whereas the capital work of Swinburne is that in which his two main impulses, the impulse of revolt and impulse of submission, so act as to bring about the maximum of tension. With all deference to this ingenuity, I am unable to believe that Swinburne, or any other master, can be adequately dealt with in terms of a formula, and I am quite certain that this particular formula altogether breaks down when *Erechtheus* is brought into question. How could it have been other than a drama of submission? Had it been other, it would have been made evident that Swinburne's rebelliousness was mere heat of blood, mere meaningless opposition to every kind of constraint. Given the ideal liberty of the Athens of *Erechtheus*, a proud submissiveness to the conditions on which alone its liberty can be perpetuated is imposed on man. We are no longer in the world of *Atalanta*, where the death of the blameless, or all but blameless, is required arbitrarily by the Gods, or it may be by a Fate which overrules even them. Here is no individual tragedy, against which there may or must be indignant protest. It is the city of liberty that is here menaced, and so that it be saved all things must be sacrificed, and the Gods be praised for the safety of the fortress and fosteress of freedom no matter how terrible the price of deliverance. Revolt, to return to the high political aspect of the matter, is against tyranny; there can be no revolt against that which secures liberty.

What turned Swinburne's attention to the theme of this tragedy I have not been able to discover. To be sure, there was the fragment of Euripides to inspire a poet desirous of a Hellenic patriotic subject. But Swinburne's hatred of Euripides renders it unlikely that he acted on an impulse derived from that, though he did condescend to utilize it provisionally, eventually discarding most of it. Whatever chance sent him to the subject, his choice was exceedingly fortunate. The Athenian setting, the descent of Erechtheus from the Earth, the fact that the menace to Athens is from the "son of the Sea's Lord", the demand that the sacrifice to save Athens shall be that of the virginal Chthonia, the opportunity thus given the poet for the expression of the maternal and patriotic emotions of Praxithea, the circumstances of the fourfold battle, the dearly won triumph of Athens, the final assurance of the eternity of that city of the spirit, made it a subject perfectly to his inner purpose. We shall return to *Erechtheus* hereafter, to consider its purely literary excellence; what is to be set down now is, that its theme and setting make *Erechtheus* a specialized work of art, an emanation from the poet who was never weary of reciting the Greek poetry of the praise of Athens, not the expression of every side of the poet who sought to rally the forces of modern liberty under the auspices of Landor, Hugo, and Mazzini. We cannot, when we desire to apprehend the political, or, as I almost prefer to call it, the religious, thought of Swinburne fully, concentrate on *Erechtheus* and wave aside the *Songs before Sunrise*. But *Erechtheus* represents, not only with a uniform majesty of temper, but also with a lucidity far from usual with Swinburne, the ideal towards which his imagination was moving when he composed the *Songs before Sunrise*. It is our chief warrant for rejecting all criticism which would attribute the enthusiasms and agonies of the *Songs before Sunrise* to the disconnected, spasmodic responses made by an over-strung poet to the accidents of contemporary politics and the promptings of Landor or Hugo or Mazzini. In no writings of those his masters, nor anywhere else, is there to be found the ideal of which *Erechtheus* is the expression.

Chapter VI

THE TROUBLED YEARS

WITH the publication of *Songs before Sunrise*, in 1871, there closed for Swinburne, at thirty-four, the period of the vehement blossoming of the aloe. Much, indeed rather too much, was to come from him in the thirty-eight years of life that remained, and amongst many things of little value to us not only masterpieces on the great scale, *Bothwell*, *Erechtheus*, *Tristram of Lyonesse*, *Balen*, but a really considerable number of lyrics little or not at all inferior in poetical quality to those of his splendid April, though mostly, in Rossetti's sense, less " amusing ". But languor and dejection, not, as will presently be shown, without some fortunate poetical consequences, had begun to affect his natural ardour and confidence.

One source of the trouble was physical. Unwarned by the severe epileptiform seizure in 1863, by what he himself called the " really dangerous " attack of 1867 at Lord Houghton's, and other of these experiences, so terrifying to everyone but the victim, who indeed sometimes seemed, after a few days, the better for them, Swinburne had continued a mode of life most perilous to one with so highly strung a nervous system. With Charles Augustus Howell, with Simeon Solomon, with a much more reputable but hardly safer companion in George Powell, with the journalist Purnell, who was perhaps no worse than ultra-bohemian, and with the incomparably nobler but for him very mischievous Burton, he was too near a too rapidly replenished wine-cup. He had, as he admitted in one of those apologies it was sometimes necessary to write to Lord Houghton, no vocation to the service of Bacchus, but periodically, though only when in London, he sought to emulate companions hardened in that service.

In 1870, in consequence of the school-boy indecorum of his conduct, he had been obliged to resign from the Arts Club, and he never again belonged to any social institution. From his older and more distinguished friends he had somewhat fallen away, or they from him. In particular, from 1872, he lost the benefit of that easy affectionate authority which Rossetti, with the British bluffness so curiously overlying his Italianate subtlety, had exercised over him since 1860, but for the exercise of which Rossetti by this time was becoming unfitted by chloral, insomnia, suspiciousness, desire for solitude. Despite the abruptness with which Rossetti, having earnestly sought Swinburne's companionship in 1862,[1] had ended their joint occupation of 16 Cheyne Walk, an occupation which Swinburne had not supposed to be terminable at the mere caprice of either party, their relations had continued to be cordial till 1872. When, in 1869, Rossetti wrote to tell him of the exhumation of the poems buried with Mrs. Rossetti, Swinburne replied in what must surely be one of the noblest and most delicately sympathetic letters ever penned. When, presently, the recovered pieces were being prepared for the press, Swinburne was assiduous in minute and sagacious counsel, especially with reference to " Jenny ", suggesting with levity and acumen reasons for altering " double-bedded " to " double-pillowed ", protesting

[1] The main facts were stated by Swinburne on Rossetti's death, in " A Record of Friendship ", written in 1882, but printed only in 1910, for private circulation. This pamphlet, however, does not contain a passage of some importance the manuscript of which was not discovered till later. In this additional passage he describes the surprise with which he received Rossetti's intimation, and concludes " but the ultimate result could only be an amicable separation ".

against proposed deletions ("I do not want to see 'Jenny'—whose life has not been such as to call down in lightning from heaven *les malheurs de la vertu*—incur without deserving it the doom of Justine"), upholding the great plain line which he was afterwards to praise in his very generous review of the volume in the *Fortnightly*. And this was by no means the only time at which he assisted Rossetti. It was Swinburne who, when his friend was held back from continuing "The Bride's Prelude" by the difficulty of devising a conclusion, proposed, with admirable dramatic logic, that the brothers should kill Urselyn the moment he had made an honest woman of Aloyse. For this piece Swinburne had a sustained enthusiasm, holding it to be Rossetti's "finest and most pathetic invention", and to it he returned when Rossetti had passed away, after nine years of estrangement, in the beautiful and affecting tribute, "After Many Days".[1] Nor, as the reader of volumes published by the poet himself is aware, was this the only posthumous tribute. Swinburne, in short, after Rossetti's death recalled only the intimacy which had endured from 1860 to 1872, not the years of alienation which began when Rossetti took peevish exception to the mildest criticism offered him by the most enthusiastic admirer and helpful counsellor he ever had.[2]

At the time Swinburne was mystified, and continued in perplexity after Rossetti's death, as may be seen from a letter of 1882 to W. Bell Scott about "the sufferer who survived the man we knew and loved". Per-

[1] Privately printed in 1918 in *The Italian Mother*; the original holograph manuscripts of the two drafts of the poem are in Mr. Wise's collection, the later bearing the title "Written after reading the Proofs of 'The Bride's Prelude'".

[2] The final rupture remains somewhat obscure, but a certain amount of light is thrown on it by a letter from Rossetti to Swinburne inserted by Mr. Wise in "A Record of Friendship".

manently separated from Rossetti, seeing less of Morris and Burne-Jones, less also of Whistler, Swinburne in the early 'seventies had perhaps only two new friends, Walter Theodore Watts and the critic whom we now honour as Sir Edmund Gosse, such as those concerned for his health, his dignity, and his work could have desired for him. There began to be periods, however, when neither desirable nor undesirable friends saw much of him. Under the influences of drink and nerves, he turned aside into very strange places, as he had also done in earlier years, or retired into the loneliness of his own rooms, to brood, to drink, to question the worth of what he called the monotonous puppet-show of his life. At times he was missing, and it taxed the ingenuity of the admirable Dr. Bird, of Welbeck Street, his intelligent, indulgent friend as well as physician, to find him. Periodically he was lost, found again, taken to the country by Admiral Swinburne, where he would recover swiftly and behave perfectly, only to revert to dangerous living on return to London. Once, at least, after his father's death, Lady Jane Swinburne was totally ignorant of his whereabouts.

Drink, or rather Swinburne's exceptional incapacity for it, accounted for much. There were other causes for languor, dejection, feverish excitement. There was that in him which could find no natural satisfaction. It was not merely in the spirit in which he had joined the Cannibal Club that he went to certain resorts, not merely in the spirit in which he had written "The Cannibal Catechism" that he returned at intervals from 1862 to 1881 to his epic of flagellation, the unpublished and, of course, quite unpublishable composition entitled *The Flogging-Block*. Interest in this subject had been shown as early as 1859, in his Fletcherian comedy *Laugh and Lie Down*, in which one character, Frank, is so frequently under the scourge; raptures over birching

ORIGINAL HOLOGRAPH MANUSCRIPT OF
"AT A MONTH'S END"

appear in work so late as *The Sisters*, 1892. The matter is not one into which I desire to enter: students of a certain department of human behaviour will readily deduce what is implied by the persistence of this interest, harmless as the references to it in Swinburne's published works are.

It would be shallow, however, to suppose that drink and some sexual aberrations fully explain the physical and mental condition to which Swinburne was reduced, in spite of several and astonishingly rapid temporary recoveries of bodily and intellectual vigour, by 1878. There can be no doubt that at times during the 'seventies he was deeply troubled by a sense of isolation. From the first he had been set apart from his fellows by his extraordinary appearance, his extraordinary nervous constitution, and, above all, by a genius which was so very far from being representable as the result of normal faculties raised to an immensely high power. But, in the beautiful simplicity which distinguished, it seems, his boyhood, and certainly his early manhood, as also his old age, he had never displayed consciousness of his difference from other boys and young men born in his class, educated as he had been, and taking an interest in the things of the mind. Deliberate eccentricity in dress or manner was utterly impossible for him, pose and gush and rant at all times foreign to him: never did he seek to accentuate his divergence from the normal, well-born, cultured Englishman. But in the 'seventies he evidently became aware that he was different, and the knowledge induced both depression, and, in reaction from it, an occasional arrogance from which his youth had been and his old age was to be free. Worse, he began, now and then, to feel a loss of contact with real life, an incapacity for normal experience; and, worst of all, doubt of the validity of his specialized, though extremely intense, experience.

Who shall say whether, if his parents had allowed him years earlier to enter the Army, for which he had no qualifications except absolute courage, or if he had been thrown by the necessity of earning his livelihood into the general scramble, or if the brandy and the myrtles and the birch-twigs had not been so accessible, he would or would not have passed through this phase, in which there were several brief intervals of renewed youth and recovered confidence? But in these years from time to time, and especially from 1876 to 1879, the wings drooped, the bright, defiant head was bowed, the wild eyes were turned inwards questioningly, sorrowfully.

Our chief poetic evidence that Swinburne in these years was conscious, as never in youth or in old age, of the great gulf between him and other men, even his brothers in art, is that idealized autobiography, "Thalassius", which has hardly received the attention due to it. It has, as a poem, some of the weaknesses which grew on him; it is in parts diffuse and vague, and perhaps only in the magnificent passage of the Bassarides and in the Sun-God's blessing of the poet does it rise fully to the height of the subject; but as autobiography it is far more suggestive than has generally been seen. For here is Swinburne, at the close of this period, representing himself as in every respect set apart from mankind, though pledged to the service of humanity. He is the child of the Sun and of the Sea; he is, in the final benediction,

"A fosterling and fugitive on earth
Sleepless of soul as wind or wave or fire,
A manchild with an ungrown God's desire";

he is, in a certain sense, and the poet's perception of this is astonishing, in early middle age still pubescent, destined to remain a manchild, an ungrown God; he has forgone his chance of sharing in the central human experiences, " sold life and life's love for song "; he lives only in his poetry,

" Being now no more a singer, but a song."

With all this, take certain passages in the contemporaneous " On the Cliffs ", outpourings to Sappho and the nightingale:

" My heart has been as thy heart, and my life
  As thy life is, a sleepless hidden thing,
  Full of the thirst and hunger of winter and spring,
  That seeks its food not in such love or strife
  As fill men's hearts with passionate hours and rest....

         The best of all my days
  Have been as those fair fruitless summer strays,
  Those water-waifs that but the sea-wind steers,
  Flakes of glad foam or flowers on footless ways
  That take the wind in season and the sun,
  And when the wind wills is their season done....

  We were not marked for sorrow, thou or I,
  For joy nor sorrow, sister, were we made,
  To take delight and grief to live and die,
  Affrayed by pleasures or by pains affrayed,
  That melt men's hearts and alter; we retain
  A memory mastering pleasure and all pain,
  A spirit within the sense of ear and eye,
  A soul behind the soul, that seeks and sings
  And makes our life move only with its wings
  And feed but from its lips."

The writer of these two poems wrote out of a poignant sense of what was exceptional in his spiritual situation; but with a pride in it which Swinburne in the 'seventies was far from feeling continuously. Look at certain pieces in the second series of *Poems and Ballads*, published in 1878 but written appreciably earlier, and you will find the moods of dejection, of wistfulness, of pensive acquiescence most characteristic of Swinburne in the middle and later 'seventies. The subdual and spiritualization of the hitherto clamorous music, the new delicacy which distinguish the extremely beautiful " A Forsaken Garden " and those other poems, " The Year of the Rose ", " Relics ", " A Ballad of Dreamland ", " A Vision of Spring in Winter ", remind us that they are the work of hours in which the poet was drooping under burdens of which he had earlier been unconscious, or gently reviving after dejection. These things have about them some suggestion of the maladive or of convalescence.

Their author's mood and condition varied very frequently during the 'seventies. A few weeks in his London rooms, in Great James Street, where he would so often sit solitary and idle among his books and his queer treasures, his serpentine candlesticks and the table with the mosaic top, brooding till the impulse to brandy or another distraction took him out, and he would be over-wrought, his natural vividness dimmed, his natural unsuspiciousness replaced by the belief that all manner of evil was being plotted against him in various quarters. A few more weeks and there would be excruciating mental agitation, ending in physical collapse. But his father had only to get him to Holmwood, the house near Henley which Admiral and Lady Jane Swinburne had taken in place of their Isle of Wight home after the death of his sister, Edith, and the invalid would speedily become serene, active, discreetly behaved. Visits to Jowett at Oxford, and, much more, sojourn with him in successive autumns from 1871 in Scotland or elsewhere, were also highly beneficial. A visit to the Channel Islands with John Nichol in the late spring of 1876 had a magical effect, though within a few weeks he was once more ill, and Holmwood was once more the cure. But in March 1877 his father, who may not have understood his son's work, but who had repeatedly shown affectionate indulgence and much good sense in dealing with a very difficult case, passed away, mourned in one of the simplest and most touching of Swinburne's many elegies.

Swinburne left Holmwood after the funeral, declined to return thither, and entered on a long and nearly unbroken course of reckless living. He had behind him, as the work of the 'seventies, two solid and great achievements, in both of which he had enjoyed Jowett's encouragement and advice, *Bothwell*, completed, after immense labour, in 1874, out of which, as he once gratefully declared, flinging himself at Jowett's feet, the Master had helpfully cut 4,000 lines, and *Erechtheus* begun while staying with Jowett at Malvern in July 1875, and completed while staying with Theodore Watts at Southwold in September and October of that year. Now, *Bothwell* is the most tremendous thing, except Mr. Hardy's *Dynasts*, done in dramatic form in modern English literature. The historical scholarship, the elaborate and almost incredibly patient working out of its enormous plot, the sustained ardour of this immense drama afford the highest proof we have that Swinburne was no mere brilliant improvisor, but a student and artist capable of planning greatly and executing with minute finish. And *Erechtheus*, the most rapidly and confidently written of all his major works, is the most exactly organized. But consider as a whole the work done by Swinburne between 1871 and 1878, and you will observe signs that quite often in these years he was provoking himself into intellectual activity.

Through almost the whole of this period he was glad to have his flagging spirits raised by controversy.

Opportunities were provided by Buchanan, Furnivall, and his own readiness to search for them.

In October 1871 there appeared in the *Contemporary Review* under the title, "The Fleshly School of Poetry", and over the signature, Thomas Maitland, an attack on Rossetti and Swinburne. Before the end of that month Rossetti was informed that Thomas Maitland was Robert Buchanan, and proceeded to improvise a limerick on

" Buchanan,
Who the pseudo prefers to the anon,"

taking the matter at first, as William Michael wrote to Swinburne, "in a reasonable spirit of disdain". Presently, however, it become evident that Rossetti was seriously affected, and it was out of chivalrous concern for his friend, rather than with the wish to add to the defence of his own *Poems and Ballads* already made in *Notes on Poems and Reviews* in 1866, that Swinburne now produced *Under the Microscope*. With this generous motive, however, there mingled very probably the desire to enliven himself, for earlier in 1871 he had brought himself very low by reckless indulgences, had had to be rescued by his father, and had subsequently had to be taken by Jowett to Scotland. He was greatly gratified by his father's description of *Under the Microscope* as "a cat o' nine tails", and by his former and since alienated editor's recognition, in an article on Tennyson which Hutton contributed to *Macmillan's Magazine*, that the outer satirical husk of the essay was not its kernel. Swinburne claimed, not unjustly, that it was more than a fierce reply to Buchanan, that it contributed something to the understanding of artistic questions of more enduring interest than those at issue between Buchanan and himself. But it was in too many places disfigured by elaborate and over-toppling irony, and in one passage, speedily cancelled,[1] by a quite outrageous outburst of temper against Tennyson. Quite legitimately and very delightfully, Swinburne had long protested against the taming and moralizing of Arthurian legends in which Tennyson indulged, and had been wont to refer to the *Idylls of the King* as the " Morte d'Albert ". But here he had summed up the dramatic personnel of Tennyson as " that cycle of strumpets and scoundrels, broken by here and there an imbecile, which Mr. Tennyson has set revolving the figure of his central wittol."

Buchanan was not wholly silenced; he produced a feeble satire, " The Monkey and the Microscope ", in *St. Paul's*, in August 1872; but his influence was shaken, despite the extravagances of Swinburne's pamphlet. There was a further clash in 1875, when Swinburne addressed to the *Examiner*, then edited by his friend William Minto, a letter entitled " The Devil's Due ", and signed Thomas Maitland, a signature which it amused him very much to use. This letter, which also appeared as a pamphlet for private circulation, dealt with Buchanan's " Fleshly School " article and with the Earl of Southesk's *Jonas Fisher*, and out of it arose Buchanan's libel action of 1876 against the *Examiner*. Swinburne, not unreasonably, insisted that it had been for Minto, as Editor, and not for himself, to judge of the risk of publishing it; but he obstinately refused to consult with the *Examiner's* legal defenders, chiefly, it seems, through irritation at something the paper had said in disparagement of Mrs. Lyon Linton, who was Landor's spiritual daughter and therefore above criticism.

At the suggestion of Watts(-Dunton) he made the *Examiner* a present of a short poem, but insisted that

---

[1] It would appear that only half a dozen copies of the cancelled leaf are in existence: forgers have at least twice in recent years provided copies to enhance the value of the pamphlet.

this was purely an act of grace, and recounted to his friend at length the obligation under which he had placed the *Examiner* by allowing it for a modest fee to print his article on Auguste Vacquerie, an article which, gratifying to Victor Hugo's adherents and appreciated in Paris, was by no means the kind of contribution which an editor in London would covet.¹

Buchanan made one of his slimy recantations in regard to Rossetti some years later; he never relented towards Swinburne, his chief grievance, apart from the chastisement he had received, being that Swinburne in 1867, in an article on Matthew Arnold, had mingled some contempt with pity in a reference to the ill-fated poetaster, David Gray. But Buchanan, who had no central convictions, ceased to matter.

Long before this controversy closed, Swinburne had entered into others: the controversy provoked by the publication of the fierce sonnets on Napoleon III; that arising between him and the vulgarly abusive Furnivall over Swinburne's Shakespearean criticism published in the *Fortnightly Review* in 1875-76; the angry debates excited by events in the Balkans. Letters to the Press and indignant outpourings to friends need not detain us. Nor need more than a very few words be said of the quarrel with Emerson, who was reported in American prints to have reflected on Swinburne's character, and who, having unwisely left Swinburne's request for a contradiction unanswered, became the subject of polyglot epigrams of great pungency and impropriety. The

---

¹ Swinburne's ideas of editorial requirements were often odd. Thus, he desired a friend to let the editor of the *Athenæum* see his epigrams on Lytton, and himself submitted to Knowles, of the *Nineteenth Century*, though here he confessed to a doubt of their suitability, his "Rondeaux Parisiens" inspired by resentment partly of Stead's puritanical and obscene crusade in the *Pall Mall Gazette* but chiefly of hypocritical French horror at the immorality of London.

Note of an English Republican on the Muscovite Crusade, 1876, a violent and voluble tract, is of little interest now, but has a certain importance as illustrating both the temper which was now becoming usual with him in controversy and the peculiarity of his reaction to political characters and events. I shall return to it later for the light some correspondence relating to it casts on Swinburne's hero-worship and almost insensate hatred of public characters not found worthy of worship.

Herbert Spencer found the invective of this *Note* magnificent. The magnificence is there, but obscured too often by the faults which were now more and more prevalent in Swinburne's prose. These same vices of exaggeration, of circumlocutory and over-obvious irony, of alliteration and double or treble antithesis, of inability to refrain from striking out violently to right and left when the writer's eyes should be fixed before him, appear also in *A Note on Charlotte Brontë*, 1877. There is in this a more radical effect. It shows eager sympathy and fine acumen in dealing with Charlotte, rare insight and courage in its eulogy of Emily's poetry; but too many even of its best passages seem merely incidental to an attack on George Eliot. He attacked her partly because, on the whole for sound reasons, he disapproved of the valuation of her work then general, but also because, one of the vainest of his imaginings, he supposed her to be inciting her literary following to assail him. What pretext there was for his innumerable flings, some in rather blunt little epigrams, at the viceregal poet, Lytton, no one has yet discovered. Lytton, to be sure, was an imitative writer who came near to being a plagiarist, though not without a certain talent, and even, in at least one composition, a certain personal feeling. But he had done no harm to Swinburne; his father had been kind to Swinburne. It can only be supposed that Swinburne needed a poeticule to torture. He was on edge in these years; he was provoking himself into intellectual activity.

There were, indeed, as has already been noticed, radiant intervals when Swinburne, cured by the country or the sea, and soothed by his parents or by Jowett, would reappear in London ardent and purposeful and gay and charming; but the fits of dejection, the demonstrations of arrogance, the days of dependence on excitement, the hours of lassitude, became more frequent. In 1878 he presented, he the vividly youthful, something of the aspect of an old man, grateful for help up and down stairs, tottering from his excesses. In September 1879 he was dying in his rooms in Great James Street, when Theodore Watts(-Dunton), with Lady Jane Swinburne's approval, and mingling persuasion and something like violence, got him into a cab and took him to his own rooms and then to Putney. With his almost unprecedented recuperative power, Swinburne in six weeks was as well as he had ever been. The fundamental soundness of his constitution, corresponding to the sanity which underlay all his intellectual extravagances, became evident; not for twenty-four years did he have another illness; and he lived for thirty more.

Such contact as he had had with ordinary life now ceased. Life came to him thenceforth only as a rumour. There remained his books, the sea, children, the memory of old friendships very beautifully cherished by him.

Chapter VII

PAN AND THALASSIUS

CERTAINLY one of those for whom, in Gautier's phrase, the visible world exists, Swinburne is exceptionally privileged or condemned to apprehend it, not as a series of pictures in which natural objects have their detail, are massed together, are stationed firmly in their circumstances, but under fugitive yet monotonously recaptured aspects, and with a kind of emptying of much of the scene. He sees things much as his Althæa saw the approach of the famous hunters, with half-dazzled eyes:

" For sharp mixed shadows and wind
  Blown up between the morning and the mist,
  With steam of steeds and flash of bridle or wheel,
  And fire, and parcels of the broken dawn,
  And dust, divided by hard light, and spears
  That shine and shift as the edge of wild beasts' eyes,
  Smite upon mine; so fiery their blind edge
  Burns, and bright points break up and baffle day."

There are hardly any set and full and clear pictures in Swinburne. Landscape or seascape, the effect is of haze with light breaking on or out of certain widely separated, undefined things—waves, flames, clouds, stars, flowers—as they may have existed in the general intention of God before His art gave them particularity: " bright points break up and baffle day ".

Swinburne worked constantly from a very few remembered prospects, in Northumberland, in the Isle of Wight, in Siena, on the east coast of England; but the actual scene is " scattered with light ", the moment he begins to work on it. Keats transfers nature to his pages, as it were, bodily, completely, circumscribing with a very definite outline what is to be transferred in its totality; but with Swinburne the component parts of that on which he is gazing fly asunder, and only some of them reassemble in the unity of a curiously mental composition. So far as he was observant, it was in a way unlike that of any other poet, and I do not think the result of his initial observation was ever submitted to the test of a fresh reference to nature. The quality he had primarily discerned in any natural object became for him its distinguishing, if not its sole, quality. The thing once seen was brooded over, and then, as in the classic instance of the stormy Channel crossing celebrated by him over and over again, it was drawn upon without the slightest modification from subsequent experience.

With few exceptions, his remembered landscapes and seascapes have no linear pattern to hold them together, their unity, when they have it, coming from the quite wonderful maintenance of atmosphere, the persistence of the monotonous music to which they are revealed, and, more profoundly, from the affinity which must exist between every thing in a world resolved into its elements. The world on which the reader of Swinburne looks is that of a just completed creation, a world in which the elements have not yet accommodated themselves to the routine of co-operation or to a war of attrition. It is full of excitement, which the poet cannot always communicate to the reader, but which he himself feels intensely, because the wind and the sea have not yet learned the limitations of their power. And there is another excitement, man's, in the possession of fire. Swinburne uses that word, fire, the bare, undefined word, with incalculable frequency, and as if he were the contemporary of Prometheus, thinking not of a familiar serviceable thing, but of an elemental energy newly stolen from heaven.

He goes too far, but he can afford to go farther than any other of our poets in the use of the undefined natural symbol, in saying " wave ", " flame ", " wind ", " star ", without an epithet or with only such epithets as " swift ", " bright ", because the abstract things matter so uniquely to him, and because that use of them is singularly to his purpose. If, as a rule, he refuses to define his natural symbols, it is not that he is working in a decorative craftsman's convention like William Morris, who, very properly, will not allow one stitch of the tapestry he is making in verse to stand out from the rest, but that he would preserve the primordial value of the symbol, his sense of nature, for all the complexities of his own convention in rendering her, being thoroughly primitive.

That such a poet should have been urged, and by Watts-Dunton, to directly and elaborately descriptive poetry about nature is to me unintelligible. Whatever not inexcusably irritated people may say about Watts-Dunton, he had, in general, a truly remarkable insight into the principles of poetry and the conditions of poetical production. But, not only on this ground, I am forced to the conclusion that he understood certain sides of Swinburne's highly peculiar genius less than almost any other intelligent human being can have done. It was, or should have been, obvious that, with his mode of apprehending nature, his mode of rendering his experience of her, the finest of Swinburne's nature poetry was bound to be either incidental or an attack on the problem of the relationship between the soul of man and the prime energies of nature, and not descriptive of particular landscapes and seascapes. But Watts-Dunton, whether in his anxiety to find morally safe subjects for Swinburne or with some idea of widening his friend's range, persuaded him to undertake the novel task.

One of the earliest results, let it be gladly admitted, was not altogether unfortunate. "By the North Sea", in *Studies in Song*, is too diffuse, and it contains at least one piece in which Swinburne seems to be parodying himself; but here and there, especially when inspired by what was *macabre* in the subject, Swinburne does attain to success in calling up, in this strange flickering picture, the likeness of an unpeopled and disastrous shore, of the sand-encumbered tides, of ruined coastal churches and graveyards crumbling to the sea. And there are those lines in which he acquires a wizardry to which he very seldom even aspired:

" Far flickers the flight of the swallows,
Far flutters the weft of the grass,
Spun dense over desolate hollows,
More pale than the clouds as they pass:
Thick woven as the weft of a witch is,
Round the heart of a thrall that has sinned,
Whose youth and the wrecks of its riches
Are waifs in the wind."

The world for that instant has become a fluttering thing of mere surface; and there are some other momentary successes, as in " Neap Tide ", with its crepuscular harmony of ebbing waters and fading light, and more ambitiously, in " Evening on the Broads ", which has also its technical interest as offering us the English equivalent of elegiacs. But these successes are not numerous, and they are surrounded by quantities of verse almost intolerably diffuse and repetitive.

It is a pity that if Swinburne was to be pressed to write nature poetry, instead of being left to use natural symbols in his lavish incidental way, Watts-Dunton did not cast back to that piece, solitary in Swinburne's work, which surprises and delights and soothes the more discriminating readers of the first series of *Poems and Ballads*, " The Sundew ". It may be that the like of it could never again have been produced by its writer, but assuredly less harm would have been done in the attempt than resulted from incitation to rhapsodic descriptions of vague and vast marine subjects.

" The Sundew ", though adequately marked by its author's personality, comes nearer than anything else he wrote to being in the main English tradition of nature poetry. The little marsh plant is carefully transcribed from nature:

> " Yellow-green,
> And pricked at tip with tender red;
> Tread close, and either way you tread
> Some faint black water jets between
> Lest you should bruise the curious head."

With a Pre-Raphaelite touch or two, and some Swinburnian idiosyncrasy, there is in this poem an infusion of almost Wordsworthian sentiment:

> " We are vexed and cumbered in earth's sight,
> With wants, with many memories;
> These see their mother what she is,
> Glad-growing, till August leave more bright
> The apple-coloured cranberries."

The thing is seen clearly with all its actual circumstances, and the epithets, which is unusual with Swinburne, are descriptive in the ordinary sense, directly qualifying the immediate context instead of being merely contributions to the general atmosphere.

Or Watts-Dunton might have reminded Swinburne of his early successes in creating atmosphere, as in another of the first series of *Poems and Ballads*, " August ".

The Pre-Raphaelitism which, with some tincture of Tennyson's " Palace of Art ", had earlier yielded a passage in " The Two Dreams ",

> " Some angel's steady mouth and weight of wings,
>   Shut to the side; or Peter with straight stole
>   And beard cut black against the aureole,"

may perhaps be traced in such lines of " August " as

> " The split green wood,
>   With all its bearded lips and stains
>   Of mosses in the cloven veins."

But it is the power of creating atmosphere, already foreshadowed in " The Two Dreams ", with its rendering of a sick atmosphere in which all things felt sweet are felt sweet overmuch, and colour is a tyranny, and the weight of the trees a burden on the strengthless air, it is that power which makes " August " so wonderful. The drowsy luxury of the summer evening in the orchard, the colours soothing the sense like music, the slow invasion of the mind by peace,

> " As water feels the slow gold melt
>   Right through it when the day burns mute,"

are conveyed by Swinburne to his reader as few of the excited later experiences of place were. That power over atmosphere he never wholly lost. There is no more sustained exercise of it in his work than in one of the tragedies written in his old age, *Rosamund, Queen of the Lombards*, in which the oppression of summer is felt almost physically by the reader. But in the huge and whirling movements of his later lyrical rhapsodies over the sea there was lamentably seldom opportunity for its employment.

And yet it is in a late poem, one of the productions of that decline in which we are constantly told he became wholly incapable of high poetry, that this power was used with most originality. An able critic has lately managed to write a book on Swinburne without mentioning " A Nympholept ", and the two most distinguished authorities on Swinburne that we have among us excluded it from a selection of his poems. To me it seems the finest lyric he produced in the last twenty years of his life, and in its strange way one of the profoundest nature poems in the language, striking down as it does to an experience almost incredibly primitive, to an aboriginal sense of the beauty and terror of the earth. This poem, so full of the charm and dread of the forest, of " the naked noon ", of " the strong sun's imminent might ", of the fear to which the ancients gave the infinitely suggestive name, panic, is a dealing with mysteries, and in its treatment of natural facts is to fulfil Mallarmé's demand that the poet should give us " not the intrinsic dense wood of the trees " but " the silent thunder afloat in the leaves ". And for this delicate enterprise, which would seem to require a subtle, hushed, insinuating mode of verse, Swinburne chose a metre of emphatic stresses, a stanza that openly admits its artificiality. But the Kingdom of Pan, it would appear, no less than the Kingdom of Heaven, suffers violence: mysteries can be unveiled to this assertive, almost strident music, and an involved, rhetorical style can utter what might be supposed to be barely communicable in the whisper of some confessional lyric. A more paradoxical triumph it would be difficult to call to mind.

The poet is in the forest at noon, aware of the influences of the place and hour, strung with expectation of some momentous revelation. Is it love, is it dread, that enters into him? Dread at first. But thereafter:

" I sleep not: never in sleep has a man beholden
  This. From the shadow that trembles and yearns with light,

> Suppressed and elate and reluctant—obscure and
>   golden,
> As water kindled with presage of dawn or night—
> A form, a face, a wonder to sense and sight,
> Grows great as the moon through her month, and her
>   eyes embolden
> Fear, till it change to desire, and desire to delight."

The terror,

> " The sense, more fearful at noon than in midmost night,
>   Of wrath scarce hushed and of imminent ill to be ",

has yielded to this uncertainly won joy in nature. But whether Pan be indeed of goodwill towards man must remain doubtful, when the moment's conviction, or dream, is past. The beauty of the earth is enough, taken simply. Yet, is it? Something is lost if nature have no love towards man.

> " Thee, therefore, thee would I come to, cleave to,
>   cling,
> If haply thy heart be kind and thy gifts be good,
> Unknown sweet spirit. . . .
>
> The terror that whispers in darkness and flames in
>   light,
> The doubt that speaks in the silence of earth and sea,
> The sense, more fearful at noon than in midmost night,
> Of wrath scarce hushed and of imminent ill to be,
>   Where are they? Heaven is as earth, and as heaven
>   to me,
> Earth: for the shadows that sundered them here take
>   flight;
> And nought is all, as am I, but a dream of thee."

How is it that in this poem, first published in *Astrophel*, the last but one of his collections of lyrics, and produced in years in which Swinburne often lacked the power of communication, how is it that so much, such difficult substance, has been conveyed, and through a kind of verse which might be thought incapable of conveying any such intimate experience? We shall get no complete answer to that question, except from the fact that Swinburne was a great poet to the last days of his life, though he wrote but few great poems after forty. The miracles became infrequent; the power to work them was there, latent or misdirected though it might be, and this is one of the occasions on which it was exercised. But, I think, we need not leave the matter simply at that. There is a partial explanation.

In Swinburne, metrical urgency and great prodigality with metaphor and simile combine to make the reader incurious of the suggestions so abundantly and swiftly offered and withdrawn. In a more slow-moving writer, and one more economical with imagery, each metaphor will claim attention, and should any one of them be emphasized to the degree of suggestion that it is more than metaphor, the reader's mind will question, if only to accept, the claim. But where there is so much speed, with such profusion of imagery, the reader falls into the habit of discounting metaphors, past which he is in truth carried almost too rapidly for notice of them; and when, amidst a host of them that profess to be no more than metaphors, there occur those which assert identity, no challenge is perceived, the reader acquiesces in a claim he has not measured, and has conceded what the poet demands without being aware of it. Swinburne did not always use the opportunity his method gave him, but here, in "A Nympholept", he used it with extraordinary success, and I defy any reader, during perusal or immediately on its conclusion, to say at what point the poet's strangest matter was smuggled into the reader's mind.

This way of getting past the intellectual objection while the reader is taken up with the sound and shimmer of the verse may also be studied in the rather too diffuse and exaggerated poem, " On the Cliffs ". The involution, the haste, to what destination is not clear, the apparently half-accidental approach to the main theme, the employment of mere analogies in regard to what are eventually to be felt as identities, the frequent slight ambiguity, the haze and flickering light in which the relationship between Sappho, the nightingale, and the poet himself is established—these are trying, but enable some very curious things to be done.

Swinburne could be far simpler and more direct. Instead of working out the involved claim to imaginative kinship addressed in that poem to the nightingale he could say, in his wistful and charming verses " To a Seamew ", quite simply,

" When I had wings, my brother,
  Such wings were mine as thine."

But it was that involved, diffuse way of working, under cover, as it were, of an excess of sound, of an excess of metaphors, of a veil of the glittering spray thrown up by the speed of his movement, that was most characteristic of him; for good when he used the special opportunities it gave him, for evil when he did not. And it was not only, though it was with the most of tiresome failures, in his nature poetry that he employed that method. Elsewhere he had with it both failures and successes, few of the successes more remarkable than the elegy on Burton, written about the same time as " A Nympholept ", with its strange landscape, of which the thought, twisting and toiling forward through obscure analogies, never looses hold:

" Auvergne, Auvergne, O wild and woful land,
  O glorious land and gracious, white as gleam
  The stairs of Heaven, black as a flameless brand
  Strange even as life, and stranger than a dream! "

In his youth, like any other young poet, Swinburne had joy merely from the incidental beauty of nature, from each beautiful phenomenon, of the not very many observed by him, separately considered. Such joy can never be very long-lived, must fade out as the temperature falls in the blood, as beauty comes as less of a surprise; or, if it does survive, can inspire only an infantile, though delightful, poetry like that of some minor Elizabethan or of Mr. W. H. Davies. The deeper and more durable joy proper to great poets in maturity can come only of an apprehension of some valid relationship between all the observed phenomena of nature, and between them and man. Swinburne, from a rather early stage, was concerned much less with the static facts of nature than with her prime energies, and the bias of his thought against accepted religions, together with his defiant sense of man's potentialities, led him to an imaginative conception of the universe in which the idea of man as the master of things was imposed on a pantheism closely resembling that of Emerson's "Brahma". The great poem, preferred by its author to all other of his works,[1] in which this conception was formulated, is one of those compositions which baffle the compartmental critic. It is equally, or almost equally, a political poem, a religious poem, a poem of nature.

More explicitly philosophical than anything else he ever wrote, it is the most imaginatively tolerant of all his poems, acknowledging that those things which hinder the growth of the mystic tree of life are nevertheless part of it; and, indeed, on this view of the

[1] "Of all I have done I rate 'Hertha' highest as a single piece, finding in it the most of lyric force and music combined with the most of condensed and clarified thought."—Swinburne in a letter to E. C. Stedman. It was not till very late in life that he came to prefer his odes to all his other lyrics. To "Ave atque Vale", which must share with "Hertha" pride of place, he was consistently unjust.

universe, everything that exists is justified, in a sense, by the bare fact of its existence. The folly or crime, for man, in whom the life of the tree becomes fully conscious and capable of purpose, is to seek exterior sanction, instead of looking into his own mind and heart, where he would find impulses at one with nature's.

> " There is no God, O Son,
> If thou be none,"

says nature to man, in the piece called " On the Downs ". There is nothing knowable above or below the life in which nature and we are participators; there is no goal set for evolution by an exterior and superior will; growth has no guerdon but only to grow. But man is not released from obligation to a mythical exterior authority in the interests of moral anarchy, and nature is not so much *décor* for the mere delectation of atheistic connoisseurs. The obligation laid on man is heavy and infrangible. There is imposed on him the duty of identifying himself with the general life of the universe, of giving himself freely to its service.

> " I am in thee to save thee,
> As my soul in thee saith;
> Give thou as I gave thee,
> Thy life blood and breath,
> Green leaves of thy labour, white flowers of thy thought,
> and red fruit of thy death—

> For truth only is living,
> Truth only is whole,
> And the love of his giving
> Man's pole-star and pole;
> Man, pulse of my centre, and fruit of my body, and seed
> of my soul.

One birth of my bosom;
One beam of mine eye;
One topmost blossom
That scales the sky;
Man, equal and one with me, man that is made of me, man that is I."

The duty comes to man in many forms. There is the special demand made by contemporary political events, a demand on free men to further the development of political liberty. But there is also the vaster and more continuous demand made by a more comprehensive conception of liberty. And there is the mute, subtle, insistent demand made by nature on man, the demand, that he should enter imaginatively into her activities. In the most fortunate hour of his early manhood, Swinburne, responding with the utmost ardour to these complicated obligations, and impelled to communicativeness by a motive which, in the noblest sense, was propagandist, produced a body of magnificent poetry, political in a way, religious in a way, in which the energies of man and of nature are related with singular power and dignity. Later he retired into a commerce with nature which may be thought more disinterested, but in which we are seldom enabled to be participators. We do not so much share those later experiences as watch them. It is the spectacle, certainly, of one who has attained to living in the life of the great natural energies, of moving with the great natural rhythms, a wonderful thing, but sometimes with hardly more meaning for our minds than the evolutions of the seabirds over the waters or the intricate and endless movement of the waves. The sunrise that thrilled us when it was associated, not merely with certain generous mid-Victorian hopes, but with the eternal aspirations of man leaves us moved only with a dim wonder when it is a vague explosion of light;

the sea that was so real, though so strangely abstract, when it was breasted by the swimmer with a symbolical purpose becomes almost meaningless when it is an unrelated and interminable expanse of heaving water. Swinburne's connexions with the normal man were too few for any of them to be discarded with impunity, and it was extremely dangerous for him to write of nature without the motive to bind men together in their relation to her.

Chapter VIII

IN SHELTER

SWINBURNE at Putney has inspired enough cheaply ironical writing. I do not propose to add to the mass of it. In the autumn of 1879 he was dying in his rooms in Great James Street; dying of his excesses, making a sordid end over which moralists could have wagged their heads without rebuke. Watts gave Swinburne thirty years of healthy, happy, studious, productive life. He enabled Swinburne to complete the trilogy on Mary Queen of Scots, to assemble, join, and finish the fragments of his long-meditated *Tristram of Lyonesse*, to produce a score of lyrics that we should seriously miss from his work as well as perhaps two score that we would readily lose, to shape and conclude his *Study of Shakespeare*, to round off his criticisms of the Elizabethan drama, to write *Locrine* and *The Tale of Balen*. He restored him to health, to dignity, to as much peace of mind as was possible for such a nature. If there was among Swinburne's friends another man capable of doing as much, that potential redeemer never revealed the slightest inclination to undertake the work of rescue.

Certainly there is another side to this matter. Watts benefited substantially in the long run by his guardianship of Swinburne, and even developed an unbeautiful anxiety to extract advantage in prestige, and after Swinburne's death in cash, from the relationship. He was too complacent over the success of his rescue work; he assumed airs of proprietorship which excited irritation in everyone except Swinburne himself. But it is fair to remember that in the beginning the guardianship involved some considerable sacrifice of convenience and time, some risk of domestic embarrassment, for the Swinburne of 1879 was not precisely the kind of permanent co-tenant to be desired by the womenfolk of a middle-class family living in a respectable suburb, and Swinburne was not immediately able to confine his swearing to French. A respectable solicitor, living with his sister and young nephew, can hardly be supposed to feel that all is in her eyes, and in those of the maid-servants, as it should be when the friend housed under the same roof is one whose boots have to be concealed to prevent him issuing forth in search of brandy, and who pads about in his socks crying out, " O God, if there is a God, which there isn't, where are my damned boots?" And as to the proprietorship, the implication that Swinburne was a guest, the excessive control over him when all danger had vanished, it is right to consider whether Watts did not become guilty of those things simply in a needless continuation of what at the outset was absolutely necessary. His hold over Swinburne in the early critical weeks was simply through Swinburne's fine sense of what was due from guest to host. Had the poet been allowed then to regard himself as other than a guest, he would have taken the first opportunity to relapse into old ways. The fiction might very well have been abandoned after a few months. The cost of setting up the new establishment at The Pines, which Watts now took, was met by Lady Jane Swinburne; Swinburne himself, as his financial position improved, Messrs. Chatto and Windus having replaced Hotten as his publishers, and Watts having undertaken management of what remained of the £5,000 he had received under Admiral Swinburne's will, contributed substantially; and in the end Watts and his heirs had not only the copyright of Swinburne's works, but, first and last, about £10,000 from the sale of Swinburne's library and manuscripts.¹ In retrospect, it is clear that the advantages, financially, were heavily on the side of Watts and his relations. That things would so fall out was not perhaps very evident in 1880. But Watts should have modified the attitude as of host to guest when it had served its purpose in restraining Swinburne. So also, necessary as it was to keep certain of his former associates from Swinburne, he should not have continued the quiet, stubborn opposition to intercourse with several who, whether or not " bohemian ", were in no way dangerous.

But all this comes to little more than that Watts did not perceive when the need for discipline, make-believe, and segregation had gone by. More serious was his development of a peculiar, and very likely unconscious, jealousy of Swinburne's past. Watts was not an aristocrat, not a Northumbrian, not an Etonian, and he had emerged from the provinces into literary society in London only at the age of forty. He did not relish the idea of Swinburne as an aristocrat, a Northumbrian, an Etonian, and the wonder and terror of the literary London of, say, 1865-1870. He thwarted the poet's attempts to revisit Northumberland, if they ever got beyond mere wistful dreamings of going thither. He prevented acceptance of the invitation to visit Eton on the 450th anniversary of its foundation. He discouraged reminiscences of wild days among men whom he too knew and in some instances honoured, but in whose youthful pranks he had had no share. He

---

¹ Swinburne's library, described as such, was sold at Sotheby's in 1916 for £2,593. What was called Watts-Dunton's library was sold in 1917 for £2,761. These were parts of the one collection, used jointly by the poet and Watts-Dunton, and it owed its value very largely to contributions by and association with Swinburne. The best of the MSS. were acquired earlier by Mr. Wise for £3,000.

wished Swinburne, as far as might be, to blot from memory everything earlier than the date of their first meeting in 1872, everything alien to Watts. That this jealousy sprang mainly from his real affection for Swinburne does not alter the fact that it in some degree cramped the poet, for his past was all that Swinburne, growing deaf, grown irresponsive to most new experiences, segregated at The Pines, had to draw upon.

Further, as I have come to think, revising an older opinion in the light of much material not available to me or to other students thirteen years ago, Watts in some respects failed to understand his friend's genius. It is not that Watts was a Philistine with utterly groundless pretensions to esteem as poet and critic. In his curiously compounded nature, conventionality, of which he was quite unconscious, co-existed with an enthusiasm, to Swinburne rather tiresome, for gipsies and vagabonds in the abstract, with much emotional susceptibility, with a vein of poetry, a certain bent to mysticism. Professional, genteel, suburban as he could be, he was also in his way and degree a poetic nature, even at a few moments an achieving poet; and he had more than wide reading, had a really unusual insight into the principles of poetry, a real feeling for the vital importance of poetry in life. Look at that sonnet of his on Coleridge which George Meredith justly admired. The image is of a singular propriety, the tone and quality of the writing are not unworthy of one who was Rossetti's friend and Swinburne's. But he does not seem to have suspected the true needs of Swinburne's genius in those later years. How far he might have succeeded in convincing Swinburne that a poem is addressed to readers not already privy to the author's experience, how far he might have been able to impress on Swinburne the advantages of solidity in substance, outline in execution, concision, restraint, are matters for conjecture. What he did was to encourage poetry in description of vague natural subjects, and interminable allusive odes in honour of Swinburne's literary heroes. To be fair, in the beginning he probably had, as indeed he once confessed, to praise anything the convalescent poet wrote; and it may be that it was difficult to go back on such amiably insincere opinions. But, even allowing for this, there is reason to believe that he did not realize the qualities and limitations of the genius brought under his influence.

For the artist, wisdom is making the best of his own assets, no matter how constituted or limited, without reference to any principle of what is generally desirable. Watts had a generalizing mind, with many theories, often suggestive, of the requirements of poetry. What Swinburne needed was a friend who should encourage him to accept his now nearly complete irresponsiveness to new experiences, to concentrate on the experiences of his youth, to work on them in more or less dramatic lyrics. The poetry of love, his kind of love, had by no means been exhausted in the first *Poems and Ballads*. In that great poem, in the second series, " At a Month's End ", Swinburne had magnificently shown what he could do when writing, not the ecstatic lyrics of an amorous rapture in which only the poet has any real existence, but the poetry of passion experienced by two actualized persons, of passion definitely conditioned by their characters and their situation. With no sense of the theatre, Swinburne had a true sense of drama, and other work in that kind should not have been impossible for him. It should have been possible for him also, instead of expending so much energy in reporting, without much care whether he was communicating anything to the reader, the sensations of the grown man when introduced to the North Sea by Watts, whose confidence that two such old friends of his would get on together was better justified in life than in poetry, to render more frequently, in imaginatively re-living his vivid boyhood, the effect of nature on a young and fiery creature, such as he had been. Not expansion of experience, but reversion to old experience, should have been the policy. It may be urged that it was. But though Swinburne in the last thirty years of his life so very frequently celebrated old enthusiasms, it was usually without throwing himself back into the past. We have only to turn to *The Tale of Balen* to see how far more fortunate were the results when he fully returned to his boyhood than when he did so partially and unconsciously.

But whatever Watts may have failed to do or done amiss, he gave Swinburne security. The poet's life now became one of almost mechanical regularity. Each morning, except Sunday, he issued from The Pines, rather late, for a long solitary walk, usually up Putney Hill and across the Heath, returning in time for the somewhat bourgeois lunch, to which, in his restored health, he sat down with an invariably good appetite. Watts-Dunton and members of the family or occasional guests shouted what they had to say to a charmingly courteous, smiling, not very attentive listener, till the Elizabethan drama or Æschylus or Landor or Hugo was mentioned, and then Swinburne's beautiful voice, which, unlike the voice of the typical sufferer from deafness, was very seldom raised to unnecessary loudness, was added to the mild debate and in a moment or two delightfully dominated it. The joint removed, the poet's beer finished, for he now drank only beer, and the descant on Marlowe or the Legend of the Ages concluded, he would retire to his bedroom for a couple of hours of dozing. In the afternoon, he would write in his study upstairs, where, from the window, he could see the garden and a statue which had once been in Rossetti's. His desk was the one which his mother had given him when he went to Oxford. He did not sit at it continuously, but walked round and round the book-lined room, composing the stanza or sentence in his mind, before he sat down to the task, to him always distasteful, of putting it on paper. Presently he would descend and read, Dickens by choice, to Watts. Then there would be the evening meal, and thereafter some three hours of more work in his study.

Visitors were not numerous. With the exception of Jowett, and, for a period, William Morris, and on a few occasions Burton, whose cigarette-smoking agitated Swinburne, older friends kept away, either because they were definitely banned or because they did not care to see Swinburne only by permission of Watts and in his presence. A certain number of younger writers and scholars were introduced to him. From 1886 he was periodically gratified by the visits of Mr. Thomas J. Wise, who was already collecting, with ardour and discrimination, not only his works, but those of writers dear to him, notably Shelley and Landor. Swinburne was a little impatient about the nice distinctions between tall and other copies, cut and uncut edges, but in his way he too was a bibliophile, and he appreciated to the full the compliment conveyed by Mr. Wise's assiduity. It would have pleased him greatly to know that the rarest of his productions, with so very many of his manuscripts and letters, would come eventually into the reverent keeping of so erudite, fastidious, and enthusiastic a collector. A poet or critic appeared now and then. Mr. Arthur Symons, whose early editorial and critical work on the Elizabethans was justly valued by Swinburne, once told me how Swinburne interrupted an inspection of the quartos in the study with a gleam of the old mischief, offering to quote him the most indecent line in the whole of English drama, which proved to be, " On this soft anvil all the world was made ". Mr. Max

Beerbohm and Mr. E. V. Lucas were visitors who have left valuable impressions. Mr. Cockerell, Professor Fitzmaurice Kelly, and others were congenial to the scholar in Swinburne. But Watts had a number of literary friends or acquaintances who belonged, if not exactly to Gath itself, to some outlying and only partially redeemed suburb of it, and it can hardly be pretended that any serious attempt was made to bring Swinburne into contact with the most significant of the younger generation of writers as such. He corresponded, however, with Mr. Hardy, was constantly exchanging letters of extraordinary interest with his younger brother in Elizabethan scholarship, A. H. Bullen, and had communications with others who meant something to him.

Literature was a living thing at The Pines, and to Watts as well as to Swinburne. Munro used to lower his voice when he spoke of the scandals of ancient Rome; at The Pines, Landor and Lamb and Coleridge and Shelley were felt to be still living and susceptible, and Watts had to warn visitors that Hazlitt's name was not to be mentioned.

It has been said that Swinburne's first task on the recovery of his health was the completion of *A Study of Shakespeare*. As a matter of fact, that work had been completed on the 27th August 1879, at his mother's house, Holmwood.[1] At Putney his energies were first devoted to the continuation of *Mary Stuart*, which, however, he had presently to lay aside for some months, and to the collection and completion of the parodies, most of them written between 1859 and 1877, which appeared in 1880, anonymously, as *The Heptalogia*. In 1880 he also issued *Songs of the Springtides*, which to

[1] "This morning before breakfast about 8, I put the very last touch to the very last paragraph of my book on Shakespeare."— Letter from Swinburne to Watts, bearing the date given above.

a considerable extent consisted of work done before the removal to Putney, and *Studies in Song*, the whole of which had been written in the spring and summer of that year. He then reverted to *Tristram of Lyonesse*, the prelude to which, probably his finest achievement in heroic couplets, had been written, not, as officially stated, in 1871, but towards the end of December 1869.[1] A great poem on this subject had been among his projects since his first year at Oxford; in 1869 it was now begun, the immediate impulse being intense irritation with Tennyson's latest instalment of Arthurian or Albertian idylls, but was soon dropped, and though he wrote passages of it spasmodically during the next nine or ten years, it was only in 1881 that he settled resolutely to its completion. In 1883, in an endeavour to check his excessive facility, he composed, in a form which was a compromise between that of the rondeau and that of the rondel, *A Century of Roundels*, which he dedicated to Christina Rossetti. The efficacy of the check imposed by the form may be judged from the fact that the hundred poems were written in considerably less than that number of days! In 1884 he published the weakest of his volumes of lyrical verse, *A Midsummer Holiday*. He now wisely paused in the almost mechanical production of lyrics, issuing no collection till the third series of *Poems and Ballads*, 1889, containing, of old work, certain very striking Border ballads written more than twenty years previously and embedded in the unpublished *Lesbia Brandon*, and, of new work, " The Commonweal ", the fine elegy on Inchbold, and " Pan and Thalassius ".

[1] Letter from Swinburne to D. G. Rossetti, the holograph original of which is in Mr. Wise's collection, dated 22nd December 1869. The 250 lines were written, apparently, in one day and almost at a single sitting, the most striking proof that we have of how naturally splendour and elaboration came to Swinburne.

Meanwhile he had been active in drama, producing, in 1885, *Marino Faliero*, full of dignity and eloquent semi-prophetic speeches from a highly idealized hero, and the beautifully ingenious and charming play, *Locrine*. His prose production had also been abundant: a volume of *Miscellanies* containing the great eulogy of Wordsworth and the witty transfer of sex as between Alfred de Musset and George Sand, and other excellent criticism in increasingly mannered prose, had been published in 1886; volumes on Victor Hugo and Ben Jonson followed; and in 1894 there came *Studies in Prose and Poetry*, including, alas, the article on Walt Whitman.

In 1891 he had written the finest lyric of his old age, "A Nympholept", afterwards included in *Astrophel*, 1892; in 1896 appeared the freshest, most human, most lucid, least straining long poem of his last twenty years, *The Tale of Balen*, full of his own youth and of the clean, sharp air of his native Northumberland. The tragedy, *Rosamund, Queen of the Lombards*, 1889, showed a new concentration of effort on strictly dramatic effect, with both gain and loss. Lastly there were published *A Channel Passage and other Poems*, 1904, and a tragedy, *The Duke of Gandia*, 1908, with at least one scene in which, through the curt dialogue, we feel contact between ourselves and the supreme criminal intelligence that dominates the action.

Twenty-nine years had now slipped by with hardly an event. Each year, late in the summer, Swinburne had gone with Watts, or, as from 1896 he became, Watts-Dunton, to the seaside for his favourite recreation of swimming. Occasionally they had visited Jowett, whose housekeeper no longer had to remove the bottles from Swinburne's luggage. In the autumn of 1882 they had accepted Victor Hugo's invitation to Paris to be present at the revival after fifty years of *Le Roi s'amuse*.

Hugo had been lavish in compliments to Swinburne since, in the early 'sixties, he had received his English disciple's first tributes—the five articles in the *Spectator* reviewing *Les Misérables*. In presenting his portrait to Swinburne in 1874, he had inscribed it: "*Au noble Poëte Swinburne, son ami, Victor Hugo*". In acknowledging *Bothwell*, dedicated to him in a fine French sonnet, he had alluded to Swinburne's definition of it as an epic drama: "*occuper ces deux cimes, cela n'est donné qu'à vous.*" And eventually on this occasion in Paris he was to assure Swinburne that he was happy to press his hand as that of his son. But before that there was some confusion in the incense-laden atmosphere, so that at the moment of first presentation Swinburne was hardly identified by the aged and illustrious poet; and afterwards when Swinburne, not having been able to hear the terms in which Hugo proposed his health, could not make Hugo hear his own fervent reply, there was a scene of pure comedy, the final touch to which was put by Swinburne, in the fearless old fashion, breaking the glass out of which he had drunk to the master, and Hugo emerging from his Olympian reverie to mourn the destruction of one of his best glasses.

But Swinburne's admiration, which had long ceased to be based on any of the facts of Hugo's production or personality, and was neither time's fool nor at any point corrigible by experience, continued unabated. The master's death was a very great sorrow to him, relieved by writing the long study of his works and the brief beautiful poem, "In time of mourning", in which, surprisingly, there is not a superfluous word. The production of elegies now became an important part of his poetical life. Earlier he had tried to restrain his generosity in tributes of this kind, confessing to a fear that if he wrote any more necrological poems he would be generally regarded as professionally devoted to mortuary literature. But as the years thinned the ranks of his friends, the impulse to honour them and to recall old days repeatedly proved too strong. Nor need we regret it: much of the better work of his age is in these poems. Incidentally, they confirm my contention that wholehearted imaginative reversion to his boyhood and youth invariably, in these later years, resulted in work above the average of that which he produced in expression of recent experience.

His friendships had always mattered profoundly to Swinburne and he very largely lived in them. But it should be realized his contact with his friends was now infrequent or interdicted. The peculiar quality of his emotion towards every friend but one was determined by the fact that though they lived, though occasionally he corresponded with them or even met some of them, he saw them chiefly in retrospect, loved them for what they had been to him long ago, thought of them almost as a man thinks of the lost friends of his boyhood. No man was ever less given to gush and demonstration in friendship than Swinburne. He had beautiful patrician ways, with reticence in all his volubility. But in these years there came into his feeling for his old friends a singular tenderness. Certain of his dedications, certain of his published and unpublished letters, reveal a delicacy of devotion hardly to be paralleled. And to this his friends responded. There exist, for example, letters to him from Burne-Jones in which he is addressed by the nickname of his childhood, " Hadji ", an Oriental allusion not clear to his correspondent, who sometimes spells it otherwise: " My dearest Hadji ", " Dear little Carrots ", and so forth. And Swinburne, learning of that illness which was to end the life of William Morris, writes to " My dearest Ned " a letter of sacred affection, telling him how constantly he composed in his mind messages to them both. And lastly there comes the beautiful tribute to their memories:

" No sweeter, no kindlier, no fairer,
No lovelier a soul from its birth
Wore ever a brighter and rarer
Life's raiment for life upon earth
Than his who enkindled and cherished
Art's vestal and luminous flame,
That dies not when kingdoms have perished
In storm or in shame.

No braver, no trustier, no purer,
No stronger and clearer a soul
Bore witness more splendid and surer
For manhood found perfect and whole
Since man was a warrior and dreamer
Than his who in hatred of wrong
Would fain have arisen a redeemer
By sword or by song."

Chapter IX

THE LYRICAL DRAMAS

THE prominence given long ago in criticism of Swinburne's work to *Atalanta in Calydon* will never be sensibly diminished. Despite certain small defects, that poem remains the one major thing done by him which can be confidently recommended to every type of reader. But though, except in some details, there is no reason to challenge the unanimous verdict of Victorian criticism in regard to *Atalanta*, it is very necessary to correct the general assumption that its successor, *Erechtheus*, was simply an attempt to repeat that early triumph. The two plays on the Greek model have much less in common than their structure suggests, and it is with some reluctance that I treat of them together. *Atalanta* is the work of an inspired boy: *Erechtheus*, with as real though with less readily recognizable an inspiration, is the work of a man. It is not in the nature of things that the austerer emotion of the later play, excited by a kind of patriotism foreign to the average modern mind, should evoke anything like as general and swift a response, but the greater of two things does not become the less merely because it is less charming, less easily to be taken to the ordinary bosom.

Atalanta is a tragedy of youth, full of virginal and virile young ardours. Something of the dawn is about Atalanta herself and Meleager and other of the persons of the drama. That atmosphere of youth, of matutinal beauty and energy, is so pervasive and the result of so many factors that it is barely permissible to exhibit it in any one passage or to lay stress upon any one of the means by which it is created, but it may be pointed out that Swinburne's concern for it began with the very choice of characters. For whereas in the legend as he found it Meleager had a wife, Swinburne excluded her, presenting us with a hero, experienced in arms and in the chase, but innocent of women, and acquainted with love only as the dedicated maiden Atalanta comes into his life. And everywhere, from the opening speech of the Chief Huntsman in supplication to the maiden goddess, and the rapturous first chorus of spring, to the darkening of day with the feast turned funeral, the lights and colours are those of morning and April. Candour, brilliance and speed, blossoming beauty, and strength that has yet to reach its utmost development, all the attributes of youth, are in this play, and in the writing of it a young poet's delight in his lately discovered command of the instrument of verse, a lovely exuberance, not yet become extravagance.

Naturally enough it was the novelty of the lyrical utterances, the choruses, that attracted most attention in 1865, but it is more than time that justice were done to the peculiar excellence of the blank verse, which, if less obviously stamped with its author's personality, was really as novel, and in which, for the two earlier plays, *The Queen Mother* and *Rosamund*, showed it much less and were unheeded, there was first fully revealed to the reading public this poet's art in the employment of lines made up mainly or wholly of monosyllables.

" Pray thou thy days be long before thy death,
  And full of ease and kingdom; seeing in death
  There is no comfort and none aftergrowth,
  Nor shall one thence look up and see day's dawn,
  Nor light upon the land whither I go.
  Live thou and take thy fill of days and die,
  When thy day comes! and make not much of death,
  Lest ere thy day thou reap an evil thing."

Mastery of blank verse was later to be even more strikingly shown by Swinburne in *Bothwell* and elsewhere, but it may be doubted whether in any other work of his he displayed greater naturalness in transition from this kind to that which accords with the more usual idea of eloquence. The whole of that long and great final speech of Meleager from which I have quoted deserves the most careful examination, for it, with many other passages of his blank verse certainly, but perhaps more conclusively than any other, answers those who, thinking of the most mechanically stressed portions of his lyrical, or rather of his rhapsodical verse, deny him the finer kind of variety, which is lacking, which is generally regretted, but which would have been an error in the single-hearted and austerely lofty *Erechtheus*.

Atalanta is in many respects the most balanced, using that term in the strict sense, of Swinburne's ampler works. It offers us, for one thing, the most nearly perfect balance between his classical and his romantic tendencies. Again, it comes nearer than any other work of his on the great scale to striking a just balance between the sense of a dominating and inexorable fatality and the impulse to challenge it, though the attentive reader cannot fail to notice that in one choral utterance defiance is carried to the point where it not only disturbs this balance but for a moment vitiates the dramatic atmosphere. Then, too, there is in the structure of *Atalanta* an admirable concern for the correspondence of parts, even though within each part there may be something of that delicate excess of which I have already written. This last merit, perceptible as it must be to every competent reader, is not now likely to receive quite its due applause. The most of us have forgotten, and some to-day may not ever have known, the ideals which prevailed when the amorphous and drifting compositions of Dobell and of the author of *Festus* were in favour;

we can hardly realize how surprisingly shapely and how resolutely directed *Atalanta* appeared to those who first held in their hands the handsome cream-coloured quarto of the original issue, and felt that here at last was found, and despite a charming exuberance, the restraint of a definite and dramatic purpose. On the other hand, we to-day may be supposed to be much more generally alive than the public of sixty years ago to the poet's failure to give certain of his choruses the dramatic value they should have possessed, and to insecurity in his conception of the fate which at times seems identifiable with the will of the gods and at others to master even them.

Familiar as *Atalanta* may be presumed to be to all possible readers of these pages, it is well to remind ourselves of the course of its action, which is ordered from the outset with a fine skill in preparing for conquest of the chief difficulties of the subject. That Althæa is doomed to destroy her son by setting fire to the quenched brand on which his life depends is a thing we may accept with a willing suspension of disbelief; but whatever the celestial explanation of the tragedy, it is essential that the poet should trace on earth also the causes of it. He provides it in Althæa's exceptional tenderness of memory. She is one, as she says, who remembers what others forget:

" For what lies light on many and they forget,
   Small things and transitory as a wind o' the sea,
   I forget never."

Those words are from her speech, early in the play, to Meleager, warning him against the peril of loving such a one as Atalanta. By emphasizing this tender devotion to the past, and in this particular form of devotion to remembered childhood, her own son's here, presently her own and her brothers', Swinburne does much more than provide a means whereby, on the human plane, we may reconcile Althæa the infinitely loving mother with Althæa the destroyer of her son: he also intensifies the tragedy by making her vengeance spring from that in her which makes her so perfect a mother.

In words which might well be cited in support of Swinburne's contention that great poets are bi-sexual, so intimately do they express the emotions of maternal retrospect, she says there, while the hunters are assembling, to Meleager:

" I have seen thee all these years
A man in arms, strong and a joy to men
Seeing thine head glitter and thine hand burn its way
Through a heavy and iron furrow of sundering spears;
But always also a flower of three suns old,
The small one thing that lying drew down my life
To lie with thee and feed thee, a child and weak,
Mine, a delight to no man, sweet to me.
Who then sought to thee? who got help? who knew
If thou were goodly? nay, no man at all. . . .
But fair for me thou wert, O little life,
Fruitless, the fruit of mine own flesh, and blind,
More than much gold, ungrown, a foolish flower."

But not less tender are Althæa's memories of the childhood of her brothers:

" I would have died for these;
For this dead man walked with me, child by child,
And made a weak staff for my feebler feet
With his own tender wrist and hand, and held,
And led me softly and showed me gold and steel,
And shining shapes of mirror and bright crown,
And all things fair, and threw light spears, and brought
Young hounds to huddle at my feet and thrust
Tame heads against my little maiden breasts
And please me with great eyes. . . .

There were no sons then in the world, nor spears
Nor deadly births of women; but the gods
Allowed us, and our days were clear of these."

It is not of the violent folly that precipitated the ending of their lives, but of their loving chivalry to her long ago that Althæa thinks, and it is out of this passion of remembrance, for which we have been admirably prepared by her earlier utterances, that she sets fire to the fatal brand after the Messenger has related to her the slaying of Toxeus and Plexippus by her son.

That narrative and, even more remarkably, the narrative of the Herald who brings news of the destruction of the boar, are masterly in triumph over a difficulty inherent in the form of the play. It was barely possible that the two recitals should escape flatness, and it might have been expected that the poet would have set himself to that evasion by which is so easily earned praise for restraint. Swinburne, that is to say, might have been expected to rely on the telling effect of the bare fact in each event, instead of which he gave us, with extraordinary spirit and brilliance, a full story. The narrative of the Herald, especially, is a marvellous achievement, with its vivid description of Plexippus silenced amidst his boasting by the sudden sight of the boar,

"Where the green ooze of a sun-struck marsh
Shook with a thousand reeds untunable,
And in their moist and multitudinous flower
Slept no soft sleep, with violent visions fed,
The blind bulk of the immeasurable beast";

of the wounded boar crashing through the reddened brake; of Meleager braced to the encounter,

"Right in the wild way of the coming curse,
Rock-rooted, fair with fierce and fastened lips,

Clear eyes, and springing muscle and shortening limb,
With chin aslant indrawn to a tightening throat,
Grave and with gathered sinews, like a god;"

and, by an exquisitely managed transition, of the place of the hunters' repose, where,

" Much sweet grass grew higher than grew the reed,
And good for slumber, and every holier herb,
Narcissus, and the low lying melilote
And all of goodliest blade and bloom that springs
Where, hid by heavier hyacinth, violet buds
Blossom and burn; and fire of yellower flowers
And light of crescent lilies, and such leaves
As fear the Faun's and know the Dryad's foot;
Olive and ivy and poplar dedicate."

This kind of poetry may be out of fashion now, but there is not anywhere in even our literature finer work of anything like the same sort. It has dignity in energy, a beautiful, proud, young step, rapid and confident, with brief, lovely pauses as of one whose speedy foot would now and then prolong the luxury of contact with the sward of spring.

But indeed throughout this play, till night comes with such tragic prematurity, there is that sense of youth, of morning, of vernal impulse. And when his doom has been dealt out to Meleager and his body is wasting with the burning of the brand, those same motives are worked into the conclusion with rare art. The alternation of the Second Messenger's three-line speeches in blank verse and the half-quatrains of lyrical verse uttered by the semichorus has, perhaps, little more than technical interest. But the great lament, so novel and beautiful in its stanzaic form, to which Meleager himself, Atalanta, and the chorus contribute, uses with delicate pathos those old associations as the chorus mourns over the dying man,

" O the grief, O the grace,
As of day when it dies ",

as Atalanta wishes that death had come to her ere she beheld him made dark in his dawn; and the great farewell speech of Meleager, in its outpouring of filial devotion, reviving memories of parental love towards him, reaches back into the morning of his days.

To say of so noble a play that it is yet, under the severest tests, inferior to *Erechtheus*, may well seem almost blasphemous. And indeed the assertion of its inferiority needs to be qualified. *Atalanta* issues from the totality of Swinburne's genius; *Erechtheus* issues from what was specialized in it. The later play is a tragedy of citizenship in the purest and sublimest, but, it must be added, rarest conception that men have had of it, whereas *Atalanta* is a tragedy of humanity. Unquestionably there is a narrowing of the appeal, a peculiar limitation of the range of emotion, in *Erechtheus*, and with that a concentration in the writing on uniformity of effect without the slightest relief. Man may be a political animal, but he is seldom quite so political as all that. Also, the average intelligence, nourished on romantic and realistic literature, grows uneasy when page after page makes the one steady demand on it, when the central subject is never allowed to be forgotten, when there are no episodes of a more obviously human and, in the Rossettian sense, amusing quality. But all this does not affect the truth that nowhere else in Swinburne is there a body of verse so evenly magnificent, that nowhere else is there in him work so minutely and firmly organized by the intellect. We could never have too many plays like *Atalanta*; we can hardly wish for more like *Erechtheus*; but we, or those of us who have learned to approach it in the right temper, can never be sufficiently grateful that we have *Erechtheus* itself. A more conclusive, though unintentional, reply to those who urge that Swinburne had no intellectual centre cannot be imagined. For what, from the point of view of detractors, is the trouble with *Erechtheus* but that it is all inexorably related to an intellectual centre, that it is rigid, and allows no opportunity for the pettier and more gusty of the human passions, no scope for the growth of mere idiosyncrasy in its characters?

I cannot hope that any arguments of mine will secure justice for *Erechtheus*. People in general long ago made up their minds that it was an attempt to repeat the success won with *Atalanta*, and, finding it colder and more specialized, they concluded that it was less inspired. Actually, it is full of passion, of a white heat of passion for something remote from the minds of most men indeed but worthy of the utmost worship that man can give an ideal.

The plot of the play may seem, and some years ago I myself was unimaginative enough to describe it as being, intolerable in its cruelty. Athens is menaced by the Thracians. Twice before has the city of Pallas been in peril, in consequence of the inveterate animosity of the god not honoured there; now is imminent the final assault. The oracle has declared that salvation is possible only through the sacrifice of Chthonia, daughter of Erechtheus and of Praxithea, and in view of the origin of Erechtheus, which it is necessary to remember, daughter of the very earth for which she is to die. The horror of the maiden sacrifice is not diminished by the poet, who indeed uncompromisingly allows the chorus, of old men, not of girls as in *Atalanta*, to expatiate on it with ferocity. But when I thought it intolerable I was guilty of thinking of the thing in itself, not of what it is in the atmosphere of a play in which every Athenian

Emery Walker, Ltd., Photo

ALGERNON CHARLES SWINBURNE
*From a Drawing in The Fitzwilliam Museum, Cambridge
attributed to Simeon Solomon*

character is uplifted to regard sacrifice for the dear and sacred city the loftiest of privileges. The necessary note has been struck very early in the play, in the first speech altered by Erechtheus in prayer to Pallas:

> " Fare we so short-lived howsoever and pay
> What price we may to ransom thee thy town
> Not me my life; but thou, thou diest not, thou
> Though all our house die for the people's sake,
> Keep thou for ours thy crown our city, guard
> And give it life lovelier that we died."

That note is heard again and again, when Erechtheus brings to Praxithea the terrible mysterious message and she supposes herself destined to die for the city, when she tells Chthonia who it is that must be sacrificed and her daughter accepts her doom,

> " This my doom that seals me deathless till the springs
>   of time run dry ",

and glories in it:

> " That I may give this poor girl's blood of mine
> Scarce yet sun-warmed with summer, this thin life
> Still green with flowerless growth of seedling days
> To build again my city; that no drop
> Fallen of these innocent veins on the cold ground
> But shall help knit the joints of her firm walls
> To knead the stones together, and make sure
> The band about her maiden girdlestead
> Once fastened, and of all men's violent hands for
>   ever...."

Chthonia sacrificed, Athens is saved by the victory which Erechtheus wins over the invader, Eumolpus, losing his own life in the moment of triumph. And then, while the chorus with changed note is bewailing the stain of innocent blood on the freedom of Athens,

Athena herself appears to comfort the stricken Praxithea, who answers:

"There is no grief
Great as the joy to be made one in will
With him that is the heart and rule of life."

And the chorus breaks into the song of the glorious future of Athens, with its prophecy that the enmity of the sea towards her shall be allayed.

"And the sons of thine earth shall have help of the
    waves that made war on their morning
And friendship and fame of the sea."

Erechtheus is far more Greek than *Atalanta*, both in spirit and in the construction of its choruses, which follow the classical arrangement into strophe, antistrophe, and occasionally epode. That, though hardly negligible in a composition professing to be on the Greek model, is of very much less moment than the merits for which Swinburne is beholden to no exemplar. The sustained loftiness of the emotion, the grave ardour of expression, the unfaltering speed with which the action is conducted, the exactitude with which the whole material is organized, the continuous relation of all of it to the chief motive of the play, these are merits more greatly to be honoured, by those who can apprehend them, than any incidental splendours, any episodical appeals to the softer sentiments. Of the choruses, perhaps not one remains in the memory as naturally as most of those of *Atalanta* do; but not even Swinburne has written with more brilliance in lyrical attack than in the chorus which tells of the North Wind's wild wooing of Oreithyia or with more elaborate splendour than in the chorus of storm and battle. The gain from adherence to the classic model may be exaggerated, though it does seem to me that there is more gain here than in those odes, of which his ode to Athens may here be most pertinently cited, and which Swinburne in his old age decidedly over-valued. But in several of the choruses of *Erechtheus*, as indeed in many passages of the blank verse, we have, unhappily for almost the last time, a chastity of language and gravity of temper to which Swinburne never attained with any frequency earlier than *Songs before Sunrise* or later than the second series of *Poems and Ballads*. For all the release of his lyrical frenzy he has in this play, and in these two volumes, weight as well as wings, direction as well as impulse. Here, too, he has concision amidst the ordered exuberance, whether in curt often antithetical phrases or in condensed imagery:

" For the womb
Bare me not base that bare me miserable; "

" Old men, grey borderers on the march of death;"

" Who bear but in our hands
The weapons not the fortunes of the fight;"

" Man, what thy mother bare thee born to say Speak."

The old art in the use of monosyllabic lines is frequently evident, but there is also something much less familiar to the reader of Swinburne, a kind of tautness in the blank verse, with certain movements which clinch a high argument weightily.

No other of the greater works of Swinburne flowed from him so evenly. The original manuscript shows indeed no small number of corrections and deletions, and it may be worth while to glance at two typical pages, though they and others not to be commented upon here do but confirm the feeling that from first to last, whatever details needed reconsideration, the aim never altered and the hand never hesitated.

The initial speech of Erechtheus is corrected only in the interests of more vivid and condensed expression. Where the King alludes to his taming of, till then, masterless horses, the line originally written

" And first bow down to bear man's curb and rein "

became

" And first bow down the bridled strength of steeds ";

and its successor,

" And bend their necks beneath them and endure "

became

" To lose the wild wont of their birth and bear."

The line originally written

" Or fourfold pace beneath his chariot (?) "

was changed into

" Or fourfold service of his fire-swift wheels."

And so on and so forth. As to what things, too beautiful to be spared but by the demands of so high a subject, were eventually rejected by the poet, let this one example testify. Towards the end of the chorus which immediately precedes the speech of the Athenian Herald, coming with news of the dear-bought victory, the expression of nascent hope in the hearts of the waiting elders was originally followed by these lines:

" So now may the wind that the rose-months know
  Breathe gracious and low,
With a fair breeze filling the full sail spread
That hardly for storms could at all make head

Till the hour that is come now in season to birth
With a song in the beat of its westward wings
That earth may be full of the word it brings,
For a grace to the children of earth."

They are not to be found in the printed text.

For all the revision the play underwent during the few weeks of its writing, there were during that fortunate period no false starts, no hesitations as to the course of the action or the general temper of the play, and *Erechtheus* may rightly be regarded as that work in which Swinburne was most completely master of all his resources and most resolutely bent on securing through them a single effect. It is also, as I have elsewhere said, the work which most fully and nobly embodies his political, or, as I prefer to call it, his religious ideal; and it is not the poet, majestically at home in that rarefied atmosphere, but we who are to be condemned if the ideal is too foreign to us for complete appreciation.

Chapter X

THE TRAGEDIES

AS a dramatist, Swinburne "wrote for antiquity". With his very uncertain feeling for the public, he would have come no nearer to satisfying it if he had striven to write for the contemporary stage, in which he took no interest, though he did get as far as once discussing with the taciturn Irving the possibility of a production of, presumably some fraction of, *Bothwell*. For one type of mind, the dramatic pretensions of Swinburne are at once and completely discounted by the fact that his are not acting plays. To me, if I may venture to say so, the description of his tragedies as closet-drama is not finally decisive of his claims. The poetical drama that cannot be produced on the modern stage is not necessarily an illegitimate thing. The question is whether the form is justified by the results, whether something of emotional and imaginative worth has been produced which could not have been brought into existence by the adoption of any other form.

There are dramatic poets who can compromise with stage requirements, with more or less of gain in some respects, more or less of loss in others: there are others with whom compromise must mean total loss. Swinburne had but little of the power, proper to the pure novelist, the pure dramatist, of solving a human problem in action. He had, within certain limits, a real feeling for character, and he had an extraordinary sense of historical and emotional atmosphere, with a rare eloquence in the expression of erotic and of patriotic passion. To complain of him that he did not, in quest of a merit to which he could not have attained, sacrifice all the opportunities he secured by ignoring the conditions of the contemporary stage is surely foolish. *The Queen Mother*, *Chastelard*, *Bothwell*, *Marino Faliero*, and, apart from these, the singularly charming *Locrine*, are works of art in which we have presented to us certain vivid characters in an appropriate atmosphere. It is reasonable, it is necessary, to say that in no one of these do we feel that curiosity about the progress of events, that suspense, that profound final satisfaction which the complete dramatist gives us. But each offers us character, atmosphere, the expression of passion, and in no form other than that which he has used could the poet have given us these. We may not be at the centre of that world in which the complete dramatist works, but assuredly we are not merely in the province of the writer of dramatic soliloquy. In each of the plays there are effects of contrast and co-operation; the persons influence each other powerfully; the picture unrolled before us is not one in which we may be content to note one figure at a time without heed to the significant grouping. *Bothwell*, indeed, owes much of its effect to the host of personages who contribute to the tragedy, not knowing what the remote consequences of their words and gestures will be. The conclusion of *Mary Stuart* throws back, in the finest of Swinburne's dramatic inventions, to the sin against love in *Chastelard*, and the Queen dies in expiation. There is construction in these plays, which, in truth, though this is forgotten in the now general contempt heaped on all quasi-Elizabethan drama, are protests against the lax exercises in what was then supposed to be the Elizabethan form or an improvement on it. Take the conventional view of Swinburne as a dramatic poet, and he might be expected to applaud Beddoes: he had, in fact, a hearty detestation of the dramatic work of that poet.[1] Exuberant as much of Swinburne's own dramatic work may be, it is ordered, and the vastness of *Bothwell* comes not of digression but of an extreme, possibly excessive, anxiety to do justice to every part of an enormous subject.

In the tragedies, and that is one of the reasons why they should receive more attention from the student of Swinburne, there is visible a development which continued to the end of his life. As a lyrist he wrote very little after 1875, and scarcely anything after 1881, which expresses new interests or a modification of technical ambitions; as a dramatic poet he was still evolving when he died. I do not profess that his progress as a writer of tragedy was of any startling kind, that it involved any sudden and violent break with his past, or that it has extraordinary intrinsic importance. But, having regard to the general stiffening and setting of his mind in early middle age, it does concern us to note that in this one department of his imaginative activity there was progress.

He began with those selfless exercises in the manner of Fletcher done at Oxford. Before he left the University he had produced what, with much revision, eventually became the less valuable of the two plays issued, to an entirely unheeding world, in 1860. *Rosamund*, with a substratum of Elizabethan drama, is superficially Pre-Raphaelite, echoing Ros-

---

[1] There is possibly an echo of Beddoes, as an eminent critic has suggested, in one line of *The Queen Mother*:

"Naked as brown feet of unburied men."

Possibly, not probably; Swinburne, it must be remembered, in early life had a certain taste for the *macabre*, which was evident in his talk until Watts-Dunton frowned upon it.

setti, touched here and there by the influence of Browning. There are charming verses in it, and already there is a feeling for atmosphere, but its persons are exhibited, with some delicate distortion, as on a tapestry or canvas, in graceful languor, decoratively, without appreciation of the angularities of character, and without energy. *The Queen Mother*, still disgracefully neglected, is quite another affair. With still more feeling for atmosphere, it has a real hold on character; the speeches of Catherine are personal; pungency has come into the writing, with vigour; and the verse, which in *Rosamund* wandered down every tempting garden-path, is resolutely shaped, with a constriction it was seldom to have afterwards. No doubt the writer is still, in some ways, a disciple. There is the general Elizabethan temper, there are the careful reminiscences of Shakespeare and of George Chapman, with some recollections of his newly discovered hero, Wells. But this is the work of a man with an imagination of his own and an independent ambition.

In *Chastelard*, the product of immense labour, but in its final form so swift and song-like, there is achievement. No tragedy of Swinburne's is easier to read or more definite in effect. One thing only, but effectually, prevents it from being generally enjoyed as no other of his tragedies ever could be: the nature of its emotional content. Expressing so ardently a passion for passion which but few can share, reviving with such subtle sympathy the fantastic and fanatical devotion characteristic of the persons and the period with which it deals, it is too far removed at once from the modern mind and the usual English conception of love to find general favour. Yet to us, some few of us, to the present writer, at any rate, it is a peculiar treasure. We may, and in our seriously critical moods we must, admit that it is the masterpiece not of a broadly human poet but of a specialist in a particular, doubtless both exceptional and perilous, kind of emotion; but the union in it of luxury and energy, the swiftness with which it moves for all its exuberance, the art with which, for all the variability of mood, its beautiful monotony is preserved, delight us long after we have lost instinctive sympathy with such cries of the youthful as " happy days or else to die " and of the connoisseur of life as *qualis artifex pereo*. And it is not only a lovely, exciting poem: it is, in its way, truly a dramatic poem. One aspect at least of Mary Queen of Scots has been seized with complete success; Chastelard, that exquisite and disastrous idolator of love, has been understood, in every nerve of his being; and the poet has seen and used to the full the opportunities for contrast given by the introduction of Mary and Chastelard and other sophisticated figures into the Scotland of that time, where the women, as Sir Edmund Gosse has said with brilliant exactness, " rustling in their bright emptiness like so many dragon-flies, are presented to us caged in a world of violent savages and scarcely less acrid ascetics ". And there is at least one scene, the last between Mary of Scots and Chastelard, which is in the full sense drama, with its great stroke of irony as she has forboding that she will somehow die sadly and he bids her think how the axe's edge would soften to such a neck.

It is in Chastelard that we become aware of the scholarship which Swinburne brought to his historical tragedies. His knowledge of Mary herself was then incomplete, but the period he already knew to perfection; and, correcting the impression of Swinburne as at that time an irresponsible romantic, it is to be noted that he had studied minutely not only the court whence Mary came, the extravagant culture which Chastelard represented, but also all that was embodied by Knox and hostile to his hero and heroine. Swinburne's recapture of the spirit of the lesser writers about Ronsard in the French lyrics of his own composition which he introduced into the play is not more remarkable, more eloquent in testimony to his power of entering into past modes of feeling, than his recapture of the spirit of the Scotland of that epoch.

With *Bothwell*, probably the most arduous task that any English dramatic poet has ever undertaken, there was at once a great broadening of interest, the assumption of enormously heavier obligations towards a complicated and in part obscure body of historical facts, and the adoption of greater sobriety of style. It is, of course, his chief work as a dramatic poet, stupendous in ambition, unflagging in energy, and it has his greatest scenes. We cannot say of it as a whole that it works steadily upon our curiosity about what is to come, but think of those pages in which apprehension deepens in the doomed Darnley! There is nothing in English drama, except the supreme scene in Marlowe's *Edward II*, which arouses such terror as that portion of the second act of *Bothwell* in which Darnley recognizes the song the Queen is singing, the song which Rizzio sang immediately before his murder. Every circumstance heightens the horror, every line tells, and at last, when Darnley has asked the dreadful, revealing question, " How do men die? " and cries out——

" Mary, by Christ whose mother's was your name,
Slay me not! God, turn off from me that heart!
Out of her hands, God, God, deliver me!——"

the reader comes out of a terrible, convincing night-

mare infinitely relieved that the act is at an end.
And this vast and magnificent play, unlike most work
on a great scale by its author, has things to set in
relief against its fieriest ardours, its most tumultuous
passages. There is modulation; there are moments
when some deeply involved actor in the tragedy is
visited by a doubt of the urgency, even the reality,
of the cause to which he is irrevocably pledged. Thus
Bothwell muses:

> " I am wrought
> Out of myself even by this pause and peace,
> In heaven and earth, that will not know of us,
> Nor what we compass: in this face of things,
> Here in this eye of everduring life,
> That changes not in changing, fear and hope,
> The life we live, the life we take, alike
> Decline and dwindle from the shape they held,
> Their import and significance; all seem
> Less good and evil, with less hate and love,
> Then we would have them for our high heart's sake."

After *Bothwell*, *Mary Stuart* may seem somewhat
flat. Swinburne himself decidedly over-valued it,
supposing himself to be justified by the praise
bestowed on it by Sir Henry Taylor, who, admirable
in its sort as is his own, once-famous drama, was
hardly the critic to feel the absence of the shock and
sting of life in work so highly skilled. That which
Swinburne had to do in *Mary Stuart* was extremely
difficult; he did it extremely well; and I doubt
whether it would be possible to point to any dramatic
composition in our literature in which, having much
prose matter to handle, the author has so consistently
succeeded in transforming it into poetry. But however delightful the sense of difficulties overcome may
be to the author, his readers can only say that *Mary*

Stuart, on the whole, inspires respect rather than enthusiasm. It is only at its conclusion, in the fine invention whereby Mary is sent to her doom because she fails to recognize Chastelard's song, that the poet gets free from the merciless pressure of history.

Yet in its sobriety *Mary Stuart* is something of a development from its predecessors. *Marino Faliero*, too declamatory, perhaps, though with a really noble rhetoric, has, in its very different way, something of that continuous onward lyrical sweep which *Chastelard* possessed. But more to my purpose, as illustrating the modification of Swinburne's aims in tragedy, are the two late plays, *Rosamund, Queen of the Lombards* and *The Duke of Gandia*. In this *Rosamund*, published when Swinburne was sixty-two, for the first time the bones of the play are allowed to emerge through the poetry. Much is sacrificed that it is difficult not to mourn. The old exuberance has been replaced by a taut, for Swinburne almost naked, way of writing; but the gain in sheer dramatic quality will not be disputed. The curt speeches have in certain instances a beauty that would be perceived even in quotation, but more than the speeches in the earlier plays they tell in their context as they cannot when excerpted. Take that utterance by Almachildes under temptation:

" I cannot. God requite thee this! I will."

It is a great line in its place, almost too bare for quotation. Restraint, with reliance on the situation to give significance to few and simple words, could hardly go further than in that, or in this:

" *Hildegard.* Hast thou forgiven me?
 Almachildes. I have not forgiven God."

In *The Duke of Gandia*,[1] perhaps planned much earlier, not completed till 1908, this brevity, with the old art in making blank verse out of monosyllabic words, is carried much farther. It is not merely that there is severe, and even excessive, restraint put on the lyrical and rhetorical impulses of the writer: for the first time, he has learned to make unsaid things terribly eloquent to his readers. It is a very slight piece of work, and it is not, any more than its predecessors were, drama in the full sense, but there is now a strange, baleful power in suggesting the secret heat of hatred, the deadly unuttered thoughts, of the dreadful creatures that front each other, wary and venomous as snakes. From the very nature of the work, no quotation can do it other than injustice; but take this from that fourth scene in which almost every word seems to be distilled reluctantly out of passion that would conserve its poison for still further concentration.

"*Alexander.* Thou hast done this deed.
Caesar. Thou hast said it.
Alexander. Dost thou think
 To live, and look upon me.
Caesar. Some while yet.
Alexander. I would there were a God—that he might hear.
Caesar. 'Tis pity there should be—for thy sake—none.
Alexander. Wilt thou slay me?
Caesar. Why?
Alexander. Am not I thy sire?

[1] Whatever may first have set Swinburne thinking of this subject, it may be recalled that he had, though chiefly on account of its one lovely incidental song, an admiration for Nat Lee's *Cæsar Borgia*, the hero of which, of course, is this very Duke of Gandia.

ALGERNON CHARLES SWINBURNE
*From the Painting by G. F. Watts
in The National Portrait Gallery*

THE TRAGEDIES 179

Caesar. And Christendom's to boot.
Alexander. I pray thee, man,
 Slay me.
Caesar. And then myself? Thou art crazed, but I
 Sane.
Alexander. Art thou very flesh and blood?
Caesar. They say,
 Thine."

It is as if the speakers were grown misers of their hate.

I do not say *The Duke of Gandia* is a great thing, but it is a very extraordinary thing, and that Swinburne should have come to write like this is astonishing. Disconcerting readers who expected, though the most of them would have been bored by, the old ample eloquence, the volume received scant attention, but it deserves it, especially from those who are quite certain that Swinburne, from the moment he went to Putney in 1879, wholly ceased to develop.

Locrine and *The Sisters* lie apart from the rest of his tragedies, experiments of very unequal value, the one a most happy, the other an entirely unfortunate exercise in virtuosity. As a piece of literature *The Sisters* is falsely based, showing us Swinburne, of all improbable experiments, striving for realism. Now the theory of realism is that the ideas and emotions of people are to be rendered only in such words as they themselves would use, that is, inexpressively, without expression of the finer part of their thought, their feeling, since people in general are dumb, or inadequate, in the moments when they make a fatal decision or challenge fate or bow to it. Well, even in the prose drama, by which I mean not merely drama that happens to be written in prose, but the drama of the prose intelligence, and even at its finest, as in Ibsen, whom Swinburne disliked, the aim at realism, it might be argued, is an error. But when we turn to the poetic drama, there is nothing to argue about. The quest of realism is now not only of doubtful wisdom but bound to fail, the adoption of the form of verse having inevitably put the play a certain distance from the use and wont of daily life. To seek for the immediate illusion of reality, while employing an instrument which precludes creation of that illusion—how extraordinary an error, and how surprising that Swinburne should have been guilty of it!

All the same, *The Sisters* is not to be wholly thrust aside. Little as the critic must think of this *tour de force*, in which early nineteenth-century persons talk a conversational, and occasionally slangy, blank verse, it has some value for the biographer, giving us as it does Swinburne's own view of his boyhood. He made, as he pleasantly boasted in private, rather a nice young fellow of the boy he had been, but he did more than that, and there must have been irony in his profession that he was simply reproducing the lineaments of a well-bred, high-spirited young Englishman. For hidden away in *The Sisters*, to be discerned only by those who have been set on the alert by passages in the correspondence and unpublishable writings of Swinburne, are strange things, evidence that, looking back on his boyhood, he saw there a boy destined never to come to full normal manhood. There are traces of a restrained self-pity, traces of a self-knowledge with which Swinburne is seldom credited. He looked back and saw himself in the bloom and brilliance of a wonderful and enchanted youth, but without failing to see what was perverse in himself.

Of *Locrine*, under reproof, I decline to speak critically. Granted that it is not what, from the moment its form, on a hint, it may be supposed, from *Selimus*, was decided upon, it never could have been made, it remains an ingenious and delightful work of art. No doubt, it might be asked whether there is in the substance at this stage or that any absolutely convincing reason why this or that metrical form should be adopted; but how can we wrangle in that spirit over a play in which the most complicated rhymed forms can yield such natural and happy effects as this, where a child chatters so freely in intricate easy verses:

" That song is hardly even as wise as I—
Nay, very foolishness it is. To die,
In March before its life were well on wing,
Before its time and kindly season—why
Should spring be sad—before the swallows fly—
Enough to dream of such a wintry thing?
Such foolish words were more unmeet for spring,
Than snow for summer when his heart is high,
And why should words be foolish when they sing? "

Skill and grace and charm are everywhere in this dramatic poem. It is without edge, without profound significance, but for my humble part I should as soon think of assailing Day's happy and lovely *Parliament of Bees* because it does not compete with Marlowe or Webster or Ford as of attacking *Locrine* for not being what it could not have been, a competitor with *Chastelard* or *Bothwell*. Mild heaven condemns that critical care, though wise in show, that would with superfluous burdens load John Day or make portentous demands on *Locrine*. Surely to God, there is a time for eating honey with grateful lips, without complaint that it is not something else.

Chapter XI

THE POET AS CRITIC

I DO not know that ordinarily one would regard Mr. George Moore as the spokesman of the general public or even of that smaller public which takes its literature critically, but he undoubtedly spoke for an almost unanimous public opinion when he declared that Swinburne wrote the worst prose of any poet. Mr. Moore, in the admirable development of his genius, is very far from being simply the author of his early books grown old, and here he expressed an animosity towards Swinburne's prose that has certainly increased with the passing of the years, and is now, I gather, all but universally felt. For myself, though I am depressed by a sense of loneliness in this position, I cannot accept the unqualified condemnation of Swinburne's prose. He had, certainly, and from the first, a number of unfortunate mannerisms, and after the publication of *Essays and Studies* they were accentuated lamentably. That weakness of the wrist making penmanship so uncomfortable, causing him to elaborate his sentences and paragraphs before pen touched paper, explains part of the trouble; but verbosity, a passion for alliteration, a still stronger passion for complicated antithesis were evident in much of his prose long before his work was conditioned by that physical distress in writing. At no time could he be depended upon to write a dozen successive pages without weakening the effect by voluble, alliterative, antithetical outbursts. The preface which he drafted for the collection of Border Ballads on which he was engaged in his twenty-second and twenty-third years contains a passage about Scott as circumlocutory as anything he produced late in life, together with a splutter of irritation as ineffective as any to be discovered in his final essays. The root of the trouble was in him from the outset; in the ultimate ramifications of what grew up from it, reading him sometimes became like forcing one's way through tropical jungle.

It was not merely, by the time he was producing his last studies of the dramatists, that he annoyed all readers not habituated to his peculiarities and very many who were. Certain of his tricks aroused unjust but not altogether surprising doubt of his sincerity. Could a choice of epithets seemingly dictated by the desire for alliteration be possible for any writer with a real zeal for the finer truth, the *vraie verité*? Could the sort of antithesis in which Byron and Buonaparte were contrasted with Scott and Wellington come from a writer entirely in earnest? And then there were passages, even whole pages, which had a kind of obscurity, for though the sun was strong above and the ground firm and familiarly known to this guide, the density of the tangled umbrage dimmed the illumination, and his habit of pacing needlessly to left and right before crashing impetuously forward caused bewilderment.

But, with all this, Swinburne, if not exactly a great prose writer, was from time to time a writer of great prose. Allowing that he wrote the worst prose of any poet, he wrote also some of the best. In the *Notes* on his first miscellaneous volume of lyrics, in the *William Blake*, in several of the *Essays and Studies*, notably in the pages on John Ford, on Byron, on Rossetti, on the drawings at Florence, and here and there in later volumes, there are passages in which the manner is worthy of the matter, in which a splendid vocabulary is used, if not with all the restraint that might be desired, at least with a regal magnificence, in which the rhythms are noble and those proper to prose. The famous passage on the death of Byron is, I believe, accepted as wellnigh flawlessly beautiful by even the most hostile, who are reduced to representing it as wholly exceptional. Very unusual it is in the degree of its restraint and the delicacy of its rhythms:

" His work was done at Missolonghi; all of his work for which the fates could spare him time. A little space was allowed him to show at least a heroic purpose, and attest a high design; then, with all things unfinished before him and behind, he fell asleep after many troubles and triumphs. Few can ever have gone wearier to the grave; none with less fear. He had done enough to earn his rest. Forgetful now and set free for ever from all faults and foes, he passed through the doorway of no ignoble death out of reach of time, out of sight of love, out of hearing of hatred, beyond the blame of England and the praise of Greece. In the full strength of spirit and of body his destiny overtook him, and made an end of all his labours. He had seen and borne and achieved more than most men on record. ' He was a great man, good at many things, and now he had attained his rest.' "

But if unusual, such prose is not altogether unmatched in the remainder of Swinburne's work. Here are some passages, likely enough not the best that could be put forward, but surely of a quality which must silence all detraction:

" Once only in my life have I seen the likeness of Victor Hugo's genius. Crossing over when a boy, from Ostend, I had the fortune to be caught in mid-channel by a thunderstorm strong enough to delay the packet some three good hours over the due time. About midnight, the thundercloud was right overhead, full of incessant sound and fire, lightening and darkening so rapidly that it seemed to have life, and a delight in its life. At the same hour, the sky was clear to the west, all along the sea-line sprung and sank, as to music, a restless dance or chase of summer lightnings across the lower sky; a race and riot of lights, beautiful and rapid as a course of shining Oceanides along the tremulous floor of the sea. Eastward, at the same moment, the space of clear sky was higher and wider, a splendid semicircle of too intense purity to be called blue; it was of no colour nameable to man; and midway in it, between the storm and the sea, hung the motionless full moon; Artemis watching with a serene splendour of scorn the battle of Titans and the revel of nymphs from her stainless and Olympian summit of divine, indifferent light. Underneath and about us the sea was paved with flame; the whole water trembled and hissed with phosphoric fire; even through the water-sparks. In the same heaven, and at the same hour, there shone at once the three contrasted glories, golden and fiery and white, of moonlight and of the double lightnings, forked and sheet; and under all this miraculous heaven lay a flaming floor of water."

After that, take this rather too fanciful, and more than once too nearly metrical, but unquestionably beautiful passage from the *William Blake*:

" There is, in all these straying songs, the freshness of clear wind, and purity of blowing rain; here a perfume as of dew or grass against the sun, there a keener smell of sprinkled shingle and fine-bleached sand; some growth or breath everywhere of blade or herb leaping into life under the green wet light of spring; some colour of shapely cloud or moulded wave. The verse pauses and musters, and falls away as a wave does, with the same patience of gathering form and rounded glory of springing curve, and sharp, sweet flash of dishevelled and flickering foam, as it curls over, showing the sun through its soft heaving side in veins of gold that inscribe, and jewels of green that inlay, the quivering and sundering skirt or veil of thinner water, throwing upon the tremulous space of narrowing sea in front, like a reflection of lifted and vibrating hair, the windy shadow of its shaken spray."

And then, since these are elaborately descriptive passages, savour this consummately witty and acutely critical excerpt from Swinburne's treatment of Alfred de Musset and George Sand:

" Few, probably, will admit the suggestion that this was a simple case of moral outrage perpetrated by George Lovelace on Clarissa de Musset. As few who know anything of either will fail to admit that the usual parts were obviously inverted or reversed in the action of this dolorous tragi-comedy; that at least during their luckless residence in Venice, he was a woman and she was a man—in that kingdom by the sea. Not a very lovable woman—but assuredly not a very admirable man. I cannot think, in a word, that M. George behaved like the gentleman he usually showed himself to be—though doubtless a gentleman of whom it might be too often said that he loved and he rode away—in his affair with poor misguided Mlle. Elfride. And surely, when the unhappy girl was dead, it was scarcely manly on the part of her old keeper to revive the memory of her frailties."

Writing of Swinburne's prose in my former book on him, I remarked that since it derived in the main whence his verse did, it would be rather idle to seek its origins in the work of earlier or contemporary masters of prose. But it now seems to me that it is possible to put my hand on two sentences, in writers greatly cherished by him, which will show us the source of certain peculiarities familiar to the reader of Swinburne. Look at that wonderful sentence in which Charles Lamb has given us the equivalent of a Titian:

" Precipitous, with his reeling satyr rout about him, re-peopling and re-illuming suddenly the waste places, drunk with a new fury beyond the grape, Bacchus, born in fire, fire-like flings himself at the Cretan."

" Reeling satyr rout ", " re-peopling and re-illuming "—are not those the models of scores of phrases in Swinburne? Is not " born in fire, fire-like flings himself " the hint on which Swinburne, who in his verse also would frequently use a device like

" Came flushed from the full-flushed wave ",

took to a particular pattern of repetitive phrase?
And then look at this sentence from Charlotte Brontë:

" The sway of the whole Great Deep above a herd of whales rushing through the livid and liquid thunder down from the frozen zone."

Is it not from that sentence that Swinburne had the hint for bringing an effect of echo into his epithets?
On the whole, however, the springs of his prose are identical with the springs of his verse. Something in elaborate descriptive passages he owed to the earlier Ruskin. I used to think that, widely as his rhetorical, emphatic utterances differs from the gentle insinuation of Walter Pater, he owed something, at any rate when he was writing the admirable notes on the drawings by Old Masters at Florence, to that critic.[1] But it is now

[1] Swinburne was in this matter a pioneer. When he wrote of these drawings, and for long afterwards, there was no catalogue of

beyond doubt that it was Pater who was under obligation to him. Swinburne's study of the drawings, with its finely imaginative treatment of Leonardo, was made in 1864. When Pater's subtle and beautiful and delicately distorting essay on Leonardo appeared in the *Fortnightly Review*, Rossetti at once saw a certain resemblance, amid very many differences, between the style of it and Swinburne's, and Swinburne himself wrote, " I confess I did fancy that there was a little spice of my style as you say ".[1]

Of the influence of Landor on Swinburne's thought and feeling there is the amplest evidence, but the student will search long before he can detect much trace of Landor's influence on the structure, colour, and rhythms of Swinburne's prose. Indeed, it would seem that, simply as a writer of prose, Swinburne learned next to nothing from Landor, from whom he could have learned so much. My attention was drawn in conversation a few years ago by Mr. Arthur Symons to a single line of Landor's verse which perfectly anticipates, though it may not actually have influenced, Swinburne's verse:

" And weary with strong stroke the whitening wave."

But, except that Swinburne is known to have reflected, with ill-founded satisfaction, on the likeness between his irascibility in prose and Landor's, he might, as regards the general manner of it, never have given Landor a serious thought.

the drawings, and though some of his ascriptions would not now be accepted, his criticism retains a value which has never been warmly enough acknowledged.

[1] Letter from Swinburne to Rossetti, dated 28th November 1869, in Mr. Wise's collection. There is extant also a letter from Swinburne to Morley in which the poet alludes to Pater's frank avowal of obligation.

The better prose of Swinburne belongs to that remarkable, not quite indisputably justified, prose of which, when not at their best, De Quincey and Ruskin, in their several ways, were eminent producers.[1] He has less strangeness of imagination and orchestral gift than the former, less opulence and exquisiteness of colour than the latter, but he is in some ways of their order, not content with prose that can be spoken on the natural level of the voice. The curious thing is that, amidst all that volubility, all that elaboration, there are occasional phrases so concise and trenchant that we seem to feel a sudden transition as from Johnson the writer to Johnson the talker. It is difficult to conceive of a prose more wasteful than the bulk of Swinburne's, or of a phrase more packed than that which gives us the Venus of the Horselberg as " grown diabolic in ages that would not accept her as divine ".

And in the criticism to which nearly all of his prose was devoted we find, similarly, an immense waste in long-winded rhapsodical praise or over-elaborated and far too obvious irony with all sorts of petulant irrelevances, and yet, from time to time, the terse and telling phrase that the concisest and most single-purposed writer might envy. Thus though the prose of Swinburne might seem at first sight a prose which must exclude the *vraie verité*, it is, in fact, only the prose of a man whose right hand grasps it firmly while his left scatters alien or confusing matter round it. His definite judgments, though they do not imply a critical philosophy as profound as Coleridge's, are less fallible, and might indeed be described as infallible if it were not that he insisted on the supreme worth of virtually

[1] In saying this I do not forget that Swinburne protested with amusing energy against incursions into "the detestable as well as debatable land of pseudo-poetic rhapsody in hermaphroditic prose". Pseudo-poetic his prose was not: hermaphroditic it was apt to be.

everything written by Hugo. But often enough they need to be extracted from a context in which the strutting and fretting and fuming, the waving of censers and flourishing of cudgels, are at best distracting, at worst exasperating.

Part of the trouble comes from a chivalry that takes no heed of propriety. Dealing with some great or exquisite work of art in a temper of faultless responsiveness, he suddenly remembers that such a poet or commentator at some time was guilty of irreverence towards some one of the Swinburnian divinities, and in a spurt of anger he breaks from the high argument to pursue the offender. Or with really a very just sense of the worth of a writer, as he has shown elsewhere, he approaches that writer in the wrong temper simply because some critic has grossly over-praised or under-praised him. Cool correction of an erroneous estimate is very rarely possible for him. Look at that essay on Byron and Wordsworth. There is scarcely anything said in the furious protest against over-valuation of Byron that is without a considerable measure of truth, but under provocation he presses the attack beyond all reason. The result is a remarkable piece of invective, but for a view of Byron we must turn to the earlier essay, which is a little too generous here and there, yet substantially just. Look at the attack made late in life on Walt Whitman.

When Whitman learned of the attack, he is said to have snapped out, remembering the splendid lyrical eulogy published in 1871, " The damned simulacrum! " The late Mrs. Meynell thought she had disposed of Swinburne, as a coherent intelligence, when she had contrasted his dedication of a volume to William Bell Scott, as " poet and painter ", with his subsequent chastisement of that rather clumsy and jealous person as " rhymer and dauber ". Mrs. Meynell's case, such as it was, might have been strengthened if she had been able to quote certain unpublished lines of Swinburne on W. B. Scott:

" The infinitely little ghosts
Of sprats deceased on unknown coasts;
And many a long putrescent prawn,
Preserved unfit for human victual,—
Prince, lord of flies' and rhymesters' spawn,
That scarce deserve a strong man's spittle,
Beelzebub, thou hast in pawn
The less than infinitely little! "

But the explanation is other than she supposed. Swinburne's real judgment of W. B. Scott is to be found in the elegy he wrote on his death, a poem which very remarkably combines warmth of feeling with cool measurement of Scott's achievement:

" Scarce in song could his soul find scope,
Scarce the strength of his hand might ope
Art's inmost gate of her sovereign shrine,
To cope with heaven as a man may cope. . . .

None that can read or divine aright,
The scriptures writ of the soul may slight
The strife of a strenuous soul to show
More than the craft of the hand may write."

It is frequently necessary for the reader of Swinburne to do what Swinburne should have done for him, to relate the scattered eulogies and denunciations till he has Swinburne's real opinion of a writer as a whole. There are inconsistencies in Swinburne, but they are fewer than is commonly supposed.

Nor are his extravagances, except in regard to the minor works of Hugo, so extreme as the casual reader may take them to be. Almost all his criticism is very high-pitched, but he who has accustomed himself to this hyperbolical mode of expression will find that there is really, beneath the surface, far less confusion about the comparative values of writers than at first sight there seems to be.

More serious than the defects conventionally attributed to Swinburne as a critic is his rather frequent failure, especially in later life, to expose fully the basis of his appreciation, to choose sufficiently precise terms of eulogy or condemnation. There are a good many passages of the later prose which, taken by themselves, tell us little more than that to him such or such a book seemed above praise or beneath contempt. Loud-mouthed assertions that all but the spiritually stillborn children of dirt and dullness must immediately unite in worship or derision of the book in question are not criticism. The failure may be found in his fervent critical elegies as well as in his prose; it is extremely difficult to recollect the grounds on which in the verbose odes to Hugo that writer was promoted to the company of Æschylus, Dante, and Shakespeare, and, except for one most admirable couplet in definition of Landor's *Hellenics*, it would not be easy to find in the vast centenary poem material from which a portrait of Landor could be composed. Yet on occasion in his panegyrical verse he could attain to an almost incomparable truth and vigour of critical portraiture. Thus in that early sonnet on Landor which he wrote after visiting him but never published, though it declines into mere vague declaration of the master's immortality, there are such lines as these:

" The stateliest singing mouth that speaks our tongue,
The lordliest and the brow of loftiest leaf,
Worn after the great fashion close and brief."

The noble English elegy on Théophile Gautier, though

perhaps not free from the surplusage of which Swinburne strenuously endeavoured to rid it,[1] is rich in admirable criticism. The still nobler elegy on Baudelaire, with less particularity of allusion, has stroke after great stroke of critical portraiture. There are exact and vivid touches in many of the poems on the Elizabethan dramatists; nobody can add anything essential to the characterization of Rowley as " rough Rowley handling song with Esau's hand ". And finally, passing by other excellent things, there is that late poem on Burns in which the lesser and the greater Burns are discriminated with the utmost decision and lyrical energy.

> " But love and wine were moon and sun
> For many a fame long since undone,
> And sorrow and joy have lost and won,
> By stormy turns,
> Full many a singer's soul, if none
> More bright than Burns.
>
> And sweeter far in grief or mirth
> Have songs as glad and sad of birth
> Found voice to speak of wealth or dearth
> In joy of life.
> But never song took fire from earth
> More song for strife."

And in the prose, for all the passages which, with a few trifling changes, might be shifted from an essay on one idol to an essay on another, again and again there are pages of precise and profound criticism, in which the distinguishing qualities of the work under consideration are noted and valued brilliantly.

It is altogether absurd to deny discrimination to a writer who, from early youth, exhibited, though intermittently, so exceptional and resolute an independ-

[1] Letter to Morley.

ence in fastening on the neglected best in known and unknown writers. The boy of thirteen who went to the Elizabethans and to Landor, and to the latter at the attraction of a piece so unlikely to charm a boy's taste as " The Song of the Hours "; the undergraduate who, compiling an edition of the Border Ballads, at once fastened on to the great, beautifully moving, " The broom blooms bonnie and says it is fair ", a piece to this day left out of the anthologies; the young critic who, in 1862, was writing with high intelligence and judicious enthusiasm of Théophile de Viau; the editor who first firmly drew the line between the best and the worst of Coleridge's poetry; the critic who confidently preferred Collins to Gray and Stendhal to Mérrimée—it is nonsense to assert that such an one did not possess the rarest gift for pouncing on fine work however neglected or confused with less valuable matter or frowned upon by his contemporaries. But there is no more striking evidence of the soundness of his instinct and the determination of his obedience to it than is afforded by his *William Blake*. When he was elaborating it from his review of Gilchrist's book, he was subjected not to pressure from outside his own circle, to which he might well have been indifferent, but to persuasion by so dear a friend, so admired a poet, so zealous an admirer of Blake, as D. G. Rossetti. Gabriel was insistent that minute examination of the prophetic books was waste of time; Algernon, with all deference, was obstinate in pursuing a line of inquiry hardly to be expected of him. It can scarcely be necessary to say which of them has been justified by time.

It was with an effect of great novelty that Swinburne's criticism came to readers in the late 'sixties, the early 'seventies. It was not merely that his subjects were often unusual; the attempt to reproduce the whole emotional experience of commerce with great writers was new, and the excitement of this critic was then contagious. Later on, the novelty faded, for immensely wide as was Swinburne's range of reading and sympathy, it did not widen, and indeed, with the passing of the years, he came to seem to some readers rather tiresomely concentrated on the Elizabeth dramatists, while the intensification of certain of his mannerisms made it more and more difficult to respond immediately to his appeal. But though this is a secondary consideration, apart from the great intrinsic value of much of his criticism, it will eventually be seen to possess no little historical importance, as having markedly affected the development of that kind of criticism in which the aim is to reproduce, with the utmost vividness, the shock of delight with which an eager mind first experiences a work of art.

Of his criticism of the English dramatists it must always be said that it constitutes the chief part of his work as a writer of prose, but to the present writer it seems that, with all its erudition, insight, and enthusiasm, it is open to an objection not commonly levelled at it. That it is not, as a rule, quite what the general reader would desire, is a small matter: if the five or six major poets be excluded, the dramatists, however reluctant one may be to admit it, are subjects for the specialist. But if Swinburne's criticism be regarded, and no doubt it must, as being addressed to specialists, certain of his essays can hardly be pronounced other than too summary. The trouble here, and very often elsewhere, with Swinburne was the vagueness of his conception of the public. As a boy the present writer incurred obligations to Swinburne's criticism of Shakespeare and Marlowe, Webster and Ford, Beaumont and Fletcher, which he must acknowledge with profound gratitude; but in a critical capacity he is forced to ask himself precisely what audience that critical work of Swinburne's presupposes, and is puzzled to find an answer. As incentives to the reading of Elizabethan drama the earlier essays, with some indeed of the later also, are incomparable, and in maturity one may return again and again to scores of passages, hundreds of phrases, in which Swinburne has surprised the secret of a tragedy. But for a full, patient, evenly just exposition of a dramatist, comparable, let us say, with Pater's essay on Wordsworth, one will have to search long. In this, as in several other respects, the essay on Ford is probably his finest single study. It is not wholly free from some of Swinburne's faults, but its merits are not incidental, and it addresses itself, if I may venture to judge from my own experience, equally well to the reader as yet only superficially acquainted with the subject and to the reader who comes back to it many years later after a recent study of the dramatist with whom it deals.

On the whole, it seems likely that the great mass of criticism produced by Swinburne in lifelong devotion to the dramatists will survive, not as a perfect body of interpretative and appreciatory writing, but as a series of stimulants for young minds and a treasury to which every worker in this subject will resort for a large number of highly authoritative judgments.

In regard to what Swinburne did for particular dramatists, it is doubtless to George Chapman that he rendered the greatest service. Not only did he produce the long essay, somewhat confused and extravagant, but containing deeply sympathetic and nobly eloquent passages; he lavished great pains on the corrupt text for which R. H. Shepherd was nominally responsible.[1] The purified text and the enhanced

---

[1] Shepherd deserves some credit for his assiduity in reviving neglected writers, and I cannot refrain from mentioning his endeavour to get a posthumous hearing for Ebenezer Jones. But as an editor

reputation of Chapman, and especially the increased prominence ever since given to that dramatist's great connected French plays, were due to Swinburne's generous efforts. At the other end of the scale, he was able to reinstate such minor dramatists as Yarrington, Mayne, and the nameless authors of *Doctor Dodypol*, *The Tragedy of Nero*, *Nobody and Somebody*. His familiarity with the least of these was and must remain astonishing. It cannot be rivalled unless there should be born another being who unites the scholar's tireless devotion with so amazing a faculty of lightning-like apprehension.

In sheer scholarship, though this has been questioned, Swinburne went beyond any of our greater poets. In the academic sense, he may not have been an eminent classical scholar, but only Milton and Landor match him in capacity to use the classical languages for poetry, and they wrote no French poems and possessed no such exhaustive knowledge of any period of literature as Swinburne had of the Elizabethan. His criticism, impetuous as it was, proceeded from a mind that had been nourished on all that was best in five literatures, and that for all its apparent or actual recklessness was always aware of the standards set up by the supreme masters in each. Beneath the specialization and eccentricity there was the indefatigable student of Æschylus and Shakespeare, and the inflamed amateur of the curiosities of perverse literature passed no day without calling to mind the achievements of the greatest and most universal of writers.

he was both incompetent and unscrupulous. He it was who peddled as a rarity *Unpublished Verses*, by Swinburne, a wretched little leaflet containing merely an excerpt from the published "Hesperia". He declared that only twelve copies of it had been printed by him, but as a matter of fact reissued it whenever he could find ignorant collectors. His laxity as nominal editor of Chapman entailed labours on Swinburne's part which temporarily affected the poet's eyesight.

It is no exaggeration to say that the sweep of Swinburne's mind over literature makes most other great poets seem dwellers in an intellectual parish. From the Greek dramatists to Baudelaire, from Catullus to Christina Rossetti, from the early French romances and chroniclers to Stendhal and Dickens, from Villon to Gautier, he ranged unwearyingly and with perfect naturalness. Certain of his theories, such as that of the division of great writers into Olympians and Titans, or that of the threefold character of the medieval poetic intelligence, were put forward perhaps too often, and with certain phrases, such as " spirit and sense ", he toyed too often; but constantly, and perhaps more frequently in conversation than in his writing, he attained to high success in the summary definition of great writers. What could be better than the summing up of Swift, which I take from one of his letters, as " a bastard of Dante begotten on a daughter of Rabelais "? It is worthy of being set beside Coleridge's great epigram on Swift.

If, as has so often, and not without some truth, been said, Swinburne's experience was of literature rather than of life, it is well to remember the breadth and intensity of that literary experience. He had some few prejudices; he was hypnotized by Victor Hugo once the 'sixties were passed; his raptures over Sappho were barely related to what we have of her poetry; his hatred of Euripides, though not unintelligible, was fantastic; but when allowance has been made for these, it remains true that no English critic has been more catholic in mind or more ardently responsive to every manifestation of beauty. Nor has any English critic more decisively known his own opinion. It is, of course, the phenomena of contemporary literature that cause most indecision. Well, there was only one contemporary about whom Swinburne found it difficult to make up his mind. For

years he alternated between uneasy admiration and
dislike of Carlyle; and came to a settled opinion only
when, learning how Carlyle had blasphemed Coleridge
and Wordsworth and Lamb, he wrote, besides the two
indignant sonnets published in the volume which
contained *Tristram of Lyonesse*, a series of more virulent
pieces withheld from publication, " Old Malignity ",
" The Carlyliad ou les Mille et un Crachats ", " A Poet
to a Puritan ", and the rest. Reading these things
together with the nobly tolerant sonnet on the deaths of
Carlyle and Newman, and with various of his more
amiable references to the former, it can hardly be
contended that he fell into any very serious error about
Carlyle. Of his truly lamentable misconception of
Coventry Patmore I have already written. For the
rest, there was no considerable writer at work between
1850 and 1880 of whom Swinburne did not form a
substantially just opinion, though it must be added that
there was no writer arising after 1880 to whom he paid
more attention than courtesy demanded. But, and this
is the point, it was by no means the generally admired
Tennyson or Browning or Matthew Arnold to whom
he gave his warmest admiration; in each instance he
went past the effigy to the artist, and if, as regards
Browning, he somewhat over-emphasized the importance of *Fifine at the Fair*, that at least shows that it was
not merely what, on the conventional view of him, would
be called Swinburne's part of Browning that he was
capable of honouring.

With admiration went mockery, that other mode of
criticism: parody. The *Heptalogia* shares with James
Hogg's wonderful and almost entirely unknown volume
the foremost place that can be accorded to genuinely
poetic parody. Neither has much of what people in
general would call fun, each is consummate in the
reproduction of the originals. " Our divine and dearest

Mrs. Browning ", as Swinburne liked to call her, our " sea-eagle of English feather ", unconsciously parodied herself often enough, and has had attention from many parodists, but never has there been produced anything so preposterous and yet so intimately resembling some of her best work as " The Poet and the Wood-louse ". There are other unpublished parodies of her by the devoted and mischievous Swinburne. One would, I fear, scorch this paper if I ventured to transcribe it in all its gay indecency; but here is a sample of one quite blameless, with its recollection of her absurd

" Will you oftly
Murmur softly ".

Like most of his parodies, it is rather early work.

" There's a picture—Saint Cecilia
Is, I think, the Saint designed,
If you look at it you feel your
Eyes had better far be blind.
Such a duncely
Painter oncely
Drew that portent of insipid ease,
Dull, O duller, than Euripides!!! "

And Browning himself, elaborately parodied in the unpublished

" Wanting is—all,
Jargon abundant,
Verbiage redundant,
Splutter and squall. . . ."

Nor does the parody of Swinburne's own peculiarities in the *Heptalogia* stand alone: there are several unpublished self-mockeries, one of them of work so late and so congenial as the Eton ode.

The element of mischief, in regard even to work

Augt — 91

My dear Mr Swinburne,
I am & always have been your admirer, & in your Birthday Song I find metre & diction as lovely as ever; but the touch of kindliness toward myself — implied in your praise or overpraise of what I may have accomplished in Literature — moves the heart of the old Poet more, I think, than even the melody of your Verse.
Accept my thanks before I post away & believe me Yours ever
Tennyson

TENNYSON'S LAST LETTER TO SWINBURNE

which he profoundly admired, must never be overlooked in considering Swinburne. Not even Hugo was altogether exempt, and if we would understand the curious duality in a mind that has been declared too simple to be worthy of analysis by the subtle young critics of to-day, we must remember that, even while he treasured Hugo's tremendous compliments to him, he was now and then merry about the magnificent terms in which the master was wont to acknowledge donations of books which he could not read.

In criticism proper it can hardly be claimed that Swinburne's humour issued fortunately. Too often it took the form of a ponderously elaborated irony, the more deplorable because it proceeded from a writer who, under pressure of dramatic necessity, had achieved the edged elegance which diverts the reader of *Love's Cross-Currents*. Humour, it has perhaps not generally been realized, inspires certain of the pomposities of his critical prose, passages in which the grandiloquence is deliberate, and in which it amuses Swinburne, though not always his reader, to develop alliteration to the utmost of even his capacity for it. It must be regretted that the infusion of vigorous colloquialism and the suddenness of ironical reference to his own notorious moderation which enlivened the talk of Swinburne were rare in his critical writing; and though I see no reason to believe that *Love's Cross-Currents* was more than a brilliant *tour de force*, a success not to be repeated, I find myself lamenting that Swinburne's prose was developed so almost exclusively in writing on subjects which encouraged solemnity and fierceness. Simply as discipline, it would have been well if the study of social manners, the writing of prose dialogue of a mundane kind, had occupied more of his time in the years in which his prose was beginning to swell and stiffen.

But take him as he was, and he is, with all his

inequalities and mannerisms, at least the writer of certain passages of great though troubled beauty. And for all the gustiness of his criticism, the dust-devils that spring up almost causelessly and obscure that view of the subject which he is really capable of giving us, he has said profound and final things on almost every great writer. The *William Blake*, probably, is the book in which there will be found the finest of his criticism. It is not faultless; to say nothing of some of the mannerisms of the writing, it betrays the fact that between its inception and its completion ampler knowledge modified his opinions of Blake. But it is a great book, with pages of exposition in which Blake himself seems to be declaring his secret aims, with pages of noble and as yet not conventionalized eulogy. The *Study of Shakespeare* has this weakness in common with the *Blake*, that it is not precisely what Swinburne set out to write; yet is it not in its settling of the spiritual if not the chronological succession of the plays, and in its treatment of *Lear* and *Cymbeline*, quite masterly? The volumes of essays contain matter of every degree of merit, from the pages on Ford, which I cannot desist from praising, to the quite intolerable assault on Whitman, but a volume of great criticism could be made out of them. Indeed, that is what Swinburne as a critic needs; he needs editing. Judgments of the highest value are to be found in all but his very worst work, and when the task to which I have pointed has been carried out, he will stand as a critic far higher than he does to-day. And as to the quality of his prose, though probably nothing can, and certainly nothing should, silence protest against the verbosity, involution, and artificial elevation of his worst passages, two now obscured merits will then be more visible: the often happy employment, in his earlier prose, of words with reliance on their legitimate but less usual meanings, and the terseness of individual phrases in a prose which on general view is so diffuse. That a great deal of his earlier prose, and some of even his later, the less excited portions of it, has these merits will, no doubt, be denied by most readers of these lines. The claim assuredly cannot be justified by a vague recalling to memory of its average. But he who will examine it with unprejudiced attention, and excerpt as he proceeds what he may at the time suppose to be very exceptional phrases and sentences, will be surprised eventually by their number. Swinburne was not a great prose-writer, but he contained one.

Chapter XII

LAST DAYS

HIS seventy-first birthday found Swinburne much as he had been for years. A certain delicacy of the lungs remained with him from the very dangerous attack of pneumonia he had had in 1903, but he still took his long morning walk daily, without heed of the weather, still brightened instantly at every opportunity of oral tribute to his beloved Elizabethans and Hugo and Landor and Lamb and Shelley, still read Dickens to Watts-Dunton, still worked into the night in his study with the little statue of Hugo and his quartos to stimulate him. Four days before his seventy-second birthday, going out, as usual without a coat, into a wet and windy morning, he caught a severe cold at a time when the entire household was prostrated with influenza. Next morning he had an order from Watts-Dunton's sick bed not to venture out; but it was too late. Symptoms of pneumonia had shown themselves. His illness was brief and not very painful. His delirium had in it no dreadfulness; only the sweet, frail voice went on and on, repeating the choruses of Æschylus and of Sophocles. On the 10th April 1909 he died.

To the end of his days he had rejected every form of Theism. The very last lines he had written had been an appeal to eternal justice to determine which was worthier of chastisement, God as the maker of man or man as the maker of God. At some time, years earlier, he had exacted from Watts-Dunton a promise that no Christian rites should be performed over his grave. Of this promise Watts-Dunton was now obliged to inform the poet's sister, Miss Isabel Swinburne. Watts-Dunton added, no doubt correctly, but perhaps needlessly, that Swinburne had thought of Christianity, or perhaps of the devout High Church Anglicanism to which his mother and sisters were attached, as separating him from those he loved. But Swinburne had ceased in middle life to regard death as extinction. As he had written to William Bell Scott after D. G. Rossetti's death, he had attained to something more than a hope, if not quite to a fixed conviction, of the survival of human personality. He had relied more steadily on that other immortality, whereby something of every great man lives on to influence the aspirations and acts of humanity. Thirty years before his own death he had written of this persistence of personality in " Thalassius ":

" Seeing that even the hoariest ash-flake that the pyre
Drops, and forgets the thing was once afire,
And gave its heart to feed the pile's full flame,
Till its own heart its own heat overcame,
Outlives its own life, though by scarce a span,
As such men dying outlive themselves in man,
Outlive themselves for ever."

For the rest, he had kept at heart always those high, stoical words to him of the aged Landor, that whatever was to be was best. It was not without faith of a kind that Swinburne faced the end.

He was buried at Bonchurch, next to his parents, near his former home, near the sea. The rites of the Church were precluded by his wish, but the Church had its spokesman by his grave to say, briefly, that those who had charge of that consecrated place were glad he should lie there.

With the exception of a wreath from Eton, there were no formal tributes from institutions. Swinburne had belonged to none, and had steadily declined honours from them. To Lord Curzon's offer of an honorary degree from Oxford in 1907 he had replied as, with his dislike of the University, might have been expected; in 1908, he had refused the Civil List pension of £250 a year offered him by Mr. Asquith; and there was now no token of national mourning. The newspapers published long tributes, mostly rather more enthusiastic than could have been anticipated, since for many years his work had been received with no more than respect. His own generation spoke only in the voice of George Meredith:

"That brain of the vivid illumination is extinct. I can hardly realize it when I revolve the many times when at the starting of an idea the whole town was instantly ablaze with electric light. Song was his natural voice. He was the greatest of our lyrical poets—of the world's, I could say, considering what a language he had to wield."

Reversionary in many ways, as I have already pointed out, and for all his assimilative and mimetic tendencies very strangely rigid beneath the surface, he had long been almost as remote from the age as Shelley. In his later volumes of verse, too, with very fine things, still under-valued, there had been a good deal to chill or weary readers. For all his influence on the two rather tenuous poets who prolonged Pre-Raphaelitism, O'Shaughnessy and Marston, and the work he had done in preparing the ground, by moral revolt and by introducing Baudelaire into England, for certain writers of the 'nineties, one of whom, Ernest Dowson, showed direct obligation to him, Swinburne had founded no school. Up to a point the most imitable of poets, he had been proved, not least by his own failures to imitate himself, beyond that point inimitable.[1] Whatever writers in the late 'seventies, the 'eighties, the 'nineties owed to him, it had become plain that he closed the great romantic epoch, and was to be reckoned the last of an old, not the first of a new, dynasty. In the act of homage to him as what was mortal passed beyond further salute, his eulogists stood afar off. Meredith might mourn " a part of our life torn away ", but they could not. He had so long been so aloof, and from his distance latterly so uncommunicative. What they had to lament was hardly more than the loss of that spectacle of a sea-bird impending over the changeful and monotonous and tireless movement of the sea, the play of light on wings seen almost intolerably brilliant against the haze that always filled so much of his heaven, an effect of dream or mirage with scarcely any meaning for their intelligence.

[1] " The high Gods spot in a minute
It isn't the genuine thing,"

as H. D. Traill made Swinburne say in a very happy parody.

Chapter XIII

CONCLUSION

IT is interesting, and may really be useful, to consider a poet's approach to his subjects, but the finally important thing is what he makes of his subjects when he has reached them. Swinburne approached almost all of his subjects through literature, and it has stupidly been assumed that therefore his experiences were second-hand. The latest and one of the ablest of my predecessors has retorted, justly, that Swinburne's experiences of literature were not less sincere or vivid than Wordsworth's of nature, and it is proper when dealing with what seems derivative in Swinburne to remember the breadth and intensity of his literary experiences. But this, obviously, is not an adequate reply. It is mitigation, not refutation. It does not take into account the distinguishing peculiarity of Swinburne's mind, the singularity of his response to life through literature.

Swinburne, it seems to me, differed from those whom we call derivative poets not merely in degree but in kind. Highly, and it may be excessively, responsive as he was, he was also in a sense inattentive to the phenomena of nature and the events of the life about him, incurious till in some work of art their significance was thrillingly revealed to him. When he came on the Elizabethan dramatists, on Hugo or Shelley or Baudelaire or Rossetti, it was as if one passing through life swiftly, in an abstract ecstasy, had suddenly had laid on him an electrically stimulating hand, and had heard a voice saying, "Look!" But when he looked, it was with his own eyes; on a hint from another it is true, but on his own part of the spectacle, with a really individual as well as perfectly sincere reaction to the beauty and strangeness of things.

A careful writer has produced a book on Swinburne and Landor, perhaps to no great purpose, though it is delightful to have those two proud names brought together. I wish someone duly qualified would produce a book on Swinburne and Victor Hugo. We should see then how, even when the English poet seems to be writing under dictation from the French, he is entirely himself, the political poems, often on Hugo's own subjects, often written from the same point of scornful view, being as thoroughly differentiated from what might seem to be their model as the poems on children, in the beauty of so many of them and the fond silliness of a few, are from those of "The Art of being a Grandfather".

For Swinburne, as a rule, to establish contact with life there was needed a connexion supplied by some other writer; but the contact was individual, and from the moment it was achieved he became, in a profound sense, independent. He needed, and constantly accepted, introduction; he did not need guidance! His intellectual obligations, so incalculably great if you consider them superficially, are not really in the aesthetic region very much more than those in the social region of a man who should owe the beginnings of most of his permanent friendships to a hostess. Of this or that subject frequently treated by Swinburne, we may say that he would hardly have turned to it if Landor or Mazzini or Hugo had not given him the hint; but it is not as their disciple or slave that he has dealt with it. He sees the thing first in a mirror, but he goes thereafter to the thing itself, with his own " nerves of delight ".

The initiatory process, if we may speak of a process where all is done in a flash, is worth noticing for its strangeness, and we may amuse ourselves, idly, with speculating what manner of poet Swinburne would have been if born before certain of those from whom he had most hints. But what really matters, as I must reiterate, is the result, the sincere and original work of art that Swinburne makes, in his own way, out of his own part of material which, likely enough, he would not have found till later or at all without that hint.

Look at his work in *pastiche*. Much of it is so much more than *pastiche*; the adoption of a certain temper, a certain form, awakening in him that poet of another age acutely divined by Guy de Maupassant as existent in the very modern Swinburne. With the challenge to himself, there comes into play something that would otherwise have remained latent in him, but that was genuinely there. The boyish work left aside, here is a great deal more than mimicry; here, and I am not being cheaply paradoxical, is original poetry, because in the act apparently of mere reproduction Swinburne has established an imaginative relationship with subject matter which he would not have touched in his more evidently original work but which becomes his own. The French lyrics in the manner of Ronsard's group; the early sonnets in the manner of 1600; the perfect Caroline lyric in *Love's Cross-Currents*; the Morality he wrote for his cousin, Mrs. Disney Leith; the best of the Border Ballads: these, and some other things, which a thoughtless criticism might brush aside as no more than unprecedentedly good imitations, can scarcely be studied too closely by any who would understand

CONCLUSION 211

how through literature Swinburne entered tracts of experience else closed to him, not to play the mere mimic but to make what, I must insist, is original poetry.

I have sometimes dallied with the fancy of a selection of Swinburne's poems so chosen and arranged as to exhibit him as the poet of many periods: Hellenic, Hebraic, old French, Elizabethan, the contemporary of Shelley, of Hugo, of Baudelaire, of Rossetti. It would be amusing, and it would be instructive; and I should pray Sir Edmund Gosse, who has the fancy and the touch as well as the scholarship for so delicate a task, to prefix to it a plausible essay on the successive incarnations of Swinburne down the ages, with such biographical particulars as the lives of rebel poets like Catullus, Villon, Théophile, Marlowe, Shelley, and Baudelaire might suggest. Three poets in three distant ages born: say, rather, thirteen, each very much of the particular period, each very definitely Swinburne.

And just there, in the persistence of Swinburne's personality through all the changes of influence on him, is the fact most awkward for those who find him merely derivative. So responsive, so rigid, he is a paradox among poets, and because we cannot entirely explain him we are not justified in pretending that there is nothing to explain.

When I ask myself why it is that the peculiar result of Swinburne's approach to life through literature has so seldom been appreciated, why the originality of his work has so constantly been doubted where his discovery of the subject has been due to another poet's instigation, I seem to find part of the explanation in the fact that real things were so abstract to him, abstract things so real. At the touch of some other poet, he has suddenly become aware of the existence of a particular subject, and it is evident enough, in certain instances, that without that touch he would have passed it by; what is not evident at first glance is that his experience of it, however brought about, is his own. The thing really seen for himself, once he has been turned towards it, though felt in a really personal way, appears on his page so abstract, so unlike the outcome of direct contact with nature and humanity. We know what turned him towards it, however, and it is easy to assume that he has but borrowed an experience.

Only, if real things were abstract to him, abstract things were real. The bare fact, wave, or wind, or flame, the bare idea of liberty, of childhood, puts rapture into him. The actual associations, which may have stirred him as much as they would a more normal poet, have disappeared from his mind by the time he has translated his experience into poetry, but an extraordinary wealth of eternal associations has gathered round the stripped fact, and it is with a full, passionate sense of the eternal significance of the sea, of liberty, of childhood, that he expresses himself. Take his poems about children. In some he attempted portraiture, to little advantage. In one, he thought, for a change, perhaps, since we must not suppose that Watts-Dunton dictated everything we dislike, to become realistic, with the very dreadful consequence of the lines on a baby's face in a bonnet of plush. His art had no room for plush bonnets, any more than it had for the topography of Loch Torridon. Particular as his experience of children or of a specific sea might have been, it needed to reappear as experience of all childhood, of the everlasting sea, if he was to produce his true work.

Swinburne's is a poetry of abstractions, saved miraculously, though not always, from the great danger of such poetry by the vivid reality of abstractions to him. The epithets that would be so nearly valueless in other poets have value with him because to him they meant so much, " swift ", " bright ", and other such words being words of power for him. The bare ideas of speed and brilliance mattered to him as they have mattered to no other of our poets; he thrilled to them, and when he is himself we thrill with him. But it is the peril of this way of writing, with the eyes which have really seen the object taken off it, that there is no constantly recurrent challenge to be true to the original experience. A kind of formula is found, a beautiful formula, admirably expressive when it is first used; and when the poet has a very similar, but not identical, experience, it tends to be used again, without regard to the slight inadequacy of it. And with Swinburne there is a further peril. The original formula will have been made to suit the original metrical scheme. Let a similar subject begin to be treated in a similar metre, and the pressure to use the formula once more will be almost beyond his power of resistance. You will get then both a certain lack of freshness in expression, for all the freshness of the experience, and a slight misfit; you will get Swinburne's worst work.

He came to write, in later years, though by no means so often as has been hastily asserted, and in his tragedies hardly at all, with a technique which, considered simply as technique, is impeccable, but with too little reference to the precise nature of his substance when it was similar to substance previously expressed by him. With an astonishingly copious vocabulary, he was too easily content to repeat his phrases; with an unparalleled metrical science, he was too willing to repeat movements without asking himself whether they were exactly appropriate.

But this unfortunate monotony must be distinguished from the admirable monotony of his best work. There, in the best things in the three series of *Poems and Ballads*, in the *Songs before Sunrise*, in *Atalanta* and *Erechtheus*, in *Tristram*, and *The Tale of Balen*, despite an occasional lapse, there is a thoroughly justifiable, because expressive, monotony. The recurrence, in any of the greater poems, of particular words and phrases is due to no such weakness as we have just noticed, but to a determination to maintain a certain musical atmosphere. It is true that it is carried to a point to which no poet eager for immediate intellectual effect would carry it. In the result, there is, especially though not exclusively for fools, an appearance of comparative poverty of meaning. But the selection of language is really made with consummate art, out of vast resources, in the service of a very firm conception of the subject; only, the epithet belongs less to its neighbouring substantive than to the stanza, which itself exists less to say any separable thing with immediate effect than to sustain the music, to contribute to the creation of the atmosphere, till the mind of the reader shall be saturated. Swinburne, in his great successes, is not working with the single word, the phrase, the line, for the intellectual impression he can at once make with them on the reader's intelligence. Rather is he on his guard against that jab of too definite meaning into a mind that may retain it when the line has swept by, rather is he deliberately dimming the individual word, speeding the line on, maintaining the endless undulation of the verse. His concern, often, is less to say incidental things memorably than to avoid saying them too memorably, and his art is in keeping up the movement and the shimmer of his peculiar imagery till the general effect has been secured.

Take it hardly matters which of his greater lyrics, and ask yourself, not what this or that line has said, but whether there has anywhere been admitted a word that is not in accord with the atmosphere and emotional life of the poem as a whole. There, in that exclusion of every word that would be out of tune, every phrase that would persist too long in the memory with its separate message, every image that would not accord with the general atmosphere of the poem, is his triumph, and the evidence that he has completely and vividly conceived a work of art. It is an exceptional way of writing, and not necessarily to be preferred to that more normal way in which the poet takes the risk of incidental discords in the confidence that they will be resolved in the ultimate effect. But Swinburne's success in it is proof of "fundamental brainwork", for the thing to be expressed must have been fully and energetically grasped if every phrase and line is to be kept in accord.

It is a method for lyrical rather than for narrative or dramatic work, and it is instructive to study its application to other than lyrical substance. Take, for, I suppose, the most suggestive contrast available, *Erechtheus* and *Tristram of Lyonesse*. Each is remarkable for uniformity, for the persistence of its own particular note and atmosphere. Why is it that *Erechtheus* is a masterpiece, whereas *Tristram*, so full of magnificent poetry, is a sort of sublime failure? Some secondary explanations might be offered. *Erechtheus* was written on a single impulse at one of the most fortunate periods of Swinburne's life, whereas *Tristram* was worked at by fits and starts over a decade and finally pieced together at a time when Swinburne's inspiration was apt to flag. But the essential fact is that the subject of *Erechtheus* demanded monotony and the subject of *Tristram* did not. The real trouble with *Tristram* is that, to the extent to which it is narrative, it postulates lapse of time and succession of events, but that in spirit it is an ecstatic hymn to changeless and timeless love. So far as it is a narrative, though it is a succession of scenes rather than an uninterrupted story, it needs light and shade; but as that hymn it needs to burn throughout with the one flame. The prelude to it is, for unchecked rush of energy and splendour of imagery, one of the greatest things in English poetry; the seascapes are unmatched; the vigil of Iseult, with the refrain of wind and sea, is presented with extraordinary power; the conclusion is of the utmost nobility:

> " So came their hour on them that were in life
>   Tristram and Iseult: so from love and strife,
>   The stroke of love's own hand felt last and best
>   Gave them deliverance to perpetual rest. . . .
>   There slept they wedded under moon and sun,
>   And change of stars: and through the casement came
>   Midnight and noon girt round with shadow and flame
>   To illumine their grave or veil it: till at last
>   On these things too was doom as darkness cast:
>   For the strong sea hath swallowed wall and tower,
>   And where their limbs were laid in woful hour
>   For many a fathom gleams and moves and moans
>   The tide that sweeps above their coffined bones
>   In the wrecked chancel by the shivered shrine:
>   Nor where they sleep shall moon or sunlight shine
>   Nor man look down for ever: none shall say,
>   Here once, or here, Tristram and Iseult lay:
>   But peace they have that none may gain who live,
>   And rest about them that no love can give,
>   And over them, while death and life shall be,
>   The light and sound and darkness of the sea."

Great lines are common in *Tristram*: but almost every line aspires to greatness. In *Erechtheus*, consistently lofty as it is, there is no search for brilliance: in *Tristram*, except for a very few graver passages like that just quoted, every line would be a blazing jewel.

And the final effect, I say it with great reluctance, is one of fatigue. One puts down the poem with dazzled, aching eyes. The fate of *Tristram* was settled when Swinburne wrote the prelude to it, not realizing that no narrative or quasi-narrative poem could possibly maintain that pitch without losing hold on the ostensible subject. If, treating the legend of Tristram and Iseult on its own level, and in his handling of the scene where the dying Tristram asks whether the sail of the incoming ship is white or black there is some evidence that he could have done so, Swinburne had reserved for an epilogue the glorification of love itself! It is doubtless illogical that he should have suffered for putting the horse before the cart instead of behind it, but with Pegasus logic is at a discount.

Swinburne's usual method required a more careful choice of subject than his impetuosity always permitted. He should, as a rule, have selected subjects which demanded, in his conception of them, that monotony of which he was so great a master. He was not incapable, under dramatic obligation, of dealing with other subjects. *Bothwell* is a very impressive proof of his ability to adapt himself to changing requirements. But if he was to do that he needed to feel a duty to something outside art, to historical truth, as in *Bothwell*: it was perilous for him to venture on the treatment of legend, which he had liberty to shape to his own will, unless it was of a nature thoroughly suited to his customary method. And no poet should have been more timid of returning to subjects similar to those he had already treated, for with him it was only too probable that he would re-employ metres, phrases, a whole method suited to his first experience of the subject but not precisely suited to the experience he was then expressing.

It can never be easy for a poet to choose from among his own poems. He will know, as no one else can, his

intention in this poem or that, his choice will be affected by his sense of success in doing what he set out to do rather than by a dispassionate consideration of the value of the thing done. Given Swinburne's method, however, the difficulty of self-criticism is immensely increased. He surveys the mass of his work, in which best and worst are up to a point so very much alike, and he finds, let us say, two poems in each of which tune and atmosphere are perfectly maintained. Into neither has anything incongruous with the general effect been admitted, and each, we will suppose, is on a subject dear to him. They will seem to him equally successful, as in a way they are. But in the one poem there is hardly anything more than the negative success of having excluded all that could clog the metrical movement or disturb the general atmosphere; and in the other the negative success is subsidiary to positive success in the energetic expression of great emotion. Or, proudly conscious of his metrical science, he will judge between his poems with reference to that. There can be no question of outright failure in the mere use of any metre, since he is master of all, so he will begin to consider which has the more complexity of metrical art, and then he will declare his preference for one of the odes of his maturity over even " Hertha " or " Ave atque Vale ".

" The ode or hymn—I need remind no probable reader that the terms are synonymous in the speech of Pindar—asserts its primacy or pre-eminence over other forms of poetry in the very name which defines or proclaims it as essentially the song: as something above all less pure and absolute kinds of song by the very nature and law of its being. The Greek form, with its regular arrangement of turn, return, and after song, is not to be imitated because it is Greek, but to be adopted because it is best; the very best, as a rule, that could be imagined for lyrical expression of the thing conceived or lyrical aspiration towards the aim imagined. The rhythmic reason of its rigid but not arbitrary law lies simply and solely in the charm of its regular variations. This can be given in English as clearly and fully, if not so sweetly and subtly, as in Greek: and should, therefore, be expected and required in an English poem of the same nature and proportion. . . . It seems strange to me, our language being what it is, that our literature should be no richer than it is in examples of the higher or at least more capacious and ambitious kind of ode."

But should not the comparative rarity of the stricter and ampler ode in English, even when allowance has been made for the prevalence of the pseudo-Pindaric models, inspire caution? Is it not possible that the instinctive reluctance of great English lyrists to use the form otherwise than very exceptionally has been wise?

Correspondence of parts is indeed a necessity as well as a virtue, an irregular ode being a contradiction in terms, but the question arises whether, even in Swinburne, whose major odes are technically the best that we have, it is always fully felt by the reader or listener. We *know* that in his odes on the true classical model there is perfect correspondence, but do we always *feel* it?

The early ode on the insurrection in Crete, which Swinburne grew to dislike, is somewhat formal, and perhaps not entirely sincere; it does not come into the argument. The ode on the proclamation of the French Republic begins superbly, with its pealing rhymes:

" With songs and crying and sounds of acclamations,
  Lo, the flame risen, the fire that falls in showers!
  Hark: for the word is out among the nations:
  Look: for the light is up upon the hours:

O fears, O shames, O many tribulations,
Yours were all yesterdays, but this day ours.
Strong were your bonds linked fast with lamentations,
With groans and tears built into walls and towers;
Strong were your works, and wonders of high stations,
Your forts blood-based, and rampires of your powers:
Lo now the last of divers desolations,
The hand of time, that gathers ghosts like flowers,
Time, that fills up and pours out generations:
Time, at whose breath confounded Empire cowers."

But when, after five more long strophes, we return to this music, it is a purely mental logic that is satisfied; there is no sensual satisfaction.

Turn to the ode by which he himself wished to be judged " as a lyric poet in the higher sense of the term ", the ode on Athens. It is, as he claimed, " absolutely faithful in form to the strictest type and the most stringent law of Pindaric hymnology ". Its form is wiser than that of the odes in which wide intervals occur between the corresponding parts. We are aware in it, as in most of Swinburne's other odes, of a special ambition of aim and a special elaboration of means. It has splendid eloquence; and if the finest poetical rhetoric produced on a resolutely observed scheme were the finest poetry, it would be a masterpiece. But it is a thing wonderfully made, not a thing miraculously born. " The Armada ", which he put beside it, may no doubt also be regarded as an ode, of a novel kind. It, too, has magnificence, half lost in the volubility for which odes seemed to give Swinburne an excuse. That it abounds overmuch in diatribes against the God of Spain, with something of the effect of having been written less by a patriotic poet than an inverted and enraged theologian, is beside our present purpose. The point is that the scheme of it, though perceptible,

> My dear friend
>
> So totally am
> I exhausted that
> I can hardly hold
> my pen, to express
> my vexation that I
> shall be unable ever
> to converse with you
> again. Eyes and
> intellect fail me —
> I can only say that
> I was much gratified
> by your visit, which
> must be the last, and
> that I remain ever
> Your obliged
> W Landor

LANDOR'S LAST LETTER TO SWINBURNE

is simply not felt pleasurably in the actual reading. This composition comes, in the third series of *Poems and Ballads*, immediately after " The Commonweal ", and it is impossible not to think that its intricacy and extravagance are rebuked by the curbed energy and solemn patriotism of that poem, impossible not to wish that it had been written as a comparatively brief lyric relying on a simple stanzaic form.

The odes of Swinburne deserve to be placed between Shelley's and Coleridge's, but he was deceived in thinking that it is by them that his station will be decided, and his own preference for Coleridge's ode on France over " Dejection " shows the extent to which his opinion was influenced by regard for regularity of structure. The true basis for judgment of Swinburne as a lyrist is such a volume, and it would not be a small one, as might be produced by bringing together nearly the whole of the contents of the three series of *Poems and Ballads*, nearly all the pieces in the *Songs before Sunrise*, the principal choruses of *Atalanta* and *Erechtheus*, and a certain number of isolated later poems.

Such a selection would need to be made with heed to something else besides these qualities which are at once and everywhere recognized as peculiarly Swinburne's. It would somewhat diminish the prominence given to the clamorous, though often quite irresistible, music and wonderful, often excessive, exuberance of the first series of *Poems and Ballads*. From that volume it would gather " Laus Veneris "; " The Triumph of Time "; " A Leave-taking ", one of the clearest and most exactly communicative of all his early poems; " Itylus "; " Anactoria "; the " Hymn to Proserpine "; " Anima Anceps "; " In the Orchard "; " Before the Mirror "; " A Match "; " Ilicet "; " Stage Love "; " Faustine "; " In Memory of Walter Savage Landor "; " Dolores "; " The Garden of Proserpine "; " Hesperia "; " The Sundew "; " Félise ". To these would be added a poem which, though it is perhaps not much more than a curiosity of beauty, Swinburne was mistaken in holding back, " Cleopatra ". He wrote it very rapidly, to oblige Frederick Sandys, whose drawing it was to accompany, and modestly acquiesced in Meredith's description of it as a farrago of the commonplaces of his poetical style. Actually, though precluded by its temper and method from competition with his greatest lyrics, which arise out of far profounder emotion and spread far more powerful and rapid wings, it is a little miracle of perversity, a minor masterpiece of decadent poetry, not without influence on a famous reverie of Pater's, or, if that be worth noting, on Wilde's " Sphinx ".

> " Her mouth is fragrant as a vine,
> A vine with birds in all its boughs,
> Serpent and scarab for a sign
> Between the beauty of her brows
> And the amorous deep lids divine. . . .
>
> Under those low large lids of hers
> She hath the histories of all time;
> The fruit of foliage-stricken years;
> The old seasons with their heavy chime
> That leaves its rhyme in the world's ears.
>
> She sees the hand of death made bare,
> The ravelled riddle of the skies,
> The faces faded that were fair,
> The mouths made speechless that were wise,
> The hollow eyes and dusty hair. . . .
>
> Dank dregs, the scum of pool or clod,
> God-spawn of lizard-footed clans,

And those dog-headed hulks that trod
Swart necks of the old Egyptians,
Raw draughts of man's beginning God;

The poised hawk, quivering ere he smote,
With plume-like gems on breast and back;
The asps and water-worms afloat,
Between the marsh-flowers moist and slack;
The cat's warm black bright rising throat....

She holds her future close, her lips
Hold fast the face of things to be;
Actium, and sound of war that dips
Down the blown valleys of the sea,
Far sails that flee, and storms of ships;

The laughing red sweet mouth of wine
At ending of life's festival;
That spice of cerecloths, and the fine
White bitter dust funereal
Sprinkled on all things for a sign."

A minor poem, but to be included because it sums up so much of what was decadent in a poet too much in love with life, too full of energy, to be more than a curious, appreciative visitor of that province of the mind where love is given to beautiful things rather than to beauty.

From such a piece the anthologist would pass, with sudden exhilaration and the sense of boundless space opening before him, to the incomparable *Songs before Sunrise*, to the great movement of " Super Flumina Babylonis ", to the supreme achievement of " Hertha ", to the grave beauty of " Siena ", to the purified emotion and chastened style of " Tiresias ", to the noble arguments of the prelude and epilogue in which, as so seldom in Swinburne, the language has become translucent.

Here, in these things and such others as "The Pilgrims" and "An Appeal" and "Quia Multum Amavit", is the crowning work of Swinburne. Here there is discipline with an unsurpassed impetuosity, buoyancy with weight, an exceptional purity and lucidity of diction with all the usual splendour and speed.

Beside that body of work there is nothing quite worthy to be placed except two pieces from the second series of *Poems and Ballads*, " Ave atque Vale ", where recollection of Baudelaire has brought a certain welcome hardness, a new feeling for contour, into the verse, and " At a Month's End ". Nowhere else in Swinburne is there verse so majestically inevitable in movement as in certain stanzas of " Ave atque Vale ".

" Thou art far too far for wings of words to follow,
Far too far off for thought or any prayer.
What ails us with thee who art wind and air?
What ails us gazing where all seen is hollow?
Yet with some fancy, yet with some desire
Dreams pursue death as winds a flying fire,
Our dreams pursue our dead and do not find;
Still, and more swift than they, the thin flame flies,
The low light fails us in elusive skies,
Still the foiled earnest ear is deaf, and blind
Are still the eluded eyes.

Not thee, O never thee, in all times changes,
Not thee, but this the sound of thy sad soul,
The shadow of thy swift spirit, this shut scroll,
I lay my hand on, and not death estranges
My spirit from communion of thy song—
These memories and these melodies that throng
Veiled porches of a Muse funereal—
These I salute, these touch, these clasp and fold,

> As though a hand were in my hand to hold,
> Or through mine ears a mourning musical
> Of many mourners rolled.
>
> I among these, I also, in such station,
> As when the pyre was charred, and piled the sods,
> And offering to the dead made, and their gods,
> The old mourners had, standing to make libation,
> I stand, and to the Gods and to the dead
> Do reverence without prayer or praise, and shed
> Offering to these unknown, the gods of gloom,
> And what of honey and spice my seedlands bear
> And what I may of fruits in this chilled air,
> And lay, Orestes-like, across the tomb,
> A curl of severed hair."

These and many other verses of the poem are far too great to be regarded as a singing lesson; but what a model for any poet who should desire a supremely good example of flow and check, repetition and variation, of pure and stately diction, of phrasing that tightens on the substance without constricting it, of metrical movement precisely adjusted to the impulses and pauses and sad returns on itself of the thought!

The late 'sixties and early 'seventies were the golden years of Swinburne. Then, as seldom before, and still more seldom afterwards, he could reconcile expansiveness with closeness of expression. In the *Songs before Sunrise* restraint, what for him was austerity in expression, comes to us as a moral quality with an aesthetic consequence; in the second series of *Poems and Ballads* it is out of his wistfulness in certain pieces, his pensiveness, his realization of an isolation which he would imaginatively diminish, that Swinburne addresses himself to us with so much clarity. It is only in the second series of *Poems and Ballads* that Swinburne can be seen putting forth a hand, with a tentativeness infinitely touching in one naturally so ardent and confident and independent of the public, in the hope of finding an unknown hand slipped into his. It is not, on the whole, so great a volume as *Songs before Sunrise*, but it is the volume in which Swinburne is most communicative without any but human and aesthetic reason for being so, the eagerness to get through to the reader in *Songs before Sunrise* being in the high sense political. The anthologist I have supposed would find it difficult to leave out more than eight or nine of the pieces in that volume. It is with the third series of *Poems and Ballads* that he would be most likely to fail, judging that book not simply as an independent work but by unconscious reference to its two greater predecessors, the one so much more exciting, the other so much more charming.

Swinburne, and it is one more proof of his inability to realize and allow for the temper of the public, was singularly ill-advised in the succession, the constitution, and the titles of his publications. He thought it, if he thought about that at all, perfectly sound to follow up the sensational first *Poems and Ballads* with a long single poem so disconcerting to expectation as *A Song of Italy*; he acquiesced in the absurd arrangement whereby *Tristram of Lyonesse* was almost lost in a large mass of miscellaneous verse, some of it very different in mood; he issued in the one year two such volumes as *Songs of the Springtides* and *Studies in Song*. But I doubt if he ever did himself a worse service than in entitling the volume of 1889 *Poems and Ballads*, third series. The really capable anthologist would forget the label, and take from it, as worthy to rank with all but his very greatest things, the elegy on Inchbold; " The Commonweal "; " Pan and Thalassius "; " The Tyneside Widow "; " A Jacobite's Farewell "; and perhaps some other pieces. On other volumes he would draw less, but he would not pass over the " Adieux à Marie Stuart ", the best of the roundels, the best of the poems on children, the elegy on Burton, " A Nympholept ", certain of the sonnets on Elizabethan dramatists, the poem on Burns.

Such a selection, the basis for which has been laid by Sir Edmund Gosse and Mr. Wise, would benefit Swinburne far more than the cheap two-volume issue of his collected poems. But what is still more needed, what should forthwith be undertaken, is the production of a volume containing the substance of all Swinburne's greatest books of verse whether lyrical or dramatic or narrative, and excluding, despite the seriousness of some losses involved, those books in which he was only intermittently at or near his best. The book would not be much less bulky than the two volumes of collected poems, and it would be immeasurably more useful to his fame, giving us the dramatic poet of *Chastelard* and *Bothwell* as well as the lyrist. Even those who think less highly of the finest of the tragedies than the present writer does must acknowledge that judgment on Swinburne must take them into serious account. They exhibit far more clearly than all but a very few of the lyrical poems his feeling for character, his imaginative sympathy, his fundamental brain-work, his gift for the transmutation of prose material, his capacity for sustained emotion. They correct the impression, to which portions of his lyrical work give plausibility, of Swinburne as a fitful and erratic lyrist, a poet rarely capable of directed and resolute flight or of carrying a great weight of matter. And since he wrote but little blank verse outside the tragedies and the two plays on the Greek model, in which last, of course, there was less occasion to create the illusion of mundane speech, there is a technical reason also for insisting on the inclusion of his representative tragedies in any selection which professes to give us material for a verdict on Swinburne. Study of the blank verse of *Bothwell* would speedily show that what are often supposed to be the habitual peculiarities of Swinburne are in fact present in a marked degree only in his lyrical work, and that in writing dramatic blank verse he can pack a line as closely as any other poet. That he is of necessity dependent on spinning speed is a superstition that will not survive even half an hour spent over the tragedies. That he requires an overcharge of music to carry him forward will be disproved on any page of those plays.

Out of indolence, we speak of Swinburne's music; but, in truth, there have been few of our greater poets less concerned for the sheer musical quality of their words. Examine a few lines taken at random from different pages, and you will find that he has no fear of harshness, no shrinking from sibilants, and in blank verse no objection to over-packing the line. What one calls his music is the result not of a persistent selection of musical words but of the power and continuity of his metrical schemes. It is significant that, being so great a lyrist, he has written comparatively few songs, strictly so called, and perhaps only one, " Love laid his sleepless head ", which would immediately be accepted as in the central tradition of English song-writing. It is noteworthy that even in those not very numerous short poems in which he seems most to have abandoned himself to the dream and the music there is never that inexplicable trembling of the strings which you may hear in Shelley. Always there is the strong constraint of metre. Superficially, with his facility, he has something of the air of an improviser, but though at times there is a lack of intellectual compulsion, there is almost always, and especially in his curiously wrought blank verse, the metrical compulsion, under pressure of which the individual word or phrase is allowed little or no opportunity of making its particular musical contribution, of asserting the value it has for the ear when taken separately. Not musical value but metrical value is what concerns Swinburne as a rule.

To write in this way is natural to him indeed, the satisfaction of a deep and permanent need of his genius, and the facility with which he does so is proof of that, but it is also a highly artificial process. And here, as it happens, we are enabled to see how far it was instinctive, how far deliberate. In the second series of *Poems and Ballads* there is a piece, " A Vision of Spring in Winter ", the first three elaborate stanzas of which were composed by Swinburne in his sleep.[1] He wrote them down at once, expecting them to prove nonsense, but found next morning that no radical alterations in them were necessary, and he then added the four stanzas which complete the poem. Now in those first three stanzas, composed in sleep, though they are quite unmistakably Swinburne's as well as very beautiful, there is something unusual; the constraint has been, to a certain extent, taken off the words. They satisfy the metrical requirements perfectly, but they have a measure of independent life also, and seem to have adapted themselves graciously to the metre instead of giving up their souls to its imperious demands.

" Where has the greenwood hid thy gracious head?
Veiled with what visions while the grey world grieves
Or muffled with what shadows of green leaves,
What warm intangible green shadows spread
To sweeten the sweet twilight for thy bed?
What sleep enchants thee? what delight deceives?
Where the deep dreamlike dew before the dawn
Feels not the fingers of the sunlight yet

[1] Swinburne's statement to Miss Alice Bird, sister of the admirable doctor and friend who helped Swinburne so often in the 'seventies.

The silver web unweave,
Thy footless ghost on some unfooted lawn
Whose air the unrisen sunbeams fear to fret
Lives a ghost's life of daylong dawn and eve.

Sunrise it sees not, neither set of star,
Large nightfall, nor imperial plenilune,
Nor strong sweet shape of the full-breasted noon;
But where the silver-sandalled shadows are,
Too soft for arrows of the sun to mar,
Moves with the mild gait of an ungrown moon:
Hard overhead the half-lit crescent swims,
The tender coloured night draws hardly breath,
The light is listening:
They watch the dawn of slender-shapen limbs,
Virginal, born again of doubtful death,
Chill foster-father of the weanling spring."

There is something there, certainly not through imitation, of a way with words that we remember in some of the odes of Keats and in " The Scholar Gypsy " and " Thyrsis ". It is nearer the normal method of writing than Swinburne was wont to get. Certain words have a murmur of their own, coming up through the general metrical effect; certain phrases linger just a fraction of time beyond the allowance given them by the metre; a delicate unexpected thrill is given us by this line or that, as in the first stanza, which I have not quoted, by the line,

" Be not too long irresolute to be."

And though a poem by Swinburne is a very surprising thing, it is apt to be devoid of incidental surprises. The first stanza fixes both the temper and the precise metrical effect, and what follows, as a rule, is marvellously in accord but so exactly what would be expected that the reader, when Swinburne is not at his best, is hypnotized rather than aroused to eagerness of response.

Questions of technique go deeper than people in general perceive or, perceiving, are quite willing to allow. That Swinburne was the supreme metrician, rather than the supreme musician, that he was a born rhymer: these are fundamental facts. As a metrician he subdues the individual word to the metrical need much more than any poet anxious for immediate intellectual effect could possibly consent to do. But words with him were subdued also by the nature of his intellectual demand on them, that they should be congruous with the general scheme of the poem rather than sharply expressive in their immediate context. Then, too, his preference for undefining epithets helps to produce the haze and iridescence in which he usually moves. Highly particularized facts can gain no admission into such writing, nor can anything be steadily placed in that undulant, hastening verse. Rhyme comes in with further distraction. It is very probable, though I do not remember that this has anywhere been fully argued out, that the innovation of rhyme did as much as any change in the raw material of poetry or in the spiritual influences under which poetry was produced to give to modern poetry the qualities we call romantic. Discussion of that, however, would be beside my purpose here, which is merely to point out that Swinburne is of those poets in whose minds the answering rhyme sounds start up with an enormous wealth of suggestion, and not of those other poets whose thought, working forward largely independent of such suggestion, is but modified in expression by the necessity of rhyming. It is not in the nature of things that such a poet should habitually or often be direct and concise. The moment a line comes into his head, he is besieged by suggestions emanating from the rhyme. Alliteration is a yet further distraction. He uses it so much with better excuse than is always allowed, for he writes very frequently in anapaestic metres, and in English, from the author of

" My truest treasure so traitorly taken "

to the author of

" She has come up from the lair of the lion
With love in her luminous eyes,"

everyone who has used anapaests finely has also relied on alliteration. But it affects his thought, not least in causing him to couple things not drawn from the same category, as when "snows and sins" are brought together, in the first chorus of *Atalanta*.

The urgings of metre, rhyme, and alliteration almost suffice to make some of this poetry. Only not those great things in which, incredibly, there is a poetry that seems to exist at once wholly for its message and wholly for the gratification of its maker's technical impulse. In "Hertha", in the prelude to *Songs before Sunrise*, there is unfaltering intellectual argument with uninterrupted song, and the argument is as noble as the song is perfect. Poetry more lucid, more securely guided by its intellectual purpose, more proudly and simply adequate to its burden than the poetry of those preluding stanzas can hardly be found anywhere else in our literature:

" For what has he whose will sees clear
To do with doubt and faith and fear
Swift hopes and slow despondencies?
His heart is equal with the sea's
And with the sea-wind's, and his ear
Is level to the speech of these,

And his soul communes and takes cheer
With the actual earth's equalities
Air, light, and night, hills, winds, and streams,
And seeks not strength from strengthless dreams. . . .

To him the lights of even and morn
Speak no vain things of love or scorn,
Fancies and passions miscreate
By man in things dispassionate.
Nor holds he fellowship forlorn
With souls that pray and hope and hate
And doubt they had better not been born
And fain would lure or scare off fate
And charm their doomsman from their doom,
And make fear dig its own false tomb. . . .

He hath given himself and hath not sold
To God for heaven or man for gold,
Or grief for comfort that it gives,
Or joy for grief's restoratives.
He hath given himself to time, whose fold
Shuts in the mortal flock that lives,
On its plain pasture's heat and cold,
And the equal year's alternatives.
Earth, heaven and time, death, life, and he,
Endure while they shall be to be."

Hardly anyone, it may be assumed, is now very seriously perturbed about the morality of " Anactoria " or " Dolores ", but the personal character of Swinburne continues in some quarters to be condemned, though not in the old way. It is not that anyone is shocked, but that a good many are disposed to be patronizing towards one who, on their view of him, was a kind of degenerate with genius and had eventually to be caged in the suburbs to save his life. There was never anyone less deserving of half-contemptuous pity; and when it is proffered him one may excusably be moved to enquire whether in essential dignity he was not the better of most of his contemporaries. I, at any rate, seem to find something less dignified than Swinburne's attitude towards friends and enemies and his own fame in the uneasy postures Tennyson assumed whenever there was the slightest fear of his being attacked, recognized, or ignored. Swinburne was too easily drawn into controversy at one period of his life, and the prolonged squabble with Furnivall was both unseemly and in time tedious, but he fought, when he did fight, with exhilaration, and as a letter I have already quoted reminds us, he was never anxiously in search of signs of hostility. It was genuinely mystifying to him that Tennyson, and still more that Rossetti, should attach such inordinate importance to praise and abuse proceeding from anonymous and even obscure sources. That an artist should draw breath by leave of popular censors was to him quite unintelligible. But this is to speak only of his literary life.

I contrast him as a man with Meredith, who enjoyed so much respect in later years, and when all allowance has been made I find Swinburne very much the greater man. There is the brandy, to be sure, and we may see Swinburne, during certain unhappy years, frenzied or dejected by it in his rooms in Great James Street, while Meredith, at Box Hill, with rather too much parade of a knowledge which, having some competence in regard to wine, I venture to question, offers an epicurean, or supposedly epicurean, hospitality to friends infinitely more reputable than Charles Augustus Howell and Simeon Solomon. There is the long-maintained perverse interest in flagellation, and Swinburne writes at intervals over two decades his mock epic of it. The bibliography of Meredith contains nothing so embarrassing to the solemn student as *The Whippingham Papers*,[1] and whatever unnoted manuscripts by Meredith may exist it is safe to conjecture they include nothing as unsuited for printing as various of Swinburne's. And so on. Meredith, from the ordinary point of view, was a nearly blameless man; Swinburne was exceedingly naughty. But the moment Meredith begins to be closely scrutinized there appear in him traits of snobbery, of cruelty, of fundamentally vulgar though brilliantly contrived self-assertion, which it is impossible to observe without repulsion. On the other hand, the more minutely one looks into the life of Swinburne, the clearer become his chivalry, his delicacy of consideration, his courtesy, his amusing readiness to credit almost everyone with his own knowledge and his own high enthusiasms, his deference to every kind of merit, his loyalty, his courage.

It is not necessary to drag in Meredith or any other, though the tone of certain references to Swinburne as quite indisputably the degenerate weakling among his contemporaries excuses it. But it is necessary to insist that Swinburne, whatever his excesses and eccentricities, was never less than a great gentleman. As to morals, he may be allowed to speak for himself:[2]

" I do not want to take matters [the reference is to libels on him] too seriously or too lightly, but however many things I may have, in common with all other men, to regret on my own account that I should have done or left undone, I am conscious of nothing that should make me more afraid or ashamed that the most rigid

---

[1] *The Whippingham Papers*, London, 1888. The third " Contribution " is a poem in two parts. The manuscript of the third part of this poem exists, and has been inserted in Mr. Wise's copy to round off the printed portions. The work, needless to say, was privately printed.

[2] Letter to Watts-Dunton dated 1876; holograph original in Mr. Wise's collection.

Puritan need to stand before the world as I am. There is nothing in my life that I have more cause to wish hidden or forgotten, overlooked or kept private, than any other man who does not or who does not pretend to canonization. I admit no more right in a stranger to intrude upon my private life and report on it falsely or truly than on yours or any other man's, but I have no more reason or need to fear it."

Nothing could be manlier or more sensible.

Swinburne always showed great independence of the public with great dependence on friends. He needed more than friendship: he needed, at every stage of his life, heroes. Noble as his worship of those heroes—Landor, Mazzini, Hugo, and, on a lower level, others—was in most of its manifestations, it is idle to deny that it had in it sometimes a decadent quality, a luxurious relish of the act of prostration, just as his rebelliousness, usually born of noble indignation, had in it at times a tinge of mere perversity. To an extent that can hardly be conceived of any normal man, he lived in oscillation between worship and blasphemy; and it was with a peculiar bitterness that he discovered reasons for casting down any idol. In the whole of his correspondence there is nothing more revealing than what he wrote in the winter of 1876 about Eyre:

"I want to tell you—in case you care to know—that I, who have always at least honestly tried to think, as well as to speak, of all other men with perfect honesty, unbiassed by personal favour or disfavour on private grounds, must confess, as I do without shame or regret, to a bitter personal grudge against Mr. Eyre. He has quite unconsciously done me—and, I should think, many another man of my age and temper—one of the least forgettable or forgivable of all wrongs. He has thrown down into the dirt, broken to pieces, smashed and defiled past all chance of cleaning or mending, the living image of one of my favourite heroes, a figure which I really used to cherish and dwell upon in my mind with quite a boyish loyalty and reverence—his own."

Swinburne had been deeply moved by Henry Kingsley's account of Eyre's exploits in his " unparalleled Australian adventure ", a story to which, in his opinion, " the mightiest episode of the Odyssey is tame and unheroic ". He had felt that he would gladly have walked barefooted to London for one sight of so valiant and enduring an adventurer and martyr. But the actions of Governor Eyre made him feel that the whole breadth of the world was not enough to have between him and such a man. His bitterness is intensified by the " aftergust or afterglow " of the passionate admiration he once felt for Eyre, he says: and he utters in anguished words the pain of finding that his " whole loyal heart and soul of worship " have been given at an altar " where the god was no god at all, but a cracked and splintered and rotten idol defiled with blood and beastliness ".

The intensity of the revulsion would be more easily intelligible if the reference were to some leader in a cause to which Swinburne himself was dedicated or the most intimate of his friends. But such raptures and such subsequent execrations when inspired by a man whose life had no point of contact with Swinburne's are exceedingly strange. Thus, however, was Swinburne constituted, with a capacity for violent reaction to personalities and events utterly remote.

In that strange nature, the most abstract emotions had a certain sensuality. It is a lover's devotion that is given by him to liberty and to his heroes, and it is with the unique bitterness of love betrayed that he rounds on any hero proved unworthy. They have been poor apologists who have contended that Swinburne need never have written his erotic and perverse poems, that they were not the expression of an essential part of himself. Sensuality is largely cerebral with Swinburne, abstract thought and feeling largely sensual. What is sensual in him drives him to extremes, to almost excuseless excitements; but when the motive is adequate, it gives to panegyrics and polemics that were else but agitations of the air their reality, their human appeal. It is what differentiates him from Shelley, where they seem nearest to each other, that, for all the sincerity of his gesture, Swinburne has at times that appreciation of the luxury of it. He was in some sort a connoisseur of the sensations of worship and revolt as well as a devout worshipper and an instinctive rebel.

Belief in the collective divinity of man, that central inspiration in the *Songs before Sunrise*, came more easy than one might think to one who from youth was a worshipper of age and became a worshipper of infancy. His admiration (in that instance, it naturally stopped short of being worship) for old age began with his delight in the physical powers and turbulent character of his grandfather. Sir John Swinburne, however, as his grandson remarked after meeting Landor, had written no *Hellenics*. It was the feeling that with Landor one sort of reverence could be, as Swinburne put it, the lining for the other which bowed him in double homage to the master. The delight of a living lyrist in the coincidence of a cuckoo and a rainbow was not so rapturous as Swinburne's when he knelt in the presence of one who was crowned with age as well as laurel. It remained in some respects the greatest emotional experience of his life. But others were added to it, notably encounter with Trelawney, who, as ex-pirate and as the friend of Shelley, had powerful claims on him. He did not scrutinize poetical claims too closely when the age of the poet was indisputable, and Barry Cornwall, whose laurels were slight and dusty, was treated with the utmost deference while still living, mourned in a beautiful elegy when he passed away. Much more intimately, as time went on, he venerated the age of the mother to whom he had always been devoted, but who became the more sacred to him with the passage of years. Meanwhile his adoration of very young children developed, from about 1870, before which there was little sign of it, very rapidly and with consequences at which it is impossible not to smile. Beautiful in its tenderness of feeling, it expressed itself often enough in absurdities of conduct or eulogy. Here, too, his perversity had innocent issue, in an eagerness to be maltreated by any available infant oppressor. Watts-Dunton could not provide him with a great and aged poet to worship, but there was a child on the premises, and there were always children of very tender years on Putney Heath or Wimbledon Common. Once, at the seaside, he enjoyed the blessed and ever remembered experience of being waylaid by two highway-women who reached fully to his knee, and who extorted a halfpenny each before they would let him pass on his lawful occasions; at various times tiny strangers or children of friends indulged his taste for being bullied by irresistible weakness; and it must have been supreme bliss for him when the then infantile Miss May Morris gratified the Chastelard in him by smothering him with rose-petals as he lay prostrate in the garden, very conscious of the quality of this cruel and romantic punishment.

Under the influence of certain of those whom he particularly loved or venerated, Swinburne was so docile that it was difficult to believe him capable of the tempestuous conduct of other hours. In those perturbed years between the appearance of the first and that of the second series of *Poems and Ballads*, he had only to be translated from London to his parents' house, Holmwood, to become instantly all that their anxious affection could wish him. Brandy and the birch and the urgent duty of tyrannicide would cease to occupy his thoughts, and the radiant and serene, though of course still high-strung, Algernon would appear as the perfect son, the perfect brother, accommodating himself graciously to every domestic demand. In another way, but to almost the same degree, he had only to join Jowett on some reading party to become as sane and self-controlled as an impetuous young poet could be expected to be. With Watts-Dunton, except in a very few matters, he was from 1879 to the end almost self-effacing. " I think, and my friend Watts agrees with me ", became a formula for expressing his acquiescence in virtually everything Watts-Dunton suggested to him. In regard to business matters, he passed them over wholly to his friend, and was content to sign anything he was told to sign, except that he retained in his own hands all his dealings with his publishers. Towards them he could be very definitely assertive of his own opinion, and I have seen a letter of his in which he informed them that if they had any difficulty in changing their printers he would have none in changing his publishers. But, this and his inner life apart, he was invariably and perfectly ready that everything should be decided for him by Watts-Dunton, or Watts-Dunton's sister, or Watts-Dunton's wife, and punctilious in acknowledging the service they did him by freeing him from the obligation of dealing with the problems of daily life. A humourless record of the *ménage* has made it ridiculous, but there is nothing absurd in Swinburne's care to thank Mrs. Watts-Dunton for a judicious choice of soap, and I can conceive of the poet's mind as better employed than in attention to the lavatory arrangements. His personality was not obliterated at The Pines; simply, his inner became his only life. His position was much that of a child for whom everything is provided, but who is allowed the amplest opportunity for dwelling in its own imaginative world.

All this docility, however, was exhibited only towards those whom he loved and respected. If Swinburne took a certain pleasure in being subservient, it was only towards those whose authority he had voluntarily and affectionately accepted. Under any attempt by outsiders to coerce him he was always inflexible. A sensitive and fierce pride co-existed with his humility, and he would acknowledge no credentials except those to which his mind and heart gave endorsement. To approach him with coercive intentions, armed merely with moral or political authority, was to set the volcano in eruption.

Roughly, it may be said that he defied all those to whom he did not defer, middle courses being uncongenial to such a nature as his; but there is one very curious exception to be noticed. With all his republicanism, all his mutinous spirit, he was on the whole indisposed to challenge the existing order in Great Britain. He had physical courage in the highest degree, as he had shown at Eton, where the tiniest and strangest of boys was never for a moment in danger of being bullied, and in climbing the reputedly unclimbable Culver Cliff, to test his nerve, when his parents had forbidden him to cherish hopes of a military career, and as he continued to show in the reckless swimming exploits of his maturity, and revealed in old age when Eric Mackay, years younger and feet taller, proposed to cudgel him on Putney Heath and was cowed by his contemptuous indifference. He had no less moral courage. No man was ever less deterred by fear of consequences from any action felt to be incumbent or congenial. Yet he made no direct assault on the political institutions of his

R

country even where they were theoretically objectionable to him.

In the *Songs before Sunrise* there is just one poem, "Perinde ac Cadaver", which reflects on the British monarchy, or, rather, on the multiplication of princelets. Years later, in *A Midsummer Holiday*, there are diatribes against the House of Lords, but these are inspired by nothing more than irritation at the snobbery of a journalist who had declared that Tennyson could not confer more honour than he received on joining that House. Monarchy in the abstract Swinburne disliked, and various past and contemporary monarchs he loathed. But for Queen Victoria he had a real respect. He boiled over with rage when a Russian writer insulted her, and he wrote with perfect sincerity in celebration of her jubilee, though with only one reference to her, "a blameless queen". In one of her sons, Prince Leopold, who called on him in the middle 'seventies, when he was staying with Jowett at Oxford, Swinburne was greatly interested, though they never met each other: it was peculiarly annoying to him that his enemy, Furnivall, called an edition of Shakespeare the "Leopold".[1] He would have his naughty jests in private about the Alberto-Victorian court, though with reference rather to Tennyson's "Morte d'Albert" than to monarchy; he would allow, for such are the consequences of being an aristocrat as well as a revolu-

---

[1] In a letter of 1877, in Mr. Wise's collection, Swinburne is very sarcastic about Furnivall's "royal-nursery edition of 'Shaxpeer'", and threatens to reply to "this attack

> Sub tegmine Leopoldiculi
> Princepes (an ne pediculi ?)
> Puelluli facto ridiculi
> Parasibuli facto turpiculi."

"I don't know", he adds, "if all the diminutives are classical, not to say Augustan Latin, but they will do for bovine verse."

tionary, some tincture of hereditary Jacobite feeling to colour his allusions to a Hanoverian dynasty; but he was not at all seriously concerned to subvert monarchy in Great Britain. He had strong opinions on certain domestic or imperial questions, and developed a violent detestation of Gladstone when Irish Home Rule was championed by the betrayer of Gordon; he was not prepared to quarrel with British political institutions as a whole.

Swinburne, in short, was not a doctrinaire in politics. If he yearned for the illimitable republic, it was only because it would, if realized, give freedom; and in the measure that British institutions gave freedom he was prepared to acquiesce in them, even to applaud them. If there were defects in the political machinery and public life of contemporary England, he was prepared to take of them much the view that was taken by a poet otherwise so utterly unlike him as Coventry Patmore:

" Integrity so vast could well afford
To bear in working many a stain."

His love of England was passionate, his pride in her as the mother of poets and of seamen was immeasurable. He might chide her for lapses which seemed to him uncharacteristic of Milton's and Shelley's and Nelson's England, but in no circumstances could he turn against her in the spirit of the Little Englander or pro-Boer. The English were an elect people, the spiritual successors of the Athenians, the guardians of liberty, " sons and sires of seamen ", a people with an incomparable heritage and an unquestionable future.

This position was constantly misunderstood by those who looked only at Swinburne's republicanism and what seemed his delight in mere *sabotage*. Thus Herbert Spencer, who had known him for some years, wrote to him suggesting that his " marvellous powers of expressing well-justified anger might be fitly used at the present time in condemnation to our filibustering atrocities all over the world ", the reference being to Afghanistan, Zululand, and other regions in which Great Britain was involved in hostilities or engaged in peaceful penetration. No invitation of that kind could possibly be accepted by Swinburne. Spencer, however, was more politely corrected than the wretched emissary of a then projected Irish Republic who waited on Swinburne with a request for a seditious ode, but descended the stairs of The Pines with extreme rapidity when Swinburne, his little body twitching with fury, released the swirling flood of invective such a proposal was bound to provoke. Disloyalty and disunion were always intolerable in his view, which was stated with perfect clearness when he said in the dedicatory epistle prefixed to his Collected Poems that " the most grinding and crushing tyranny of a convention, a directory, or a despot, is less incompatible with republican faith than the fissiparous democracy of disunionists or communalists ".

I have more than once said or hinted in the preceding pages that Swinburne's political thought should rather be described as religious. It was in part from a political basis that he assailed, for it is an absurdity of whitewashing to pretend that he did not assail, Christianity. As he wrote to E. C. Stedman, and felt always, the virtues eminently inculcated by Christianity are those most desirable in the individual, the virtues encouraged by classical paganism at its purest were those most desirable in the citizen of a free republic. That Swinburne shared in the general scepticism of his period is nothing. Sensually he recoiled from all asceticism; politically, over and above the objection just noticed, he was only too mindful, somewhat childishly so, of the historic association of one great Christian institution

CONCLUSION 245

with persecution; and, more deeply, he was bound to protest against any idea of the universe which denied the potential collective divinity of man. That man's is the supreme intelligence operative in the universe, that its development has no limits, must be conceded to Swinburne for the foundation of his philosophy, which is not debarred from consideration as a philosophy because it comes to us in rapturous lyrics without definition of all its terms and logical relation of all its ideas. With reverence towards the personal character of Christ, the full poetry of which, however, Swinburne hardly felt, his is an attack on Christianity as deliberate and comprehensive as Leconte de Lisle's, and more violent. But there is no reason why any who have imagination as well as piety should shiver away from him. All energy is divine; all images of perfection testify to the existence of an immortal and all-inclusive perfection; and those modes of liberty which Swinburne glorified are part of that supreme freedom which is also obedience to the will of God.

But tolerance of his religious position can hardly involve approval of all the extravagances in his statements of it. That he made mischief with sacred things is nothing against him. It should be a misplaced seriousness that would reject the naughty fun of his impromptu carol:

" Hark, the herald angels crow,
' Here's a boy—but not for Joe!
Not for Joseph—Oh no, no!' "

When, however, he perpetrated his, also unpublished, couplet of an address by Joseph to Mary, when he appended a ribald supplementary stanza, necessarily unprinted, to " Hertha ", when he sketched the relationship between Simeon Solomon and Jehovah, and in some other of his spoken and epistolary jests, he was guilty of things in which very little humour or wit is accompanied by Hyde Park ribaldry. Such things were inconsistent with the inverted reverence which was much more truly characteristic of him, and I cannot but regard them, since they are most frequent in correspondence with Rossetti, Howell, and others of that circle, as attempts to play up to his audience. The Pre-Raphaelites cultivated for some years a sort of schoolboy impropriety. At times, as regards Swinburne, this issued in innocent enough fooling of a broad, boisterous kind, and it is by no means disagreeable to find the usual intensity of Swinburne's demeanour relaxed while he writes " A Vision of Bags ", in celebration of the corpulent William Morris's split trousers. Again, the frequency with which Swinburne for some twenty years would make ironical allusions to the chaste masterpiece of the Marquis de Sade gave relief to many of his letters and spoken rhapsodies. His impishness was often delightful. But between these rapid and discreetly phrased indiscretions and the employment of mere smut there is a great difference. And in justice to Swinburne it must be remembered that, whatever his lapses, he had, as he claimed, a real abhorrence of nastiness, and protested with energy against the abject and solemn dirtiness of certain things in Zola.

That his opinions changed violently, in certain respects, in later life has constantly been asserted, and the responsibility is put on Watts-Dunton. Without denying that Watts-Dunton influenced him towards what would be called saner opinions in some political and literary matters, I think that most of Swinburne's revulsions are otherwise explicable, and on a very great number of matters he continued to think at fifty, at sixty, at seventy precisely what he had thought at twenty or even earlier. The classic instance of his change of attitude is in respect of Walt Whitman. But has anyone succeeded in maintaining the one attitude towards Whitman?

As I have said elsewhere, for those who are at all drawn towards Whitman, there is a time when he means much more than on any strictly aesthetic view of him he is entitled to mean, and then, his work done, he drops out of mind as no great poet does. To return to him afterwards may be, given the improbability of a revival of a former mood, and a lucky opening of *Leaves of Grass*, a renewal of the old delight; much more probably, the result will be violent disgust. Which of us has not in adolescence adored and in maturity now and then blasphemed Whitman? Swinburne, as usual, went further in both directions than we, tepid of temperament, ever go; but that he should have recanted is nothing extraordinary. It is impossible to remain in the one frame of mind about Whitman for a lifetime, and not easy to do so for a week.

It is true that it was not only in regard to Whitman that Swinburne swung away from an earlier enthusiasm. Swinburne's ardent admiration of Baudelaire weakened, and there is nothing in the greater work of Baudelaire which should make a man think less of him when youthful curiosity about the fruits of his sinister garden has been satisfied. On the contrary, with the passing of years a student of that great, and in his peculiar way heroic, artist should attain to a profounder appreciation of his tensity, of his paradoxical pity emerging as cruelty, of that spirit which would be recognized as a martyr's if it were not that Baudelaire seems to be the devil's disciple when he is really God's. Watts-Dunton may have had something to do with the cooling of Swinburne's enthusiasm; he was not friendly to that second growth of Romanticism which yielded the *Fleurs du Mal*, and he certainly discouraged Swinburne's interest in the *macabre*. But, on the whole, I think we have the explanation in Swinburne's simply announced discovery that he had very little in common with Baudelaire. The ebullience, volubility, and restlessness of Swinburne are indeed far removed from the compression, economy, and immobility of Baudelaire, in whose world almost everything is petrified; and of genuine philosophical pessimism, as distinguished from a youthful protest against the frustration of desire, there is hardly a trace in Swinburne. We know what Baudelaire thought when Victor Hugo sent him a volume with the inscription, *Jungamas dextras*. " Je connais ", he wrote to Madame Paul Meurice, "les dessous du Latin de Victor Hugo. Cela veut dire: unissons nos mains, *pour sauver le genre humain*. Mais je me fiche du genre humain." The humanitarian causes which meant so much to Hugo and to Swinburne caused Baudelaire to curl his lip, and the perfectibility of man was a doctrine as amusingly absurd to him as it was sacred to Swinburne. We need not be astonished that Baudelaire occupied Swinburne less and less after 1870, and that at the time of his death he owned of all Baudelaire's writings only a copy of the *Fleurs du Mal* and the Wagner pamphlet which Baudelaire had sent him.[1]

The case of Whistler may more reasonably be considered to exhibit a sudden and almost inexplicable change of opinion by Swinburne. In early London days he had owed a good deal to Whistler and to Whistler's mother. For some years the poet and the painter had been close and reciprocally stimulating friends, and Swinburne had continued to entertain an enthusiastic admiration of Whistler's art, to which he had paid beautiful tribute in " Before the Mirror ",

---

[1] This most precious volume, inestimable in the eyes of all who honour these two great poets, is now in the possession of the writer most qualified to own it, Mr. Arthur Symons, who kindly showed it to me some years ago.

though they had drifted apart. Watts-Dunton, though occasionally resentful of Whistler's levity, was not capable of permanent anger against him, and indeed chuckled when he received, on his change of name, the postcard inquiry, " Theodore, what's Dunton?" But he unwisely incited Swinburne to the writing of the unhappy review of Whistler's controversial prose, and the pen ran away with Swinburne. There was only too much point in Whistler's sorrowful and comparatively unpugnacious reply, that he had lost an old friend and gained the acquaintance of an outsider. Twenty years earlier Swinburne had entered with rare imaginative sympathy into the artistic ambitions of Rossetti, Burne-Jones, Frederick Sandys, Whistler, and several other of the most distinguished artists of the time. But now he dealt with Whistler wholly from without.

These few instances of modified or reversed opinion must be set against his general tenacity of opinions formed in boyhood or youth. To speak of the formation of opinions by Swinburne, however, is justifiable perhaps only with reference to William Blake, Shakespeare, and Mary Queen of Scots. In studying each of these he came to feel eventually that his original estimates had neglected important characteristics. But, in general, his mind was made up in a flash. What he gave us in middle or old age was essentially his first experience of the Elizabethans and Landor and Hugo. Years of study expanded his knowledge of his favoured authors, and might result in some alteration of belief as to the authorship of an Elizabethan play, but his Marlowe, Webster, Ford were those of his rapturous discovery at Eton. Even Hugo, though Swinburne began by writing of him sanely and ended by writing about him preposterously, was the writer who had swum into his boyish ken, a fact of which there is proof in the special stress Swinburne continued to lay on *Les Châtiments*; only, after the master had responded graciously to his early overtures, it became an article of faith that the worst of Hugo was as inspired as the best.

Where there was an important change was in Swinburne's attitude towards his own poetry, a change difficult to define accurately but perhaps to be suggested by the statement that whereas poetry had been his achievement, it became his existence. He was conscious of it, though unaware of the danger involved, for we find in " Thalassius ", which is more truthful to spiritual facts than its superficial vagueness would lead one to think, that the poet, under the sun-god's benediction, is

" No more a singer but a song."

Other poets have dedicated themselves as completely as Swinburne to the production of poetry; other poets have put themselves entirely into their poetry, though for the most part poets have cultivated but a selected tract of personality, leaving the rest wild as useless for the purposes of their art. Wordsworth lived for poetry quite as much as Swinburne did, and it is the real tragedy of Coleridge that he was not kept in the society of Wordsworth, in constant subjection to one who felt that poetry was immeasurably the supreme interest in life. Swinburne's need was other than Coleridge's. He needed to be checked from almost literal absorption in his art, out of touch, I do not say with the general contemporary public, which a poet may well despise, but with that ideal public, small as it may be, and slow in gathering, which the poet must not neglect. The highest reward of the poet, doubtless, is not the attention of mankind but that rapture in his mind in which only God is participant; but it is at his peril, at the peril of the quality of that rapture, that he becomes indifferent to the communication of his experience to at least a

To a Seamew.

When I had wings, my brother,
   Such wings were mine as thine:
Such life my heart remembers
In all as wild Septembers
As this when life seems other,
   Though sweet, than once was mine;
When I had wings, my brother,
   Such wings were mine as thine.

Such life as thrills & quickens
   The silence of thy flight,
Or fills thy note's elation
With lordlier exultation
Than man's, whose faint heart sickens
   With hopes & fears that blight
Such life as thrills & quickens
   The silence of thy flight.

ORIGINAL HOLOGRAPH MANUSCRIPT OF
"TO A SEAMEW"

CONCLUSION 251

select audience, yet unborn as it may happen, but present to his imagination. The obligation to convey his experience precisely and vividly to that audience once disregarded, the poet becomes, as Swinburne did, content with movements and phrases and words which, helped by what is in his mind, may seem adequate, but which, not having been chosen and modified under pressure of the necessity of getting through perfectly to the reader, will not have the highest perfection of which his movements and phrases and words are capable. He will be like a man who talks to himself, with a code in which words and rhythms carry the little more or less of arbitrary value he has habituated himself to attach to them, without compulsion to find precise equivalents for the things he is expressing; and it is the curse of solitude that one's ideas and emotions, no longer having to be apprehended with the utmost nicety for conveyance to others, tend to become vague.

.Swinburne, certainly, was a writer of very exceptional facility, to which he had attained after labour much more arduous and critical than has commonly been supposed, but it was not his facility that was the trouble. What is called fatal facility had much better be called slipshod haste, such as was quite impossible for a great artist and great scholar like Swinburne. He was not more facile when writing some of his worst verse than when writing some of his best, the prelude to *Tristram* in a few hours, *Erechtheus* in a few weeks. But too often in later years he sang into the void, content with having had his experience, content that his expression of it was adequate for his personal requirements, totally forgetful of the needs of any audience. That he thus deprived us of much is obvious, but he also robbed himself, for the experience that is not so expressed as to be communicated will be less than perfectly expressed, as so many of Swinburne's later experiences, though by no means as many as is generally assumed, undoubtedly were.

There, in the abandonment of the attempt to communicate with us, is the real trouble in the worst work of the later Swinburne. He was not one of those poets in whom genius is a visitant; he was in temper the most continuously poetical lyrist we have had, with the doubtful exception of Shelley. But he had not the steady instinctive desire to keep up communication, and motives for effecting it were rarely operative in him after the sensual and political rebellions of his youth and early manhood had spent themselves.

He was the poet of liberty, in the widest and fullest sense of the term; and he came to this, that at times in later years be liberated himself from humanity, leaving us to watch and listen while the strange, breathless verse evolved like wave out of wave under some barely perceptible though evidently urgent impulse. Often that impulse was one of thanksgiving, for no one else among our poets, or it may be supposed the world's, has found more to praise, felt more joy in praising. Now and then he cared, as a chivalrous propagandist, to have us know the exact reasons for his praise, to have us see the lineaments of some semi-divine human face; and then his praise was incomparably eloquent. At other times, he showed us only that he was bowed in adoration before some hero, and the generalized eulogy, for all its sincerity and splendour, aroused in us only a vague excitement at best, something like boredom at the worst. He was more precise, as we should expect, in the poems of hate.

At no period of his life was Swinburne liable to those trivial, trying ailments which harass most people; at one period only, and then simply in consequence of his excesses, was he subject to lassitude; and his poetry is the product of an energy that knows no fatigue, exerts

CONCLUSION 253

itself at times out of proportion to the task, and is even content to exercise itself in the inane. He is tireless, and can become tiring, as natural things may, a persistent wind, or birds that begin singing before we are ready for them and will not take the hint of twilight, or the unwearying waves. He has the monotony in variety of the sea, and as the physical eye will sometimes be troubled by lack of a resting-place in the interminable fluctuation of the sea, the mind's eye, in a long reading of Swinburne, will sometimes be distressed by the absence of any enduring contour, anything stationary, in the undulant, flickering expanse of his verse. Is it always his failure if we grow tired? Should we tire as often as we do if we really were " what winds and waters make us "?

The most of us are to-day more tired of all but the finest work of Swinburne than the majority of any future public is likely to be. To explain in detail why the temper of the public to-day is peculiarly unfavourable to Swinburne would need far more space than is available, and it would, after all, be a waste of effort, for what matters is not the attitude of the literary public at this or that moment but the judgment which, formulating slowly after the original hasty and superficial verdict has been discarded, will take little account of prejudices peculiar to the 1860's or the 1920's. The question is, not how far he suits this generation, but how far he satisfies those demands which are made through the ages on poetry.

A poet of high humane enthusiasms, he is not a very human poet. He is full of passion, but of a specialized passion, which some people can never fully share, and others can share fully only at a particular stage of their emotional development. He has but little of the peculiarly English gift of magic, and indeed exhibits it perhaps only once at its finest, in those lovely lines in

" Ave atque Vale " telling of the wreath of wild flowers

" Such as the summer-sleepy Dryads weave,
Waked up by snow-soft sudden rains at eve ".

He has even less of that other English gift of inexplicable music, his metres being too imperious to allow of it. Atmosphere he has, supremely, with a profound, forbidden, too eager to be merely decadent knowledge of sensation, and a marvellous art of monotony, and that inexhaustible energy.

Responsive to literary influences almost beyond computation, and our greatest master of *pastiche*, he is, to the confusion of those who would present him as merely derivative, the most difficult of English poets to bring into comparison with his insular or foreign fellows. What in him is strictly comparable with Hugo or with Shelley, on the whole the poets with whom he has most in common, always turns out, on close scrutiny, to be unessential. Thus it is easy to place certain of his odes between Shelley's and Coleridge's, but they are not his most intimate or finest utterances; and to indicate where " Hertha " and " Ave atque Vale " and " The Triumph of Time " and " At a Month's End " and " A Nympholept " shall be placed is exceedingly difficult. As a man, he was different from other men, not through a degeneracy with sublime compensations, though there was always a streak of perversity in him, but as one successfully cast in a mould never used before or afterwards: as a poet, for all the complexity of his obligations, he is unique, not merely in the sense that every genuine poet must be.

In the last resort, I suppose, our attitude towards the bulk of Swinburne's work will be determined by our willingness or unwillingness to recognize energy as an absolute good, our ability to enter imaginatively into the life of the flame that leaps up with no purpose beyond that of returning to the heavens whence it was stolen. He could harness his energy, and in *Bothwell* we have it bound to an enormous task; he could concentrate it, as in *Erechtheus*; he could give it such noble issue as we find again and again in the *Songs before Sunrise*; but oftener he was content simply to release it where it achieves hardly anything, where it must be valued simply for its existence. There it is, an astonishing thing, unrelated, like a flame floating in the air, meaningless, very likely, on the ordinary view of it, yet with its significance as a symbol of liberation, adding, despite all the technique of its display, less to the symbols which art has given us than to those we find in nature. But it is not so difficult, after all, to understand why the unrelated, uncommunicative part of his poetry made Swinburne happy in its production, contented in retrospect on it. He was no longer, for all his metrical science, producing works of art; he was simply living; " no more a singer but a song ". Not living in the very finest sense, for the poet himself cannot fully have his experience till, in the endeavour to communicate it, he has minutely realized its quality, but living, all the same, with an extraordinary energy, only in a freedom as of the void, whereas in his greatest works he had attained to that more excellent freedom in which the conditioning world is itself liberated with the poet instead of being evaded by him. But he gave us, in his great hours, the privilege of sharing with him the highest human liberty; need we make it so grave a reproach to him that he also showed us, too persistently, the spectacle of that other liberty, of the sea-bird or of a flame in mid-air? It is by his achievements that he must be judged, but all that poetry which was merely his existence has nevertheless for certain natures a certain value. Only, while every achievement added to his claim on us, one quarter of the rest of his poetry would have sufficed to do all that such poetry can do, supply us with evidence that such a way of life was possible for him.

BIBLIOGRAPHICAL NOTE

THE purpose of this Note is merely to enable the reader to follow Swinburne's development. Early writings, unpublished or printed only for private circulation after Swinburne's death in the severely limited issues for which Mr. Wise and Sir Edmund Gosse were responsible, are placed opposite the approximate date of composition, the date of publication being stated after the title or description of each item. Works published by Swinburne himself are placed opposite the date of publication, with an occasional warning when that date is long subsequent to the time of composition. Exhaustiveness being out of the question, I have selected from minor and fragmentary writings those which possess most merit, or mark the response of Swinburne to some new influence, or reveal some noteworthy trait of his character, and ignored the rest.

I would once again invite attention to the slowness with which Swinburne discovered, or allowed himself to indulge, his genius for swift, ecstatic, lyrical verse.

The titles of books or pamphlets are given in italics, those of other items between quotation marks.

1857. " A Vigil ".
>Eventually altered and expanded to make " The Leper ", in the first series of *Poems and Ballads*, 1866.

" Ode to Mazzini ".
>Incomplete text printed for Watts-Dunton in 1909, twenty copies for private circulation; complete text published in *Posthumous Poems*, 1917.

1857-58. *Queen Yseult.*
>Canto I published in *Undergraduate Papers*, 1858. Cantos I-VI printed for private circulation by Mr. Wise, in an edition of thirty copies, with an introduction by Sir Edmund Gosse, in 1918. Four further cantos were projected, but not written, though

sixteen stanzas intended for one or other of these cantos exist in a manuscript owned by Mr. Wise.

A year or two later, Swinburne returned to Tristram in "Joyeuse Garde", included in *A Lay of Lilies and Other Poems*, privately printed by Mr. Wise, in an edition of thirty copies, in 1918. He wrote the prelude to *Tristram of Lyonesse* in 1869 (*not* 1871), and published the whole poem in 1882. Thus he was occupied with thoughts of the Tristram legend from 1857 off and on till 1882.

Lancelot, The Death of Rudel, etc. Privately printed in 1918.

1858. Contributions to *Undergraduate Papers*.
(1) "The Early English Dramatists. No. 1. Christopher Marlowe and John Webster."
(2) "Queen Yseult", Canto I.
(3) "'The Monomaniac's Tragedy, and Other Poems.' By Ernest Wheldrake". A review of an imaginary volume, and Swinburne's first hoax.
(4) "Church Imperialism". An attack on the clerical supporters of Napoleon III.

The Laws of Corinth. A Play in Two Acts. Unpublished.

Translations of portions of The Decameron, and "The White Hind", afterwards developed into "The Two Dreams", in the first series of *Poems and Ballads*.

1858-59. *Rosamund.*
Published in *The Queen Mother aud Rosamund*, 1860, Swinburne's first published book, and his unluckiest.

Stories intended to constitute *The Triameron*.
(1) "The Portrait".
(2) "The Chronicle of Queen Fredegond".
(3) *Dead Love.* Published 1864.
(4) "The Marriage of Monna Lisa".

1859. *Laugh and Lie Down.* A Comedy in Four Acts. Unpublished.

Undergraduate Sonnets.
Privately printed, in an edition of thirty copies, by Mr. Wise in 1918. Seven illustrate Swinburne's skill in reproducing Shakespeare, the eighth sonnet is pure Rossetti.

1859-60. *The Queen's Tragedy.*
Privately printed, in an edition of thirty copies, by Mr. Wise in 1919. Swinburne is here seen following the William Morris of *Sir Peter Harpdon's End.*

The Loyal Servant. A Comedy in Five Acts.
The last of Swinburne's exercises in the manner of Fletcher. Unpublished.

1859-61. *Ballads of the English Border.*
An incomplete edition of the Border ballads, with notes and a brief introduction by Swinburne. It was on the abandonment of this project that he began to write his original Border ballads. Published in 1926, in a shockingly edited volume, full of gross errors as regards both text and glossary.

1861. Translation of Villon's " La Belle Heaulmyère ".
The earliest of the translations from Villon; included in the second series of *Poems and Ballads*, 1878, when, however, for obvious reasons it was found impossible to print "The Ballade of Villon and Fat Madge", which was privately issued in 1910.

La Fille du Policeman.
Like the lost *La Sœur de la Reine*, a skit at once on French travesties of English life and on English middle-class morality.

1862. An important year, the first in which Swinburne began to produce characteristic lyrics with some frequency, the first in which he (through the *Spectator*) began to address the general public.

" Faustine ".
" The Sun-dew ".
" The Triumph of Time ".
Review of Hugo's *Les Misérables*.
Review of Baudelaire's *Fleurs du Mal*. 1913.
Defence of Meredith's *Modern Love*. 1914.
" Félicien Cossu ". 1915.
" Ernest Clouët ". 1916.
> " Cossu " and " Clouët " exhibit Swinburne again as an adept in mischievous hoaxing.

Théophile. 1915.
" The Flogging-Block ".
> An epic of flagellation continued, at intervals, till 1881 ; quite unpublishable.

" Laus Veneris ".
A Year's Letters.
> Begun in 1862, completed in 1866. Published, with omissions, serially and anonymously, in the *Tatler*, 1877-78, and, with alterations, as *Love's Cross-Currents*, in 1905.

1864. *The Pilgrimage of Pleasure.*
> A Morality presented to his cousin, Mrs. Disney Leith, for inclusion in her story, *The Children of the Chapel.*

" Itylus ".
" Félise ".

1865. *Atalanta in Calydon.*
> But commenced in the summer of 1863, in Cornwall, and finished, in the Isle of Wight, in February 1864.

Chastelard.
> But in some sort begun in 1858, and worked at, on and off, for seven years.

" The Cannibal Catechism ".
> This extremely unseemly set of verses, written for an institution the dinners of which Swinburne attended regularly from 1865 to 1869, is not mere naughtiness: it illustrates both his pleasure in being "horrid" and a certain satirical side of his genius.

1866. *Poems and Ballads.*
Notes on Poems and Reviews.
Cleopatra.
> Never reprinted by Swinburne.

1867. *A Song of Italy.*
" An Appeal to England ".
> Afterwards included in *Songs Before Sunrise*.

Lesbia Brandon.
> Begun in 1859-60; taken up again with the naughtiest intentions in 1867, as appears from a letter to Burton: put into type from a muddled manuscript in 1877; never published. Noteworthy as showing how long the ambition to be a novelist remained with Swinburne.

" Ave atque Vale ".
> Written on a premature report of the death of Baudelaire.

William Blake.
" William Morris "; " Matthew Arnold ".
> Beginning of critical contributions to the *Fortnightly Review*.

1868. " Siena ".
> Included in *Songs Before Sunrise*.

Notes on the Royal Academy Exhibition.

1869. "Hertha".
Included in *Songs Before Sunrise*.

1870. *Ode on the Proclamation of the French Republic*.
"Rossetti" in the *Fortnightly Review*.

1871. *Songs Before Sunrise*.
Act I of *Bothwell*.
Set up in type for Swinburne by Locker-Lampson. A year later Swinburne sought and secured Watts-Dunton's aid in re-composing the play, but found great difficulty in "revising the revision" of Acts II and IV.

1872. *Le Tombeau de Théophile Gautier*.
Swinburne contributed, on the invitation of J. M. de Heredia, the English, French, and Latin verses reprinted in *Poems and Ballads*, second series, and a Greek poem never reprinted by him.
"John Ford".
Under the Microscope.

1874. *Bothwell*.

1875. *George Chapman*.
Songs of Two Nations.
Essays and Studies.
The Devil's Due.
The last blow in the controversy with Buchanan.

1876. *Erechtheus*.
Introduction to a reprint of *Joseph and his Brethren*.
To some uncertain extent based on an article written by Swinburne in 1860, when he was powerfully influenced by Wells.
Note of an English Republican on the Muscovite Crusade.

1877. "A Note on Charlotte Brontë".

1878. *Poems and Ballads*, second series.

BIBLIOGRAPHICAL NOTE 263

1880. *A Study of Shakespeare.*
Songs of the Springtides.
Studies in Song.
The Heptalogia.
But most of the parodies had been composed much earlier: the Coventry Patmore in 1859, the Browning and Mrs. Browning about 1863, except for some additions made in 1878, the Tennyson in 1877.

1881. *Mary Stuart.*

1882. *Tristram of Lyonesse and Other Poems.*

1883. *A Century of Roundels.*

1884. *A Midsummer Holiday.*

1885. *Marino Faliero.*

1886. *Miscellanies.*
A Study of Victor Hugo.

1887. *A Word for the Navy.*
The Jubilee.
Privately printed.
Locrine.

1889. A Study of Ben Jonson.
Poems and Ballads, third series.
But the ballads were taken from *Lesbia Brandon* and represent a much earlier Swinburne.

1894. *Astrophel.*
Studies in Prose and Poetry.

1896. " Robert Burns ".
Thirty copies, printed for members of the Burns Centenary Club. The poem was included in *A Channel Passage and Other Poems.*
The Tale of Balen.
Swinburne's recovery of youth and lucid communicativeness.

1899. *Rosamund, Queen of the Lombards.*
The later manner in dramatic blank verse.

1904. *A Channel Passage and other Poems.*
Love's Cross-Currents.
But written, as *A Year's Letters*, in 1862-66.

1908. *The Duke of Gandia.*
The Age of Shakespeare.

With the exception of pieces that can never be published, nearly all the writings which were in manuscript at Swinburne's death have been printed in the privately issued pamphlets edited by Sir Edmund Gosse and Mr. Wise. Certain of these have been noticed above. I may mention, as throwing light on the opinions of the youthful Swinburne, *M. Prudhomme at the International Exhibition*, written in 1862; the unpublished pendant to his essay on Théophile, dealing with that poet's persecutor, Father Garasse, and illustrating Swinburne's command of invective in the early 'sixties; *Rondeaux Parisiens*, showing his dislike of Stead's obscenity as a social reformer and his resentment of foreign cant about English morality; *Letters to the Press*, illustrative of Swinburne's tendency to let a noble indignation issue in somewhat less than noble denunciations; and *A Record of Friendship*, revealing the delicate loyalty of his devotion to Rossetti for years, to Mrs. Rossetti always.

Posthumous Poems appeared in 1917.

The great Bonchurch edition, when completed, will include almost everything that can properly be published.

The *Letters*, 1917, are derived only from his literary correspondence, and the family letters issued by Mrs. Disney Leith are mere excerpts.

INDEX

"Adieux à Marie Stuart," 227.
Aeschylus, 22, 39, 148, 192, 197, 204.
"After Many Days," 117 and f.
Albumazar, 11 f.
"An Appeal," 98, 224.
"Anactoria," 24, 62, 76, 85, 221, 233; quoted, 86.
"Anima Anceps," 221.
"Annales des Gaules," 44 f.
Arden of Feversham, 11.
Aristophanes, 39, 53.
"Armada, The," 220.
Arnold, Matthew, 55, 126, 199.
"Art of being a Grandfather, The," 209.
Arts Club, 116.
Ashburnham, Earl of, 41.
Aspromonte, 4, 99.
Asquith, H. H., 206.
Astrophel, 77, 136, 152.
"At a Month's End," 74, 75, 147, 224, 254.
"At Parting," quoted, 70–71.
Atalanta in Calydon, 1, 17, 26, 36, 55, 60, 61, 67, 108, 112, 214, 221, 232; and *Erechtheus*, 156–169.
Athenaeum, The, 52, 126 f.
Athens, 4, 7, 9, 57, 112, 113, 164, 166, 167; ode on, 220.
"August," 133; quoted, 134.
"Ave atque Vale," 75, 139 f., 218, 254; quoted, 224–225.
Aytoun's *Ballads of Scotland*, 51 f.

"Ballad of Dreamland, A," 122.
Ballads of the English Border, 51 f.
Balliol College, 38.
Baudelaire, 23, 54, 68, 76, 80, 85, 198, 206, 208, 214, 224; and Swinburne, 247–248; elegy on, 193.
Beaumont, 43, 195.
Beddoes, 172 and f.
Beerbohm, Max, 150.
"Before a Crucifix," 107.
"Before the Mirror," 221, 248.
Bird, Dr., 118.
Bird, Miss Alice, 229 f.
Blake, William, 23, 202, 249; Swinburne's *William Blake*, 26, 183, 194, 202; quoted, 185–186.
Blake, Admiral, 49.
"Blessed Damozel, The," 15.
Boccaccio, 47, 51, 52.
Bonchurch, 205.
Border Ballads, 51 and f., 182, 194, 210.
Bothwell, 115, 123, 153, 158, 170, 171, 172, 175, 176, 181, 217, 227, 228, 255.
Bourne, Fox, 50 f.
Bowdler's Shakespeare, 40.
Brawne, Fanny, 68.
"Bride's Prelude, The," 117.
British Museum, 46 f., 48.
Brontë, Charlotte, quoted, 187.
Browning, Elizabeth Barrett, parodied by Swinburne, 200.

Browning, Robt., 44, 55, 68, 69, 73, 76, 173, 199.
Bryce, Viscount, 46.
Buchanan, Robt., 22, 29, 31, 66, 124, 125, 126.
Bullen, A. H., 150.
" Burden of Nineveh, The," 15.
Burne-Jones, 41, 62, 70, 72, 77, 81, 93, 118, 154, 249.
Burns, Robt., poem on, 193; parody of, 200, 227.
Burton, 26, 39, 62, 66, 115, 138, 149; elegy on, 227.
" By the North Sea," quoted, 132.
Byron, Lord, 1, 19, 26, 29, 183, 184, 190.

Cambridge, 66.
Campbell's Anthology, 42.
" Cannibal Catechism, The," 118.
Cannibal Club, The, 118.
Capheaton, Northumberland, 33, 36, 38, 41, 50.
Carlyle, Thomas, 55, 96; Swinburne and, 199.
" Carlyliad, ou les Mille et un Crachats, The," 199.
Carrington, C., 44 f.
Catullus, 22, 39, 65, 68, 70, 80, 198, 211.
Century of Roundels, A, 151.
Channel Passage, A, 77, 152.
Chapman, George, 23, 173, 196 and f., 197.
Chastelard, 17, 23, 26, 55 and f., 60, 63, 171, 173, 174, 177, 181, 227.
Châtiments, Les, 91, 250.
Chatto (and Windus), 50 f., 144.
Chester St., Belgrave Sq., 33.
16 Cheyne Walk, 54, 61, 116.
Childe Harold, 26.

" Cleopatra," quoted, 222–223.
Clifford, Prof. W. K., 97.
" Clouët, Ernest," 54.
Cockerell, 150.
Coleridge, 146, 150, 189, 194, 198, 199, 250, 254; ode on France, 221.
Collins, C., 32, 194.
Collins, Mortimer, 66.
" Commonweal, The," 151, 221, 226.
" Complaint of the Fair Armouress," 51.
Contemporary Review, 124.
Cornwall, Barry, 239.
" Cossu, Félicien," 54.
Curzon of Kedleston, Marquess, 38, 206.
Cymbeline, 202.

Dante Aligheri, 192, 198.
Davies, W. H., 139.
Day's *Parliament of Bees,* 181.
" Death of Rudel, The," 44.
" Death of Sir John Franklin, The," quoted, 48–49.
Defence of Guenevere, The, 15, 41.
" Dejection," 221.
" Devil's Due, The," 125.
Dicey, A. V., 46.
Dickens, Charles, 82, 149, 198, 204.
" Dirae," 100, 108.
Dixon, 230.
Doctor Dodypol, 197.
" Dolores," 5, 62, 77, 78, 79, 84, 221, 233.
Donne, J., 68, 70, 76.
22a Dorset Street, 61, 62.
Dowson, E., 206.
Drinkwater, John, 1.
Dryden, 85, 89.
Duchess of Malfi, 42.

INDEX

Duke of Gandia, 52, 152, 177, 178 and f., 179.
Dumas, 82.
Dyce's Marlowe, 42.

East Dene, Bonchurch, 33.
Eliot, George, 127.
Elizabeth, Queen, 45, 49.
Elizabethan Drama (dramatists), 11, 23, 37, 42, 93, 143, 148, 149, 171, 193, 194, 195, 196, 197, 204, 208, 227, 249.
Ellis, F. S., 27, 101, 108.
Emerson, R. W., 126; his " Brahma," 139.
Enoch Arden, 14.
Erechtheus, 7, 9, 58, 67, 97, 107, 108, 111, 112, 113, 114, 115, 123, 156, 214, 221, 251, 255; and *Atalanta*, 156–169; and *Tristram*, 215–217.
Essays and Studies, 182, 183.
Eton, 36, 37, 38, 43 f., 145, 205, 241, 249.
Euripides, 22, 113, 198, 200.
" Evening on the Broads," 132.
Examiner, The, 29, 50 f., 100, 108, 125, 126.
Eyre, Governor, 236–237.

Fantin-Latour, 84.
Faulkner, Miss Jane, 72.
" Faustine," 54, 83, 221.
" Félise," 73, 74, 75, 222; quoted, 78–79
" Femmes Damnées, Les," 85.
Fifine at the Fair, 199.
" Fleshly School of Poetry, The," 124, 125.
Fletcher, 42, 43, 172, 195.
Fleurs du Mal, Les, 85, 247, 248.
Flogging Block, The, 118.

Ford, John, 181, 183, 202, 249; essay on, 11, 195, 196.
" Forsaken Garden, A," 122.
Fortnightly, the, 54, 98 f., 117, 126, 188.
" Fragoletta," 5, 85.
Froude, J. A., 30, 55.
Furnivall, 32, 124, 126, 234, 242 and f.

" Garden of Cymdoce, The," 78.
" Garden of Proserpine, The," 221.
Garibaldi, 100.
Gautier, T., 23, 80, 82, 84, 85, 129, 198; elegy on, 192–193.
Gay, D., 77, 126.
Germ, the, 15.
Gladstone, W. E., 243.
Gordon, General, 243.
Gordon, Lady Mary, 55.
Gosse, Sir Edmund, 1, 7, 39, 50, 64, 65, 97, 100, 102, 118, 211, 227; quoted, 174.
Gray, 194.
Great James Street, 93, 122, 128, 143, 234.
Green, T. H., 46.

Hardy, Thomas, 50; his *Dynasts*, 123.
Harvard, 46 f.
" Haystack in the Floods, The," 45.
Hazlitt, 150.
Heptalogia, The, 150, 199, 200.
Herbert, George, quoted, 78.
" Hertha," 75, 97, 98, 139 and f., 218, 223, 232, 245, 254.
" Hesperia," 84, 196 f., 222.
Hill, Birkbeck, 46.
Hogg, James, 199.

Holmwood, near Henley, 122, 123, 150, 240.
Hotten, J. C., 25 f., 26, 27 and f., 101, 102, 108, 144.
Houghton, Lord (Monckton Milnes), 16, 20, 40, 55 and f., 58, 61, 62, 66, 80 f., 115, 116.
Howell, C. A., 27, 115, 234, 246.
Hugh of Lincoln, 51 f.
Hugo, Victor, 4, 8, 11, 23, 34, 91, 104, 105, 113, 114, 126, 148, 152, 153, 184, 190, 191, 192, 198, 201, 204, 208, 209, 211, 236, 248, 249, 250, 254.
Hunt, Miss Violet, 27.
Hutton (of the *Spectator*), 53, 54, 108, 124.
"Hymn of Man, The," 111.
"Hymn to Proserpine," 221.

Ibsen, 179.
Idylls of the King, 125.
"Ilicet," 82, 221.
Inchbold, 151 ; elegy on, 226.
Infelicia, 82.
"In the Orchard," 221.
"In the Twilight," 100.
"In Time of Mourning," 153.
"Intercession," 100.
"Interlude," 79.
Irving, Henry, 170.
"Italian Mother, The," 100, 117 f.
"Itylus," 221.

Jacobean Drama (dramatists), 11, 37, 42.
"Jacobite's Farewell, A," 226.
"Jew's Daughter, The," 51 f.
Johnson, Samuel, 189.
Jonas Fischer, 125.
Jones, Ebenezer, 196 f.
Jonson, Ben, 152.

"Joseph and His Brethren," 23.
Jowett, Benjamin, 22, 38, 67 f., 122, 123, 124, 128, 149, 152, 240, 242.
"Joyeuse Garde," 47 f.
Justine, 80 and f., 117.

Keats, J., 68, 69, 70, 130, 230.
Kelly, Prof. Fitzmaurice, 150.
King Lear, 202.
Kingsley, Henry, 237.
Knebworth, 26.
Knight, Joseph, 20, 26.
Knowles, 126 f.
Knox, John, 175.

La Fille du Policeman, 51.
Lamb, Charles, 150, 199, 204 ; quoted, 187.
Landor, W. S., 4, 8, 11, 23, 91, 105, 113, 114, 118, 125, 148, 149, 150, 188, 194, 197, 204, 205, 209, 236, 238, 249 ; his *Hellenics*, 192 ; sonnet on, 192, 221.
Lathom, Mr., 49.
Laugh and Lie Down, 42, 118.
Laus Veneris, 64, 87, 221, chap. iv.
Laws of Candy, The, 42.
Laws of Corinth, The, 42.
Le Roi s'amuse, 152.
"Leave-taking, A," 221.
Leaves of Grass, 247.
Leconte de Lisle, 245.
Lee, Nat, his *Cæsar Borgia*, 178 f.
Legros, 25.
Leith, Mrs. Disney, 210.
Lemprière, 18.
Leonardo da Vinci, 188.
"Leper, The," 44.
Lesbia Brandon, 52, 66, 71 f., 151.
Lewes, G. H., 55.

Lingua, 11 and f.
Linton, Mrs. Lyon, 125.
Lippincott's Magazine, 27.
Locrine, 143, 152, 171, 179, 180–181.
London, 33, 61, 66, 93, 116, 126, 128, 145, 237, 240; Elizabethan, 9.
Love, in English poetry, 69.
Love's Cross Currents, 201, 210.
" Love laid his sleepless head," 228.
Loyal Servant, The, 42, 43.
Lucas, E. V., 150.
Luke, G. R., 46.
Lytton, Bulwer, 25–26.
Lytton, Lord, 126 f., 127.

Mackay, E., 241.
Macmillan's Magazine, 124.
Mallarmé, 135.
Mallock, W. H., 5.
" Marching Song, A," 105.
Marino Faliero, 152, 171, 177.
Marlowe, Christopher, 25, 42, 148, 181, 195, 211, 249; his *Edward II*, 175.
Marston, 42, 206.
Marvell, quoted, 58.
Mary Queen of Scots, 33, 34, 55, 143, 174, 175, 249.
Mary Stuart, 150, 171, 176–177.
" Match, A," 221.
" Mater Triumphalis," 99.
Maud, 14.
Maupassant, Guy de, 210; his impression of Swinburne, 21.
Mayne, 197.
Mazzini, G., 4, 8, 53, 67 and f., 92, 93, 97, 105, 111, 113, 114, 209, 236.
McColl, Norman, 52.

Menken, Adah Isaacs, early career, 81–82 ; verses to, 71 and f.
Mentana, 4, 99.
" Mentana : First Anniversary," 105.
Meredith, George, 22, 53, 59, 61, 63, 98, 146, 222; on Swinburne, 206–207 ; Swinburne and, 234–235 ; his *Modern Love*, 22, 53, 68.
Mérrimée, 194.
Messalina, 18.
Meurice, Mde. Paul, 248.
Meynell, Mrs., 190.
Midsummer Holiday, A, 10–11, 151, 242.
Millais, 16.
Milnes, Monckton. *See* Houghton, Lord.
Milton, John, 197.
Minto, W., 125.
Mirabeau, 35.
Miscellanies, 152.
Misérables, Les, 153.
" Monkey and the Microscope, The," 125.
Moore, George, 182.
Morley, John, 25 and f., 28, 29, 30, 31, 54, 64, 65, 66, 75, 188 f., 193 f. ; criticism of *Poems and Ballads* (First Series), 17–19.
Morris, Miss May, 239.
Morris, William, 15, 22, 41, 43, 44, 45, 46, 62, 77, 93, 118, 131, 149, 154, 246.
124 Mount Street, 61.
Moxon, 25, 26, 54, 64 and f.
Munro, 150.
Murray, John, 62.
Musset, Alfred de, 152, 186.
" My Sister's Sleep," 44.

Nabbes, 42.

Napoleon Buonaparte, 183.
Napoleon III, 4, 12, 92, 93, 100, 108, 109, 110, 126; Swinburne and, 7.
" Neap Tide," 132.
Nelson, Lord, 49.
Nero, 7.
Newdigate Prize, 48, 49.
Newman, Cardinal, 96, 199.
Nichol, John, 39, 46 and f., 92, 122.
Nicolson, Harold, 1.
Nineteenth Century, the, 126 f.
Nobody and Somebody, 197.
Northumberland, 9, 33, 35, 38, 71, 72, 129, 145, 152.
Note on Charlotte Brontë, A, 127.
Note of an English Republican, etc., 127.
Notes on Old Masters at Florence, 187–188.
Notes on Poems and Reviews, 28, 83, 87, 124.
" Nympholept, A," 137, 138, 152, 227, 254; quoted, 135–136.

" Ode to Anactoria," 87.
" Ode on the Insurrection in Candia," 97, 98 f., 219.
" Ode to Mazzini," 92.
" Ode on the Proclamation of the French Republic," 37, 100, 101, 108; quoted, 219–220.
" Old Malignity," 199.
" Old Mortality," the, 46, 92.
Omar Khayyam, 22.
" On the Cliffs," quoted, 121, 138.
" On the Downs," quoted, 140–141.
Orsini, 92.
O'Shaughnessy, 206.

Oxford, 22, 37, 38, 39, 40, 43, 50, 51, 54, 55, 66, 92, 100, 122, 149, 151, 172, 206, 242; the Union, 40.
Oxford and Cambridge Magazine, 15.

Paderewski, M., 56.
Palgrave, 62.
Pall Mall Gazette, 71 f., 126 f.
" Pan and Thalassius," chap. vii, 226.
Pasiphae, 18.
Pater, Walter, 187, 188 and f., 222; essay on Wordsworth, 196.
Patmore, Coventry, 68, 69, 199, 244.
Payne, B., 25 and f., 64, 65.
" Perinde ac Cadaver," 242.
Pickering, 26.
Pickwick, 11.
" Pilgrims, The," 98, 224.
Pines, The, 144, 146, 148, 150, 241, 244.
Plato, 39.
Poe, Edgar Allan, 21, 24.
Poel, W., 42 f.
Poems and Ballads (First Series), 1, 20, 25 and f., 30, 33, 44, 47, 48, 50 f., 53, 55, 62, 63, 64 and f., 65, 66, 70, 73, 77, 79, 84, 85, 87, 102, 106, 107, 124, 133, 147, 214, 221, 226, 239; criticism of, 17-19, 31; character of, 88-90.
Poems and Ballads (Second Series), 67, 74, 87, 107, 121-122, 147, 167, 214, 221, 224, 229, 240; character of, 225-226.
Poems and Ballads (Third Series), 151, 214, 221, 226.
" Poet to a Puritan, A," 199.

INDEX

"Poet and the Wood-louse, The," 200.
Posthumous Poems, 92 f.
Powell, G., 39, 66.
Praed, 77.
Pre-Raphaelites, 40, 53, 61, 246.
Putney, 9, 10, 40, 50 f., 128, 143, 151, 179.

Quarterly Review, 32.
Queen Mother and Rosamund, The, 23, 26, 51, 157, 171, 172 and f., 173.
"Queen's Tragedy, The," 45.
"Queen Yseult," 46.
"Quia Multum Amavit," 105, 224.
Quincey, Thomas de, 189.

Rabelais, 53, 198.
"Record of Friendship, A," 116 f., 117 f.
Redesdale, Lord, 38.
Redway, G., 27, 28 f.
"Relics," 122.
Reul, M. Paul de, 1.
"Ride from Milan, The," 100.
Rimbaud, 24.
Rome, 4, 99, 100, 150.
"Rondeaux Parisiens," 126 f.
Ronsard, 175, 210.
Rosamund, 51, 172, 173.
Rosamund, Queen of the Lombards, 134, 152, 177.
Rossetti, Christina, 151, 198; her poetry, 16-17; ballad to, 11.
Rossetti, Dante G., 15, 16, 17, 22, 27, 29, 40, 41, 44, 45, 54, 61, 62, 68, 69, 93, 99, 100, 101, 108, 109, 115, 116 and f., 117 and f., 124, 126, 146, 148, 151 f., 173, 183, 188 and f., 194, 205, 208, 211, 234, 246, 249.

Rossetti, W. M., 25 and f., 28, 34, 85, 101, 107, 124.
"Rudel in Paradise," quoted, 44.
Ruskin, John, 15, 55, 62, 63, 72, 187, 189; and *Poems and Ballads*, 19; and *Atalanta in Calydon*, 60.
Russell, Lord John, 51.

St. Paul's, 125.
Sablonière Hotel, Leicester Square, 16.
Sade, Marquis de, 246.
Sand, George, 152, 186.
Sandys, F., 222, 249.
Sappho, 24, 38, 85, 86, 124, 138, 198.
Sartoris, Mrs., 72.
Saturday Review, The, 17, 25 and f., 28, 31, 69.
"Saviour of Society, The," 108-109.
"Scholar Gypsy, The," 230.
Scott, Sir W., 183.
Scott, W. Bell, 117, 190, 205; lines on, 191.
Selimus, 180.
Shakespeare, 68, 173, 192, 195, 197, 242, 249.
Shelley, P. B., 53, 69, 75, 85, 149, 150, 204, 206, 211, 221, 228, 252, 254; and Swinburne, 36-37, 238.
Shepherd, R. H., 28 f., 196 and f.
"Siena," 27, 101, 223.
Simon, Sir John, 72.
Sims, G. R., 82.
"Sir Peter Harpdon's End," 45.
Sisters, The, 119, 179-180.
Solomon, Rebecca, 80.
Solomon, Simeon, 234, 245.
Song of Italy, A, 67, 101, 108, 226.

"Song of the Hours, The," 194.
Songs before Sunrise, 7, 9, 67, 88, chap. v, 115, 167, 214, 221, 223, 225, 226, 238, 242, 255; prelude to, quoted, 232-233.
Songs of the Springtides, 150, 226.
Songs of Two Nations, 100, 108.
Sophocles, 204.
Spanish Friar, The, 89.
Spectator, the, 23, 29, 53, 54, 108, 153.
Spencer, H., 55, 127, 243, 244.
"Sphinx, The," 24, 222.
"Staff and the Scrip, The," 15.
"Stage Love," 221.
Stead, W. T., 126 f.
Stedman, E. C., 34, 139 f., 244.
Stendhal, 194, 198.
Stockdale's Budget, 46.
Studies in Prose and Poetry, 152.
Studies in Song, 132, 151, 226.
"Study, A," quoted, 30-31.
Study of Shakespeare, 143, 150 and f., 202.
"Sundew, The," 18, 222; quoted, 133.
"Super Flumina Babylonis," 223; quoted, 104.
Swift, Dean, 198.
Swinburne, Algernon Charles: his birth, 33; his ancestry and his pride of family, 33-34; and his parents, 35-36; at Eton, 37-38; at Oxford, 38-50; his love affair, 30; and Jane Faulkner, 72; and Adah Menken, 80-82; verses to Adah Menken, 71; and love, 69-90; his sensuality, 237-238; his sexual aberrations, 118-119; his income, 50; and Victorian society, 14-15; and Lady Trevelyan, 15; his first book,

15-16; position in 1862, 16; legend about, 20; personal characteristics, 20-21, 56-59; responsiveness of, 7; contradictions in his literary personality, 23; want of animus in, 31-32; his religion, 6, 95-98, 113, 204-205, 244-246; illness of, 115; his death and burial, 204-205; Victor Hugo and, 91-92, 153, 208, 209, 249-250; Pater and, 187-188; Carlyle and, 199; Meredith on, 206-207; and Meredith, 234-235; and Governor Eyre, 236-237; and Baudelaire, 247-248; and Whistler, 248-249; and Landor, 188, 194, 209; and Howell, 27-28 and f.; Rossetti, Morris, and, 22, 41, 93; Ruskin and, 15, 19; Jowett and, 39-40; Nichol and, 40; Morris's influence upon, 41-46; and Napoleon III, 109-110; and D. G. Rossetti, 115-117; Maupassant's impression of, 21; and John Morley, 17-19, 31; and Watts-Dunton, 131-132, 143-155, 240-241, 246-247; his controversies, 125-128; his political opinions, 91, 241-244; his republicanism, 34, 57-58, 95-96, 243-244; his scholarship, 174-175, 197; his love for Catullus, 22; dislike of Euripides and regard for Aeschylus, 22, 148; and the Elizabethan dramatists, 11, 23, 37, 42, 93, 143, 148, 193, 194, 195, 197, 204, 208, 227, 249; and the Jacobean dramatists, 11, 37, 42; and Aristophanes, 53; his library, 145 and f.; his

mastery of blank verse, 157-158; his service to Chapman, 196-197; his selection of language, 214-215; his odes, 218-225; his tragedies, 227-228; his musical quality, 228-229; his instinctiveness, 229-230; his crowning work, 223-224; his golden years, 225; a poet of abstractions, 212-213; as a metrician, 231-233; as a dramatist, 156-181; as a prose writer and critic, chap. xi; the poet of liberty, 3, 13, 252; liberty his vital principle, 4, 105-106; his inability to understand the reader's mind, 11-12; his need of a propagandist purpose, 12; comparison with Shelley, 36-37, 238; the want in his later work, 251-252; his present-day unpopularity, 253-254; "no more a singer but a song," 254-256; his landscapes and seascapes, 129-142; autobiographical significance of "Thalassius," 120; his preference for *Songs before Sunrise*, 106; and *Poems and Ballads*, 61-66; and *Atalanta in Calydon*, 60; and the *Spectator*, 23; his attitude towards libels, 29, 235-236; *Punch* and, 25; his parody of the Brownings, 200; on Swift, 198; an intoxicant for adolescence, 2; Mallock's parody of, 5.
Swinburne, Admiral, 33, 48, 118, 122, 123, 144.
Swinburne, Lady Jane, 33, 118, 122, 128, 144.
Swinburne, Sir John, 34-36, 238.
Swinburne, Sir W., 33.

Swinburne, Edith, 122.
Swinburne, Isabel, 205.
Swinburne family, The, 33-34.
Symons, Arthur, 68, 149, 188, 248 f.

Tale of Balen, The, 10, 115, 143, 148, 152, 214.
Taylor, Sir Henry, 176.
Tennyson, Lord, 14, 22, 61, 124, 125, 134, 151, 199, 234, 242.
"Thalassius," 120, chap. vii, 151, 250; quoted, 83-84, 205.
Thomas, Edward, 1.
Thomson, 81 f., 82.
"Thyrsis," 230.
"Tiresias," 99, 223.
"To Boo," quoted, 72.
"To a Seamew," quoted, 138.
"To Walt Whitman in America," 107.
Tragedy of Nero, The, 197.
Traill, H. D., 78, 207 f.
Trelawney, 238.
Trevelyan, Lady, 15, 20, 55, 63 and f.
"Triameron," 51.
Tristram of Lyonesse, 67, 115, 143, 151 and f., 199, 214, 226, 251; and *Erechtheus*, 215-217.
"Triumph of Gloriana, The," 43 f.
"Triumph of Time, The," 71-73, 75, 224, 254.
Turner, 19.
"Two Dreams, The," 47; quoted, 134.
"Tyneside Widow, The," 226.

Uccello's Galeazzo Malatesta, 56.
"Ulalume," 24.
Undergraduate Papers, 46, 54.
Under the Microscope, 124.

Unpublished Verses, 196 f.

Viau, T. de, 194.
Vichy, 72.
Victor Emmanuel, King, 100.
Victoria, Queen, 51, 242.
Victorian society, 14-15, 61.
"Vigil, A," 43.
Villiers de l'Isle Adam, 33.
Villon, F., 22, 51, 52, 198, 211.
"Vision of Bags, A," 246.
"Vision of Spring in Winter, A," 122; quoted, 129-130.

"Watch in the Night, A," 100.
Watts-Dunton, T., 9, 26, 28 f., 27 and f., 31 f., 34, 36, 39, 50 f., 51, 80 f., 99, 100, 101, 118, 123, 125, 128, 131, 132, 133, 172 f., 204, 205, 212, 235, 239, 240, 246, 247, 249; his care of Swinburne, 143-155.
Webster, 42, 181, 195, 249.
Wellington, Duke of, 183.
Wells, Charles, 23.

"Wheldrake, E.," 54.
Whippingham Papers, The, 235 and f.
Whistler, 62, 66, 84, 118; and Swinburne, 248-249.
"White Hind, The," quoted, 47-48.
Whitman, Walt, 152, 190, 202, 246-247.
Wight, Isle of, 33, 38, 55, 122, 129.
Wilde, Oscar, 24.
Wise, T. J., 43, 44, 45, 46 f., 47 f., 51, 52 f., 71 f., 80 f., 100, 117 f., 145 f., 149, 227.
"Word for the Navy, A," 28.
"Word with the Wind," 11.
Wordsworth, W., 11, 152, 190, 199, 208, 250.

Yarrington, 197.
"Year of the Rose, The," 122.
Year's Letters, A, 36, 52.
"Young Man's Guide, The," 55.

Zola, 246.